T0307994

ANCIENT SWALLOWS

ANCIENT SWALLOWS

Nanjing,
the Legendary City
of Literature

Cheng Zhangcan

Translated by
Daniel McRyan

Books Beyond Boundaries

ROYAL COLLINS

Ancient Swallows
Nanjing, the Legendary City of Literature

Cheng Zhangcan
Translated by Daniel McRyan

First published in 2023 by Royal Collins Publishing Group Inc.
Groupe Publication Royal Collins Inc.
BKM Royalcollins Publishers Private Limited

Headquarters: 550-555 boul. René-Lévesque O Montréal (Québec) H2Z1B1 Canada
India office: 805 Hemkunt House, 8th Floor, Rajendra Place, New Delhi 110008

ISBN: 978-1-4878-1129-7

To find out more about our publications, please visit www.royalcollins.com.

We are grateful for the financial assistance of the Information Office of Nanjing City and the Information Office of Jiangsu Province in the publication of this book.

Contents

Chapter 11: In the Misty Drizzle
Amid the misty drizzle, 480 temples rose one after another in the Southern Dynasty. This is the stronghold of foreign culture and the breeding ground of new culture. There are as many mysteries and stories that enchant later generations as there are evening drums and morning bells.

Chapter 12: Riding a Crane in Yangzhou
Yangzhou is in the south of the Yangtze River, not in the north. This Yangzhou is not the Yangzhou we know. How much glory of the past is gathered in the city? We sigh that the present and the past are so alike.

Chapter 13: High Pavilion Facing the River
Waguan Temple, from the Six Dynasties to the Southern Tang Dynasty, has always been the center of the Phoenix Terrace. The tall pavilion, which faces the river, was a landmark building back then. What happened? "The Yangtze River flows alone."

Chapter 14: Fine Alcohol of Jinling
Nanjing has the fragrance of both books and wine. The tomb of Ruan Ji, the tavern of Sun Chu, the revelry of wine immortals, and the beautiful legend of Xinhua Village are all full of the fragrance of wine.

Chapter 15: Count the Falling Petals
A stubborn and lonely old man once grew up here, once rose from here, once showed his late-year romantic feelings here, and finally died of old age here. His name is Wang Anshi.

Chapter 16: Autumn Leaves at Banshan
One leaf's falling tells the coming of autumn. The autumn in the Banshan Garden is poetic and legendary. One that resides elsewhere finally returns to his native land. Banshan has a perfect home, that is, Nanjing. Banshan is his poetics and aesthetics.

Chapter 17: Love in Jinling
Dream of the Red Chamber mourns the wealthy. *The Unofficial History of the Scholars* satirizes the world and pity talents. These are two stories about the city. Open the pages of *The Unofficial History of the Scholars* and read the heart of Wu Jingzi. Cold and warm, spring and autumn. How does he write about the city?

Chapter 18: The Elegance of the Literary Celebrities

A true literary celebrity is naturally distinguished and admirable. Certainly, Wu Jingzi is one, and there are many true literary celebrities among his friends. This is how the city and these celebrities have complimented each other.

Chapter 19: Free and Content

Sui Garden comes from Sui garden. One "foot" less, the meaning is so different. Yuan Mei, who claimed to come from the same place as Su Xiaoxiao of Qiantang, had chosen to settle in Nanjing long ago because of the Sui Garden there. In fact, in addition to the Sui Garden, there was the Six Dynasties as well.

Chapter 20: Obsessed with the Dream

A dream should cause a quarrel between two old friends only because Li Xiangjun, a famous prostitute in Qinhuai, was involved. Who on earth was obsessed?

Chapter 21: Through Common Eyes

After the Taiping Rebellion, western culture invaded. *The Dianshizhai Pictorial* took photos for the prostitutes in Nanjing in the late Qing Dynasty. Inside and outside the river houses, people were bustling, not all elegant.

Chapter 22: Wine Lover

Mr. Huang Jigang jokingly summarized his life in Nanjing as "indulged in dissipation." Through the wine cup, we can see the life of a generation of scholars and their innermost feelings.

Chapter 23: The Distinguished and Admirable Wang Bohang

Hangxie is the evening mist. Wang Xie was styled Bohang. As his name suggests, the old man is erudite and elegant. He had a legendary life and unyielding pride.

Ancient Swallows

Swallows are ancient birds. They have existed since before the Shang Dynasties.

The Book of Poetry: The Sacrificial Odes of Shang mentions a sacred beginning when the Shang Dynasty rose. "By Heaven sent down, the swallow came to earth, and gave to our great Xie his mystic birth." It is linked with the mystic birth. Swallows are black and named after their appearance. Their name is naturally simple. However, being able to shoulder the mission of heaven shows that they differ from ordinary birds after all. In fact, in the classical Chinese literature, they have another noble alias, *tian nü* (heavenly maid), but it seems less well known.

The poet Shen Quanqi in the Tang Dynasty wrote *Two Petrels Came and Made a Home on the Fancy Beams* and a poem of Su Dongpo in the Song Dynasty says *Fledgling Swallows Fly into a Mansion,* as if a swallow is snobbish. In fact, it does not despise the poor and curry favor with the rich, is neither reserved nor high maintenance. Often, it is used to the company of swallows. "How can a swallow know the will of a swan?" In the eyes of Chen Sheng, a hero at the end of the Qin Dynasty, his companions who only farmed for others and believed that selling their labor was their duty were comparable to swallows, who do not have the great ambition of flying around the world, nor the ability of eagles and falcons to soar high. They live by people and get along with each other like guests. On the fancy beams in a mansion, a family of swallows get by. Leading a peaceful life, they are happy birds. "Unwilling to compete with eagles and falcons." If insipidity can be exchanged for a lifetime of peace and tranquility, it is worth it.

However, life is merciless, and times change. "We can't always get what we want." Anything can happen suddenly and change it all. This is the destiny of human beings, and swallows cannot escape it either. In such a time and world, this little bird can only accept the ups and downs of life. During the past five thousand years, one dynasty after another has risen and fallen, leaving tears and shouts.

In Nanjing, I once heard the orioles sing at dawn.
In Nanjing, I once saw the flowers bloom early on.
Who would have known that too soon was it all gone?
I witnessed him rise, prosper, and fall.

Only the swallows persist. They fly away in autumn and return in spring. It keeps on as the dynasties rise and fall. Inadvertently, they have become a witness to the vicissitudes of life. It seems to be far-sighted and prophetic, but in fact it is involuntary.

Between spring and autumn, between south and north, swallows fly, but no one can tell whether they are from the south or the north. There are so-called Hu swallow and Yue swallow in ancient Chinese documents. Their difference is not understood. It is only known that Hu means the north while Yue the south, like *Jiangnan* and *Saibei*, which are far apart. Perhaps swallows are both from the south and the north, and have seen both the southern spring drizzle and the northern autumn gale.

This is nothing because swallows are not the only birds that can travel between spring and autumn and between south and north. What distinguishes the swallows is that they can connect ancient and modern times poetically.

Where once the swallows knew the mansions of the great,
they now to humbler homes would fly to nest and mate.

From the mansions of Wang's and Xie's back then, they flew into the humble abodes of the ordinary people today. It is not so much old as it is new; it is not so much that every swallow that flies away in autumn is old, but that every spring that returns is new—it brings new days and new hope.

> The poet grows old while Yingying stays young,
> he dies but in the swallow tower she lives on.

It is uncertain that since when swallows imply something amorous. Su Dongpo wrote:

> The swallow tower is empty,
> the beauty is gone,
> but the swallows stay.

It is full of temptation and reverie. In addition to Su Dongpo, it seems that all the literati appreciate this kind of vibe. And in addition to the ancient times, today, there are still a lot of people willing to immerse themselves in this vibe. They enjoy the traces of antiquity and elegance in this vibe.

There is a shocking and meaningful legend in *Xuan Guai Lu*. In the spring of the ninth year of the Dali Period (AD 766–799) of Tang Dynasty, someone dedicated a poem to Yuan Zai, the prime minister. Yuan was on his way to the court and had no time to read it. The man couldn't wait, so he simply recited it:

> In the old residence in the east and the west of the city,
> petals dance in the air.
> A petrel wants to build a nest,
> but flies away despite the empty room is.

When the recitation ended, the person disappeared. Soon, Yuan Zai was defeated, and his wife was killed. This tragic end for them confirmed the prophecy in the poem. It turned out that the petrel in the poem came to warn Yuan Zai. There are too many similar legends about swallows. Liu Yuxi's poem has been interpreted into a legend of kingdom of swallows— *The Nobles: The Wind Blows into the Kingdom of Swallows*, which is quite fascinating.

To me, the city of Nanjing is like a swallow, one that has flown from old times to today, one that has flown from yesterday and will fly to tomorrow. It has endured thousands of years of thick and thin. I was once invited to write a few words for Nanjing's urban planning and image promotion. Here is the verse:

The towering Zijin Mountain, leave us in awe;
The broad river and sky, encourage new swallows to soar high.

The next sentence alludes to Swallow Rock, which stands on the bank of the Yangtze River, wings spread, about to soar. The so-called new swallows are actually rather old. Looking afar, do you feel the connection between the past and the present?

The ancient Chinese often quoted swallows whispering in poetry, and there are countless stories where swallows can speak. If they really could, what would they say?

Despite the absence of traces of my wings in the sky, I have flown.

ANCIENT
SWALLOWS

Chapter 1

The Qi of an Emperor in Nanjing

Wang Jun's grand warship sailed eastward away from Yizhou,
dimming the magnificent Qi of an Emperor in Jinling.*
The fire melted hundreds of meters of iron locks,
sinking them to the river bottom,
and as a flag of surrender was hoisted in the Rock City,
the Eastern Wu army was defeated.
Too many past stories sadden us,
but Xisai Mountain stands still behind the Yangtze river.
Today the nation has been united and old barriers have become ruins,
but reeds still wave in the autumn wind.

—LIU YUXI, *Nostalgic in Xisai Mountain*

Qi (also spelled chi, meaning vital energy in Traditional Chinese Medicine) is righteousness.

Everything in this world has qi. Flowers have the qi of aroma, warriors have the qi of courage, orators are full of the qi of righteousness, and passionate talents often feel the qi of sadness. Yin, yang, wind, rain, darkness, and brightness are the six qi of the universe; "Because of the qi of land, oranges become trifoliate oranges when they are transplanted north of

---

*Jinling is the ancient name of Nanjing. The Qi of an Emperor is an auspicious aura or atmosphere befitting of an emperor in Jinling.

the Huai River, the mynah birds never fly across the Ji River, and martens die if they cross the Wen River." The qi of land promotes the variation of plants and even determines the life and death of animals. It is a classical generalization of the regional cultural ecology, isn't it?

Qi is present in every city. The older the city, the stronger is its qi. This qi is nothing but a city's unique cultural ecology. And the qi of Jinling, an ancient capital, is the qi of an emperor. Nanjing has swaggered in Chinese history for more than a thousand years with a prestigious royal emotion. It is both the glory and tragedy of this city. It does not matter whether it wins or loses. After the vicissitudes of time, the legend of Nanjing is long. However, it is known to all that Nanjing is neither the earliest nor the ancient capital with the most longevity. There is Chang'an in the west, Dadu in the north, and Bianluo in the central. Where does Nanjing get the audacity to claim the possession of the qi of an emperor?

The expression "qi of an emperor" was created as early as the Western Han and Eastern Han Dynasties. Still, it was not until the Six Dynasties Period that it became associated with Nanjing. The Six Dynasties were prosperous like a dream, and there were various interpretations of Nanjing's qi of an emperor. People in this dream couldn't help but immerse themselves in the royal atmosphere. When this grand dream was about to end, Yu Xin wandered about to the north, destitute. Looking back at the Southern Dynasty, recalling the collapse of the Xiaoliang regime after Hou Jing's rebellion, he couldn't help sighing: "Is the three-hundred-year-old qi of an emperor going to die south of Yangtze River?"

Yu Xin only gave an approximation. In fact, it has been more than three hundred years.

In the 16th year of the Jian'an Regin (AD 211), Sun Quan relocated his political center from Jingkou (now Zhenjiang in Jiangsu Province) to Moling. The following year, the famous rock city was built on the bank of Qinghuai River in the west of Nanjing, and Moling changed its name to Jianye to exhibit its determination to accomplish greatness there. Allegedly, Sun Quan's major move was based on the advice of Zhang Hong, his senior assistant. Zhang Hong was a native of Guangling, present-day Yangzhou in Jiangsu Province. He once studied the *Five Classics* in the Imperial College in the capital Luoyang, and was one of the few learned scholars in the State of Wu at the time. Chen Lin, his fellow countryman and one of the

Seven Scholars of Jian'an, admired him deeply and always felt dwarfed in his presence. The relocation of the political center was too important to be taken lightly. Zhang Hong was adamant, and his reason was nothing but the fact that Moling has the qi of an emperor.

In the Six Dynasties historical record *Biography of Jiang Biao*, it is written that King Wu of Chu built the city of Jinling as early as the Warring States Period. With hills dotted around, it was connected to the Rock City. According to the legends, when Qin Shi Huang, the first emperor of the Qin Dynasty, made an inspection tour to Kuaiji in the east, he crossed the north of the Yangtze River and passed through Jinling. Those who believed the idea of the qi of an emperor reported to him that the terrain of Jinling radiated the atmosphere of an emperor's capital, which greatly vexed him, who was determined to keep the Qin Dynasty eternally prosperous. Therefore, he ordered to break up the continuous hills, thus destroying its fengshui, and changed its name from Jinling to Moling as his denunciation. From the precious *jin* (gold) to *mo* (fodder for the horses), all the mystery and nobility of the original name are gone. He believed that the qi of an emperor there would vanish and his regime's hidden dangers, but the result was disappointing. At least Zhang Hong disagreed that his attempt to remove it was successful but insisted that it radiated royalty, thus making it the first-choice location to build a capital. Sun Quan seconded that what Zhang Hong said made sense, but this was such an important decision that he had to be cautious. Therefore, he hesitated. Surprisingly, what prompted Sun Quan to make up his mind at last might have been a remark from a foreign guest. Liu Bei happened to be in the east of the Yangtze River at that time. I am uncertain of the purpose of his trip. Was it to be the beloved son-in-law of the emperor's mother of the Wu State or to negotiate an alliance against Cao Cao? Regardless, when he passed Moling, he climbed the hills, observed its topography, and realized that it radiated an extraordinary royal sensation, perfect as a capital. Therefore, he selflessly suggested Sun Quan relocate his political center to this place. Then, Sun Quan replied to Liu Bei, "Great minds think alike."

In the written documents I have seen, Zhang Hong's and Liu Bei's reasons are undoubtedly fair. Perhaps Zhang Hong's opinion is biased. Moling was close to Guangling so it would at least be much more convenient for the return to his hometown. But this was just his private matter. Even if he ever considered it, it was never wise to express it publicly. On the table and under the table are different, and there should be a distinction between public and private, of which Zhang Hong was well aware, let alone the shrewd statesman Liu Bei. Anyone with a discerning eye could see that should Sun Quan have taken Moling in the lower reaches of the Yangtze River as his political center and concentrated his resources to expand to the east of the Yangtze River, there would have been greater benefits to Liu Bei. Should he have built his center in Wuhu or Wuchang in the middle reaches of the Yangtze River, the friction with West Shu would have inevitably increased. Those who know the history of the Three Kingdoms well should also remember that in AD 221, Sun Quan relocated his capital to Hubei and changed its name to Wuchang precisely because of the strategic need to compete with West Shu for Jingzhou. Indeed, none of this was documented, and Liu Bei wouldn't admit it. He was willing to tell the moving stories only in the *Biography of Jiang Biao*.

With thorough investigation, it was found that there was no King Wu in the state of Chu during the Warring States Period. The King Wu of Chu in the *Biography of Jiang Biao* was the disguise of King Wei of Chu. In the past, Xiong Shang, the highly successful King Wei of Chu, destroyed the state of Yue and incorporated Jinling into Chu's territory. He built a city in the spot of today's Rock City and named it Jinling City after Jinling Mountain (Zhongshan Mountain). However, some people believe that it was called Jinling (golden tombs) because it connected the mausoleums of Huayang and Jintan. Such different opinions have existed since the Tang Dynasty. In the heyday of the Tang Dynasty, both views were mentioned in *Records of Jiankang* by Xu Song. Certainly, the name of Jinling Mountain may also come from the fact that it connected the mausoleums of Huayang and Jintan. These two views are not incompatible. And it doesn't matter which is correct. What matters is that Jinling was just an ordinary place name at first, and at first people had a superficial understanding of it. Later, many literary and non-literary imaginative interpretations were added to it.

As the imagination was unwrapped, there lies the core, the so-called qi of an emperor. According to legend, more than 100 years before Qin Shi Huang, the first emperor of the Qin Dynasty, King Wei of Chu heard from alchemists that there was such qi in Jinling, so he rode to search for it and found it on Zhongshan Mountain (allegedly in Jinling Ridge at the western foot of Mufu Mountain). Immediately, a pair of gold figurines were cast and buried in the ground to suppress the qi of an emperor. This is a story about the origin of Jinling Mountain and Jinling Ridge. Allegedly, a stone slab was seen on Jinling Ridge in the Northern Song Dynasty. And there was an inscription: "Not in front of the mountain, not behind, not in the south, not in the north, whoever gets it becomes as wealthy as a state." This immense wealth drove many people crazy. They dug all over the mountains and fields and found nothing but that they had been fooled by King Wei of Chu and perhaps Qin Shi Huang, too. Zhou Yinghe, a Song Dynasty writer who authored *Truth of Jinling*, called the buried gold a total fabrication. Now it seems that his words are valid. After all, this turns out to be just another story made up by the curious.

In other documents, it was not King Wei of Chu but Qin Shi Huang who buried gold to suppress the qi of an emperor. Perhaps it makes more sense that the Qin Shi Huang was indeed the gold burier because he was believed to be more paranoid than King Wei of Chu. But since the Song Dynasty, this idea has continued to be questioned. It is not uncommon that ancient emperors offered treasures such as gold and jade to the mountains and rivers for their blessings, either buried in mountains or sunk in rivers. In the 28th year of his reign (219 BC), the Qin Shi Huang buried jade in Maoshan Mountain and sunk jade in Jianghan to worship the gods of mountains and rivers. Liu Xiu, Emperor Guangwu of the Eastern Han Dynasty, also buried gold and jade on the peak of Maoshan Mountain. This history somehow makes it more believable that King Wei of Chu or Qin Shi Huang buried gold in Jinling. But it is doubtful that they did that to suppress the qi of an emperor.

Compared with the burial of gold by King Wei of Chu, the story of Qin Shi Huang digging the Qinhuai River is more widespread. *Records of Jiankang* gives a more detailed account of the story than the *Biography of Jiang Biao*. The time was the 36th year of his reign (211 BC), but it was likely to be the 37th (210 BC); it took place in Jiangcheng, along the Yangtze River in Qixia Town, Nanjing; The qi-tellers asserted more confidently: "Five hundred years later, Jinling will have the qi of an emperor." Therefore, Qin Shi Huang ordered the excavation of the Qinhuai River to cut off the earth's energy and weaken the qi of an emperor. However, Xu Song was well aware such a folk belief was never to be taken seriously, so he added a brief note to explain the actual name of the Qinhuai River and express his doubts: the actual name of the Qinhuai River was Longcangpu (meaning a river bank where a dragon resides). Although this name suggests nothing auspicious like Hetu Luoshu (mystical diagrams symbolic of the universe and believed in myth to be related to the origins of writing), it sounds extraordinary. However, it is a pity that this dragon is no real dragon, but probably just a kind of Chinese alligator common in the local area before the Middle Ages. As for the qi of an emperor in Jinling, both the *Records of Jiankang* and the *Biography of Jiangbiao* quoted old legends without confirming their authenticity. Therefore, it is unfair to call Xu Song unromantic. Even the author of the *Biography of Jiangbiao* and historian Pei Songzhi who quoted it did not believe it.

Nonetheless, this river, which used to be called the Huai River in ancient times, was renamed Qinhuai then, suggesting the legend's significant influence. The more dynasties that have passed, the more stories and the more intricate the stories. One bit of folklore in Nanjing about Fang (square) Mountain in the Jiangning District is also related to this legend. The shape of this mountain is square, like a square seal. One day, the Jade Emperor (the Supreme Deity of Taoism) was idle and bored, playing with a golden seal, but he accidentally dropped it in the mortals' world, and it became this mountain. The locals therefore also call it Tianyin (heaven's seal) Mountain. It was said that most of the land on the mountain has black soil, and only the earth around its foot is red because it is the residual red ink paste at the bottom of the seal. This story is probably made up based on the theory of the qi of an emperor. However, the fabrication must be more recent. When Zhang Dunyi of the Southern Song Dynasty wrote *Stories of the Six Dynasties*, the name Tianyin Mountain was mentioned in the *Legend of Danyang* by Shan Qian of the Southern Dynasty. And the story of the Jade Emperor was believed not to have been made up at that time.

The key to the widespread story where Qin Shi Huang ordered the Qinhuai River to be dug and weaken the qi of an emperor is that it is both half true and half false. Despite the total absence of evidence, there is a reason for its occurrence.

The eastern inspection tour of Qin Shi Huang, recorded in the *Historical Records* and *The Book of Han*, is no stranger to those with a smattering knowledge of Chinese history. The concept of qi-telling has a long history.

Qi-telling is accomplished through observing the qi of clouds and analyzing the social situation, predicting good and bad luck. At first, this was just a military technique for fighting the enemy in actual combat. In *Mozi: To Fight the Enemy*, it is written that qi-telling foresees the qi of a great warrior, the qi of a junior warrior, the qi of the past, the qi of the future, and the qi of a defeat. Those who have mastered it can tell the end. And the prophecy based on the weather for warfare, recorded in *Tong Dian*, probably retains the fashion of qi-telling. At the latest in the early Han Dynasty, alchemists who liked to predict the future transformed qi-telling into practical political magic and a piece of new knowledge in the field of ideology. There, groups of political adventurers found abundant gambling capital.

Xin Yuanping was one of the adventurers. In the 15th year of the Emperor Wen of the Han Dynasty (165 BC), Xin visited Emperor Wen as a qi-teller. He claimed to have discovered that "there is heavenly five-colored qi like a crown in the northeast of Chang'an." He said that the northeast was the house of the gods, and the west their tomb. And the qi is an auspicious omen sent from above. "It is wise to set up a temple to worship the Gods." He persuaded the emperor to set up the Weiyang Temple of the Five Emperors. He predicted that a Zhou *ding* (ancient vessel with two loop handles and three or four legs), jade, and other auspicious omens would appear. Emperor Wen, having always been relatively humble and less ambitious for greatness, was fearful after hearing those provocative words. He did not dare to go against the will of God and built the Temple of the Five Emperors in Weicheng. In the same temple, each emperor occupied a hall of different colors. One year later, the pious emperor personally visited this temple to worship the gods. And Xin Yuanping suddenly became the star official for the emperor, was promoted, and rewarded with abundant wealth. One year later, Xin secretly assigned his minion to offer a jade cup to the emperor and claim it to be dug from the ground. Before his minion came, he reported to the emperor in advance: "I have a hunch that the qi of a precious jade is coming towards the palace."

In a short while, the minion presented the jade cup, engraved with "Long live the master." This consolidated people's belief in him as a prophet. He continued his scam while the iron was hot and predicted that the sun would return to the sky. Soon, the setting sun slowly climbed back and hung high in the sky. The emperor was elated and issued an edict to change the

17th year of his reign as the first, known in history as the first year of the Houyuan Reign. Meanwhile, the emperor ordered the nation to celebrate with the people by holding a big banquet. Xin Yuanping struck another time, "Hundreds of years ago, a *ding* in the Zhou Dynasty sank in the Sihe River. Qin Shi Huang sent thousands of people to dive to recover it, but they failed. The Yellow River, which is connected to the Sihe River, is now flooding. It is a rare opportunity to find it. I have noticed steaming golden qi of treasure northeast of Fenyin. It is a sign that the *ding* of the Zhou Dynasty is coming out. We should send people for it before the chance slips away."

The emperor immediately sent messengers to build a temple south of Fenyin and performed a ritual along the river, waiting for the *ding* of the Zhou Dynasty to surface. At this time, a letter was submitted to the emperor, reporting that everything Xin said was a lie. All his deceitful tricks were exposed. He was soon arrested and imprisoned, sentenced to death, and implicated in the deaths of his three clans. After this nonsense, Emperor Wen of the Han Dynasty became more indifferent to mythical matters and even got sick of them. Although he appointed special personnel to host a worship at the Temple of Five Emperors in Weiyang and Changmen on time, he never personally attended the ritual there again.

Since Xin Yuanping claimed to be able to see the qi of the gods, jade, and gold, the qi of an emperor was certainly no exception. Although *The Records of the Grand Historian* and *The Book of Han* did not mention the so-called qi of an emperor, it would not take long for this idea to take shape. As expected, during the Eastern Han Dynasty and Western Han Dynasty, when the fight for the throne in the Central Plains began, a qi-teller Liu Xiujin claimed that there was the qi of joy in his hometown Chongling (now Zaoyang, Hubei Province). Upon closer inspection, he realized it was the "glorious qi of an emperor."

And the idea of breaking the mountains to weaken the qi of an emperor was rather popular during the Qin and Han Dynasties. General Meng Tian defended the frontier for Qin Shi Huang and made outstanding contributions. Still, in the end, he died unjustly at the hands of Qin Er Shi and Zhao Gao. In the eyes of later generations, the first merit of Meng Tian must be that he commanded the construction of the Great Wall. People at that time believed that this was not a feat but a crime: "From Lintao to Liaodong, the Great Wall extends ten thousand *li* long and breaks the veins of the earth. This is Meng Tian's crime." (*The Records of the Grand Historian, Biography of Meng Tian*). Since the construction of the Great Wall hurts the veins of the earth, it is no wonder that digging a river eliminates the qi of an emperor.

In addition, Qin Shi Huang was stubborn and perverse. It is written in *The Records of the Grand Historian: Basic Annals of the First Emperor of Qin* that in the 28th year of his reign (219 BC), he made an inspection tour to the south, sailed along the river to the Xiangshan Temple, and was almost unable to cross the river due to a gale. He believed it was Xiang, the god of Xiang water, who deliberately opposed him and flew into a rage. He immediately sent "three thousand prisoners to cut down all the trees of Xiangshan Mountain, stripping it naked" to retaliate against Xiang. He was so small-minded that he could easily lash out on such a trivial matter. When it comes to the qi of an emperor in Jinling, it is no surprise that he was more outraged. Beautiful legends can always accurately reflect the characters' personality, specifically grasp the environment and atmosphere of the times, exude a special charm, convey a unique cultural meaning, and make people believe that there is something and be unable to stop.

Beautiful as a legend is, it is merely a legend. Frankly, artificial rivers in Nanjing and its suburbs are expected, including Xu Creek (also known as Zhong River and Lishui, connecting Lake Taihu and Lake Gucheng) in the Wu State during the Spring and Autumn Period, Yundu River (connecting Qinhuai River and Lake Gucheng) excavated by the Kingdom of Wu of the Three Kingdoms, Chao Ditch, Qing Creek (also known as East Canal), Shangxin River, Zhongxin River, and Xiaxin River excavated in the early Ming Dynasty, and Yanzhi River in Lishui (in the west of Lishui District, connecting Lake Shijiu and Qinhuai River). The new rivers in Qinhuai from 1976 to 1980 were all excavated manually, either for the convenience of transportation or for urban flood control and other safety considerations. The purpose of building them was clear and realistic, so that the construction could continue from ancient times to the present. Unfortunately, the Qinhuai River does not belong to this category. In the eyes of the nosey, this is depressing.

Since the Tang Dynasty, more and more people have realized that. People peel off the beautiful appearance of historical legends and accept scientific, rational, and simple conclusions. As early as ancient times, the Qinhuai River has been a tributary of the Yangtze River and the largest river in Nanjing. It has two sources, the north source at the southern foot of Jurong Baohua Mountain, called Jurong River, and the south head at Donglu Mountain in Lishui, called Lishui River. The two rivers converge in Northwest Village in Square Mountain Dam of Jiangning District and zigzag into the urban area of Nanjing.

At Jiulong Bridge outside Tongji Gate, the Qinghuai River is divided into two branches: inner and outer. The inner Qinhuai River flows westward, enters the city from Dongshuiguan, passes through the southern part of the urban area, joins the water flow of the Wucheng Moat in Wudaiyang, and runs westward further to the Huaiqing Bridge, where it meets the southward Qing Creek, heads westward through Lishe Bridge, Wende Bridge, Wuding Bridge, Zhenhuai Bridge, New Bridge, Shangfu Bridge, Xiafu Bridge, and eventually exits Xishuiguan to converge with the Outer Qinhuai River.

After crossing the Jiulong Bridge, the Outer Qinhuai River flows south and westward, passing under the Changgan Bridge, and splits into two branches at the Saihong Bridge. Its main stream keeps heading northwards, joins with the Inner Qinhuai River, passes through Rock City, and finally enters the Yangtze River from the Sancha River; its tributary turns westward, passes Jiangdong Bridge, and at last joins the Yangtze River from Beihekou. Whether inside or outside the city, the Qinhuai River zigzags, running up and down, following the natural flow without any trace of artificial excavation. From the *Records of Jiankang* of the Tang Dynasty to the *New Records of Jinling* in the Yuan Dynasty, it is widely documented that Qin Shi Huang opened 30 *li* of Dujiangtushan west of Square Mountain, and the river channel of Shijiao Mountain also was dug under his order, which, of course, are nonsense. The Qinhuai River flows through three counties and one city, with a total length that exceeds 100 kilometers and a drainage area of more than 2,600 square kilometers.

As early as the Stone Age, human footprints have been left in the Qinhuai River Basin. There were primitive villages along the river. Fifty or sixty villages have been excavated, including the famous Hushu Cultural Site and Yinzishan Site, which prove that the Qinhuai River existed long ago.

Otherwise, it would have been difficult for the ancestors to survive far away from the water source.

How early? Geologist Li Siguang gave us the answer. In 1935, after years of field investigation and rigorous research, he published *The Geology of the Ningzhen Mountains*. This famous book mentioned that about 100 million years ago, the "Yanshan Movement," a crustal movement represented by Yanshan in Hebei, extensively affected the eastern region of China and caused the crust in Nanjing to rise and strongly fracture, thus forming Ningzhen Mountains and other significant peaks. About ten million years ago, the crust of the Nanjing area was elevated, and the surface was eroded by flowing water. The Nanjing section of the Yangtze River, Qinhuai River, Chu River, and other rivers developed during this period. Ten million years ago, how very distant! Qin Shi Huang had grand ambitions, and the curious had such rich imaginations that they linked the Qinhuai River with the Qin Dynasty.

Where there is smoke, there is fire. The emergence of each legend has its background. So, how did the idea of qi of an emperor in Jinling come to be?

Fundamentally, this was out of the actual political needs of the Kingdom of Wu to build its capital in Nanjing. The earliest historical documents that corroborate this statement include the *Biography of Jiang Biao* by Yu Pu, *Records of Danyang* by Shan Qianzhi, *Autumn of Jinyang* by Sun Sheng, and *The Northern Expedition* by Fu Tao. All were written during the Six Dynasties. And they do not seem so sure of such a political need; in terms of time, none was made earlier than the Three Kingdoms.

It remains a mystery that when Chen Shou of the Western Jin Dynasty authored the biography of Zhang Hong in the *Records of the Three Kingdoms*, why he only recorded that Zhang Hong suggested that Sun Quan should build the capital in Moling without explaining the specific reasons. Such a critical suggestion should be detailed. Could it be that Chen Shou suspected that the statement in the *Biography of Jiang Biao* was nothing but rumors and untruths often found in miscellaneous unofficial histories? Maybe. But at least this argument existed in the Three Kingdoms Period.

Political moves such as qi-telling have been performed continuously in the history of the Three Kingdoms. In AD 220, Cao Pi took the throne and changed the reign title to Huangchu; the following year, Liu Bei proclaimed himself Emperor of Shu and changed the reign title to Zhangwu. When Sun

Quan heard the news, he was deeply tempted. "Teach your child to behave like Sun Quan." Experienced and astute, he first recruited an astrologer to find out the situation of the stars above the Kingdom of Wu. Indeed, it was his move to make up excuses for his proclamation to be the emperor and usurp the throne. In the spring of AD 229, Sun Quan put on the emperor's dragon robe in Wuchang after years of keeping a low profile. In the autumn of that year, he came back to Jianye and set up the capital here.

Observing the stars was actually to check whether there was the qi of an emperor. People at that time believed that they could see it from the stars. Allegedly, when the Jin Kingdom did not stabilize the political situation of the Kingdom of Wu, there was a purple qi among the stars of Wu, and the qi-tellers asserted that Wu was in a prosperous state, and a southern expedition might end in failure. The court and commoners of the Jin Kingdom expressed noisy comments, and those in power could not help but feel a tad uncertain. Only Zhang Hua was adamant about sending troops to fight the Kingdom of Wu. After Wu was defeated, people found that the purple qi among the stars stayed and became more and more prominent. They still suspect its authenticity. Zhang Hua found that Lei Huan, a native of Yuzhang, was adept at astrology, so he hired him and finally located the real reason. It turns out that this auspicious qi was no qi of an emperor of Wu but the light of the two swords of Longquan and Tai'e buried in Fengcheng, Yuzhang City. "The light from the heavenly treasure shines directly at the stars." This famous quote from *Preface to the Pavilion of Prince Teng* by Wang Bo refers to the story above recorded in *The Book of Jin: Biography of Zhang Hua*.

The Book of Jin extensively records anecdotes, and the story above is one of them. Zhang Hua, a knowledgeable scholar, did not believe in the purple qi, but there were flocks of people who did in the Six Dynasties Period. To win Jingzhou and dominate the upper reaches of the Yangtze River, Sun Quan once moved the capital to Wuchang. Later, he was strongly opposed, especially by the Wu family in Jiangdong, and moved back to Jianye. Sun Hao, Sun Quan's grandson, also played the trick of relocating the capital. According to the *Annotations to Records of the Three Kingdoms* to the *Records of the Three Kingdoms*, *The Book of Wu*, and *Biographies of the Three Heirs*, he did that to avoid the qi of an emperor. At that time, qi-tellers reported that Jingzhou had the qi of an emperor, and it would pierce Yangzhou, which was especially a threat for Sun Hao, the king of Wu, who resided in Jianye Palace. Sun Hao relocated the capital to Wuchang while sending minions to destroy the graves of the ministers and famous families connected to the hills in Jingzhou, in order to suppress the qi of an emperor. At this time, the bandit Shi Dan gathered thousands of people in a rebellion and attacked Jianye. Sun Hao was complacent when he heard the news and immediately sent hundreds of elite soldiers from Jingzhou to attack Jianye, claiming they were coming after Yangzhou. At this time, Sun Hao was the number one believer of the qi of an emperor.

The last monarch of Wu was vain, arrogant, self-righteous, paranoid, and timid. He was suspicious of honorable officials and famous generals. Once, Sun Hao heard a folk rumor that the tomb of general Gan Ning in the northeast of Jiankang had the qi of an emperor. Immediately, he ordered the tomb be dug to destroy its fengshui and let out the qi of an emperor. As a result, a canal with a width of five *zhang* and a depth of one *zhang* (about 3.3 meters) was made, called Zhidu. In AD 271, a political swindler named Diao Xuan made up the lie that "imperial clouds were seen in the southeast, suggesting a new king would rise and rule Jingzhou and Yangzhou." This was not a novel lie.

Nearly fifty years before, when Chen Hua, a Minister of the Imperial Household from the State of Wu, visited Wei as an envoy, he mentioned to Emperor Wen of Wei the old saying of "Imperial clouds in the southeast" and quoted the idea that emperors rise in the east from *The Book of Changes*. Consequently, he won the political and diplomatic initiative and safeguarded the interests of his country. This kind of argument, at best, was just political propaganda that could cheer the people up and lift morale. It is never actual strength. Indeed, Sun Quan was happy to believe it, but he didn't get carried away. However, Sun Hao was bewitched and got carried away. He took his mother, wife, and harem along with thousands of people from Niuzhu to the west along the land road, claiming that he intended to fulfill the destiny of "Entering Luoyang in an imperial carriage." Caught in a snowstorm on the way, they were stuck, cold, and starving. The road became slippery, and even the horses refused to move. This almost triggered a soldier mutiny. This kind of self-deceptive trick did not change Sun Hao's fate to be given a lower title of nobility but has left a topic of conversation for future generations. Over 600 years later, when the poet Wen Tingjun passed by the Mausoleum of Emperor Jing of Wu, he was emotional:

> The qi of an emperor was released,
> yet talent and destiny hardly get along.
> Three thousand *li* of the Canal Zhidu was dug,
> yet his imperial carriage never made it to Luoyang.
> —*Crossing the Mausoleum of Emperor Jing of Wu*

Wu perished, and so did the purple qi among the stars, but not the qi of an emperor in the south of Yangtze River. After the Western Jin Dynasty, the idea of the qi of an emperor and its variations keep emerging one after another. During the Tai'an Period (AD 302–304) of the Western Jin Dynasty, there was a popular nursery rhyme: "Five horses cross the river, and one turns into a dragon." This "one turns into a dragon" was believed to be Emperor Yuan of Jin's rise to the throne as a variation of the qi of an emperor. In the first year (483) of the Yongming Period in the reign of Emperor Wu of Southern Qi, some qi-tellers stated that there was the qi of an emperor in Xinlin, Louhu, and Qingxi areas of Nanjing. So, Emperor Wu ordered the building of palaces in these locations and made several inspection visits there so that this qi never leaked. And he restored the old palace in Qingxi to eliminate this qi. In the eyes of Emperor Wu, the qi of an emperor was no longer an opinion whose influence needed to be expanded as when the state was newly founded; like Sun Hao, he used it to strengthen internal cohesion and prevent usurpation. It was a sign of his fear. The first was aggressive, while the second was defensive, totally different.

After the Hou Jing Rebellion, Jianye fell into decline. Emperor Yuan of Liang decided to move the capital to Jiangling, which was seconded by the officials from the Chu because, in the old capital of Jianye, the qi of an emperor had been exhausted. At the same time, in the south of Jingzhou, there still was the qi of an emperor. This was almost the time when Yu Xin sighed, "Is the three-hundred-year-old qi of an emperor going to die in the south of the Yangtze River?" More than two hundred years later, when Liu Yuxi came to Xisai Mountain in Daye, Hubei, and when Xu Hun came to Nanjing, it was the tragic history of the Six Dynasties in front of them, and the dying qi of an emperor of Jinling was firmly imprinted in their poems, never to be forgotten.

The music *The Jade Tree and Courtyard Flowers* ended as the qi of an emperor of the Chen Dynasty faded:

When the Sui soldiers gathered in Jingyang palace,
the watchtower of the frontier fortress was emptied.
Under the pine and catalpa trees around the cemetery
were the graves of countless officials in the past dynasties;
tall and short green crops filled the dilapidated palace of the Six Dynasties.
The swallows flew across the clouds. It rained, and the sun came out;
The finless porpoise danced with the waves in the river,
and a chilly wind blew hard at night.
The emperors of the past dynasties were gone forever,
and so was the luxurious imperial life;
only the surrounding green hills remained the same as before.

         —Xu Hun, *Jinling Nostalgia*

History needs to be remembered. Hundreds of years later, the idea of Jinling's qi of an emperor gained popularity again. Allegedly, before Zhu Yuanzhang occupied Jinling, Liu Bowen stood on the bank of the West Lake and saw a five-colored auspicious cloud rising from Jinling. He asserted that it was Jinling's qi of an emperor and that the chosen one he would assist had appeared. This chosen one's subordinates include three famous navy generals: Yu Tonghai, Yu Tongyuan, and Yu Tongyuan. They were heroes like the three Ruan brothers in *Water Margin*. With excellence at water wars, they made outstanding achievements following Zhu Yuanzhang fighting up and down the country. After Zhu Yuanzhang ascended the throne, it was reported there was the qi of an emperor in the house of the Yu brothers in the west of the city. Zhu Yuanzhang at first wanted to send the Yu brothers to a distant exile but adopted Liu Ji's advice to dig a well and erect a monument at the gate of their house, claiming it was to honor their contribution. Still, in fact, it was there to destroy its geographical position. Legend has it that hundreds of cats were engraved around the monument, and they would eat however many *yu* (fish) there were. Also, a bridge was built at the back door of Yu's house to block its back door, a fishing platform was built in the east, and the alley in its west was named Ganyu (chase away the fish) Alley. Some winding alleys surround the residence like an eight-diagram. In short, it aimed to kill all the *yu* (fish).

As Nanjing folklore, it may not be accurate. Still, it reflects the ordinary people's literary understanding of Zhu Yuanzhang's character. Also, it shows how deeply rooted the Jinling qi of an emperor has taken root in the literary and cultural soil of Nanjing.

Chapter 2

A Terrain of Strategic Importance

> Jinling, a terrain of strategic importance, radiates royalty,
> and the prince visited the ancient ruins there.
> The spring breeze warmed the Zhaoyang Palace,
> and the bright moon shone upon the Magpie Tower.
>
> —LI BAI, *The Fourth Song of the Duke of Yong's East Tour*

In the Three Kingdoms Period, Liu Bei accredited Zhuge Liang to Jiangdong (the eastern area of the Changjiang River). Facing the undulating hills of Moling, Zhuge Liang couldn't help but sigh: "With Zijin Mountain and Stone City, two strategic terrains of great importance, Moling is absolutely a place of royal feeling!" People can now visit the scenic spot where Zhuge Liang reined in the horses in Qingliangshan Park in the west of Jinling (the ancient name of Nanjing). There are also the remains where he gave the horses water in the nearby Wulongtan Park. Around Qingliang Mountain are Longpanli (dragon alley) and Hujuguan (tiger pass). The newly opened two east and west Nanjing City arteries are also named Longpan Road and Huju Road. Even the beer sold on the street, in addition to Jinling Beer, there is also Dragon and Tiger Beer. For thousands of years, all over China, inside and outside Nanjing City, countless people have been quoting the phrase "a coiling dragon and a crouching tiger" (a terrain of strategic importance). History, reality, legends, and tales have been thoroughly blended here. It is difficult to tell them apart. Stories of Zhuge Liang spread like wildfire among the people, becoming an appealing conversation topic over a cup of tea. Jiao Hong, the top scholar of the seventeenth year (1589) of the Wanli Period in the Ming Dynasty, was a scholar from this city. He also spread the legend of a coiling dragon and a crouching tiger. As he died centuries ago, we can never tell whether he genuinely believed it or whether the bias for his hometown clouded his judgment. Regardless, there is one alley named after him for us to ponder the past.

The first account of the dragon and tiger legend may be *Records of Wu* by Zhang Bo. This southern scholar was much less well-known than Zhuge Liang, the Prime Minister of Shu. You should know his brothers, Zhang Jiying, who quit the government and returned to his hometown of Wuzhong as the autumn breeze reminded him of the local stewed bass with a water shield (a local dish), and Zhang Han, who exclaimed that "A drink right away is better than the fame that comes later," you might feel less a stranger to him. They lived at about the same time as the two brothers Lu Ji and Lu Yun, which was decades after the separation of the Three Kingdoms. In studying Confucian classics, scholars of the Gongyang Sect interpreted the *Spring and Autumn Annals* as the world seen, the world heard, and the rumored world, each one worse than the one before. When Zhang Bo wrote *Records of Wu*, he never personally witnessed many historical events but heard rumors about them, including this anecdote of Zhuge Liang.

It is not uncommon for the various historical books handed down from ancient times in the Three Kingdoms to have different or contradictory records about the same event. When Pei Songzhi, a scholar of the Southern Dynasties, annotated *Records of the Three Kingdoms*, having copiously quoted authoritative works and compared them, he found many discrepancies in the same events. Some stories were inconsistent because they were written during different times, came from various sources of historical materials, or belonged to different genres of official and unofficial histories, written in different narrative styles. The story of Zhuge Liang in the *Records of Wu* differed from both the *Biography of Jiang Biao* and the *Records of the Three Kingdoms*. According to the latter two, Zhuge Liang had never been to Jingkou, let alone Jianye. He was ordered to persuade Sun Quan, which was in Chaisang, Jiujiang, Jiangxi Province of today. The forty-third chapter of *Romance of the Three Kingdoms* was about this mission of his, but of course, it was expected that novelists exaggerate the facts to make the story more appealing.

Liu Bei had been to Jingkou in December of the fifteenth year (AD 210) of Jian'an, intending to borrow Jingzhou from Sun Quan, as recorded in *Records of the Three Kingdoms, Records of Shu, Biography of Liu Bei*, and *The Comprehensive Mirror in Aid of Governance*, Volume 66. On this expedition, he might have passed through Moling and took the opportunity to observe its terrain carefully. He had apparently spoken to Sun Quan. In addition to the *Biography of Jiang Biao*, several other history books record that in the conversation between Sun Quan and Liu Bei, Liu once suggested that Sun should make the capital Moling. However, no sentence suggests Liu Bei ever mentioned a coiling dragon and a crouching tiger.

It is a well-known idea that dragons and tigers, especially dragons, are the exclusive royal symbols—In *The Book of Changes: Qian Hexagram* it is written that for the hexagram 9–5, a dragon flies in the sky, and a great man is coming. This is an extraordinary omen for the rise of an emperor. In *The Book of the Later Han: Biography of Emperor Guangwu*, Geng Chun, a founding hero of the Eastern Han Dynasty, wholeheartedly supported Liu Xiu and explicitly expressed his desire to assist him. He was convinced that Liu Xiu was a dragon with great potential. This was Geng's personal insight. Zhou Yu, an official helping Sun Quan, was equally insightful. *The Comprehensive Mirror in Aid of Governance* records that he convinced Sun Quan not to lend Jingzhou out, fearing that "The dragon will never only stay in a pool but soar in the sky." He believed Liu Bei was a dragon, and one day, he would rise when the time was right. At that time, it would be too late to stop him. Zhou Yu's sharp eyes saw through Liu Bei's scheme, understanding that Liu Bei was never the kind of person willing to be a nobody for long. He had to compare Liu Bei to a dragon to warn Sun Quan. It was apparent that he never wanted what he feared to come true.

Indeed, Sun Quan didn't want it to happen, either. He also compared himself to a soaring dragon and called himself the chosen one. In AD 229, Sun Quan couldn't hold back his complacency and joy when Xiakou and Wuchang reported the appearance of the auspicious omens of a dragon and a phoenix. With the support of civil servants and generals, he officially ascended to the throne and changed the reign title to Huanglong (yellow dragon) to commemorate his achievements. Subsequently, he sent envoys to formally notify Shu that he suggested that two emperors should coexist. To the surprise of the people of the Kingdom of Wu, the monarch and ministers of Shu were deadly against it, as they generally believed that this move violated the state system, thus not justifiable, and almost ended diplomatic relations with the Kingdom of Wu. Fortunately, Zhuge Liang thoroughly understood the important principle. He put the overall situation first and maintained the Wu-Shu alliance. Liu Bei had always considered himself the rightful heir of the Han Dynasty. It was understandable that he was overly sensitive about this matter.

In essence, "a coiling dragon and a crouching tiger" is a variation of the theory that there is the qi of an emperor in Jinling, or its visualization and concretization. The people of the Six Dynasties were passionate followers of this theory, and such auspiciousness is frequently discussed in historical biographies. In *The Book of Southern Qi: Records of Auspiciousness* it is recorded that the old grave of Xiao Qi's ancestors was in Pengshan, Wujin, Changzhou, where connected mountains and hills stretch for hundreds of miles. There used to be five-color clouds above the mountains, suggesting the presence of dragons. Emperor Ming of the Song Dynasty was deeply concerned about it and sent the tomb builder Gao Lingwen to inspect the spot. Unexpectedly, Gao Lingwen and Xiao Daocheng had long been close friends, so when Gao returned from the inspection, he lied to the emperor, assuring him that there was nothing special about the place and no greatness would be found there. However, Gao leaked to Xiao that it was a special place. The emperor couldn't let it go, so he dispatched people to hunt near the grave and install colossal iron nails that were five or six feet long around the tomb to suppress the possible qi of an emperor. Unlike fearful Emperor Ming of the Song Dynasty, Sun Quan, who made Jianye the capital of Wu, must have been delighted to hear that there was a coiling dragon and a crouching tiger. It might even have boosted his ambition.

However, even if Zhuge Liang and Liu Bei had been to Moling, they didn't have to compliment the Kingdom of Wu with the words of a coiling dragon and a crouching tiger. At that time, although the confrontation of the Three Kingdoms was not yet established, the three major forces headed by Cao Cao, Sun Quan, and Liu Bei all had ambitions to unify the Central Plains. A battle of wisdom and strength was waiting for them. After Cao

Pi became emperor, Sun Quan was crowned by the King of Wu. On the surface, he pretended to be loyal, but behind the curtain, it was his buffer strategy, one step back in exchange for three steps forward.

Moreover, this King of Wu had his own reign title and officials and ministers. On his own territory, he was superior to a vassal king. In front of a strong opponent, advocating the idea of "a coiling dragon and a crouching tiger" would only make the opponent stronger. At such a critical moment, both sides needed social cohesion. They needed to command the political banner of each other. At this time, touting the rival's "coiling dragon and crouching tiger" was tantamount to handing over a knife. In addition, before Sun Quan moved the capital to Moling, there was only Jinling Township and no Stone City, which meant no crouching tiger.

Zhuge Liang did not inspect the topography of Moling on the spot, so he would not say a crouching tiger; Liu Bei may have visited Moling and inspected its terrain, but even if he convinced Sun Quan to relocate his capital to Moling, his original words would be different. There is only one possibility: the self-promoting of the Kingdom of Wu, which was another intelligent political piece of propaganda. Using the fame of Zhuge Liang, of course, was the most effective advertising; even the fame of Liu Bei would do the trick more objectively and fairly. Whoever said a coiling dragon and a crouching tiger first must be from the Kingdom of Wu? In the early days of the Kingdom of Wu's founding, many things waited to be done, and even the location of its capital was undecided. The release of these words was at least conducive to building the court's and the public's confidence in making Moling its capital.

The capital of the Kingdom of Wu had been changing at first. The Sun clan rose in Fuchun (now Fuyang, Zhejiang Province), and their earliest sphere of influence was within Wujun. As they expanded, the local mountains had to be conquered first. Setting up a government in Wujun to manage Sanwu was the political and military need of the time. Wujun's geographical location was not good enough to further develop the Yangtze River's middle reaches. In the thirteenth year (AD 208) of Jian'an, to facilitate the battle against Huang Zu, Sun Quan moved the capital from Wujun (Suzhou of today) to Jingkou (Zhenjiang of today). Jingkou City was located on the Kuaiji-Jiankang communication line because it was backed up by mountains and surrounded by a river. It was advantageous in both attacking and defending. But compared with Moling, the terrain of Jingkou was slightly inferior. Moling was surrounded by mountains on the outskirts, with Zijin Mountain standing at its east, Qingliang Mountain at its west, the Yangtze River and North Lake (Xuanwu Lake) running at its north, and the Qinhuai River at its south. It had convenient transportation with a flat middle, making it a favorite spot. More than 2,400 years ago, after King Goujian of Yue eliminated Wu, he built Yue City on the southern highlands of today's Nanjing City as a position to fight against the Chu State. There were abundant and broad rivers and waterways, which were natural training grounds for naval forces. In the battle of red cliff, the most powerful weapon for Sun and Liu's coalition to defeat their enemy was their navy. At that time, to open up the traffic line to Shendu (now India), Emperor Wu of the Han Dynasty ordered the digging of a Kunming Pool in the suburbs of Chang'an, with a circumference of 40 *li* and an area of 320 hectares, as a training ground for his navy. In Moling, the local conditions were enough so that an expensive project could be avoided. Allegedly, Sun Quan only wanted to use the Qinhuai River, which stretched for more than ten *li*, to train his navy. After the Eastern Jin Dynasty, Xuanwu Lake was used as the training ground. During Liu Song's reign, not only did the navy train on the lake, but he also inspected infantry and cavalry on the west bank of the lake. It really became a natural training field. No wonder it was called Training Lake at that time.

In the sixteenth year (AD 211) of the Jian'an Period, Sun Quan relocated his capital to Moling, and in the following year, it was renamed Jianye. For the sake of security, the Kingdom of Wu built a stone city at the estuary of the Qinhuai River in the west of Jianye to prevent the enemy from attacking from the land and constructed the Ruxu Dock in the south of Chaohu to guard against military threats from upstream. Tian Yuqing thoroughly analyzes this point in *The Politics of a Family of Power in the Eastern Jin Dynasty*. Sanwu was a relatively developed area in the south of the Yangtze River at that time. With the Taihu Lake, Yangtze River, Qinhuai River, and other water systems in southern Jiangsu, Sanwu products could be conveniently transported northward to supply Jianye. Setting the capital in Wujun would help dominate one area at best, similar to what the feudal princes of Yue in the Spring and Autumn Period achieved. Moving the capital to Jianye would allow the emperor to control Jingchu in the west and to have the chance to conquer the Central Plains in the north, thus achieving hegemony. These were real advantages, and in addition to immediate gains from the capital relocation, Sun Quan must have been tempted.

To choose the best place to build a capital, weighing the pros and cons from the political, economic, military, and other aspects is necessary. Under different circumstances, the balance between pros and cons naturally changes. The Kingdom of Wu pursued a pragmatic policy and moved its capital many times, first from Jianye. In the second year of the Huangchu Period (AD 221), Sun Quan moved it from Gongan to Echeng and changed its name to Wuchang (now Ezhou in Hubei Province) to be able to compete with Liu Bei for Jingzhou. In September of the first year of the Huanglong Period (AD 229), it was moved back to Jianye from Wuchang. At the same time, General Lu Xun was ordered to stay to assist Crown Prince Sun Deng in guarding Wuchang, and a group of ministers to protect also stayed to strengthen the defense of the middle reaches of the Yangtze River. Sun Quan believed Wuchang was at least the second capital, as pivotal as Jianye. He stayed in Wuchang for eight years; before that, he had lived in Moling for ten years. This was the most prolonged capital relocation in the history of the Six Dynasties.

This was not the only relocation of capital for the Kingdom of Wu. In April of the second year of the Taiyuan Period (AD 252), Sun Quan died, and Zhuge Ke was at the helm of the state. The dismissed Crown Prince Sun He was in Changsha as the King of Nanyang at that time. Zhuge Ke was the uncle of Sun He's concubine Zhang, and Sun He sent Huangmen (the emperor's valet) Chen to Jianye to contact Zhuge Ke, intending to covet the throne. Zhuge Ke sent people to Wuchang to repair the palace again, pretending that he would move the capital to Wuchang. Rumor had it that he was going to welcome Sun He. In fact, it was more likely that Zhuge Ke made that move to get rid of the powerful influence of the Wu gentry. This time, the capital relocation didn't succeed due to the opposition of the gentry. After Sun Hao, the last son of Sun He, ascended the throne, he moved the capital in AD 265. But it didn't take long for complaints to be heard everywhere. As a result, the capital was moved back to Jianye. The failure was because, firstly, the river was long and rapid, making it difficult for the people of Yangzhou to supply goods upstream from the lower reaches of the Yangtze River. Secondly, the clans in the east of the Yangtze

River, who were the pillars of the Kingdom of Wu, such as the Gu, Lu, Zhu, and Zhang families of Wujun (Suzhou), the Zhou family of Yangxian (now Yixing), and the Shen family of Wuxing (now Huzhou), were accustomed to the life of Jianye being the capital for decades. They were reluctant to leave their hometowns and stayed far from their sphere of influence. These big clans represented the powerful Sanwu local forces, and their opinion mattered naturally.

On the other hand, when not at war in the past few decades, Jianye's urban outlook improved significantly. *A Prose Poem about Wu* by Zuo Si shows that this city at that time had wide roads, lush trees on both sides of the road, lucid water all around, dense houses, and government offices. And the Changgan area was so thriving that it earned itself the reputation as the rich and populous zone of southeast China. Gu, Lu, Zhu, Zhang, and other high-level clans in Wuzhong lived on both the Qinhuai River and Qingxi Riverbanks. They indulged themselves in pleasure and forgot about home and duty. Therefore, the Left Prime Minister Lu Kai lashed out at the topography of Wuchang, saying it was not a good choice as the state capital. He even quoted a nursery rhyme:

I'd rather drink Jianye water than eat Wuchang fish,
And would rather die in Jianye than live in Wuchang.

The Wuchang fish was probably *megalobrama amblycephala* (Wuchang bream) from Fankou of Echeng County. It was as delicious as the bass from Wu. However, these people would instead drink Jianye's freshwater than taste the delicious food of a foreign land; they would rather die in Jianye than live in a big house in Wuchang. Nobody knows if they made up this nursery rhyme, but we can tell there is not only a strong nostalgia but also a strong political resentment; it is no romantic expression of homesickness but a dangerous eruption of rebellious emotions.

The subsequent capital relocations of the Kingdom of Wu were mostly to Wuchang, that is, in the middle reaches of the Yangtze River, while Jianye was in its lower reaches. The competition between Wuchang and Jianye was actually the beginning of the regular competition between Jingzhou and Yangzhou in history after the Eastern Jin Dynasty. Relocating the capital meant changes in strategic thinking and the competition for the political control of the Kingdom of Wu by different local interest groups. The emergence of political legends like a coiling dragon and a crouching tiger embodied the political interests of Jianye and the Sanwu groups.

During the Six Dynasties, which lasted 332 years, except for the eight years when Sun Quan moved the capital to Wuchang, the one year when Sun Hao moved it to Wuchang, and the three years when Emperor Yuan of Liang moved it to Jiangling, Jinling [renamed Jianye (建业 Jiànyè), Jianye (建邺 Jiànyè), and Jiankang successively] served as the capital for 320 years. Its status as the imperial city south of the Yangtze River has never been shaken. After the Jin and Song Dynasties, the strategic position of Jingkou became increasingly important, and it grew into a military center in the lower reaches of the Yangtze River. Still, it had always been the gateway to Jiankang, guarding the safety of this capital in the east. After years of construction and repair, Stone City became increasingly strong. Xie Tiao believed that it was genuinely impregnable. The beacon tower on the mountain stood high on the riverside, occupying the commanding heights in the city's southwest. When the weather was pleasant in spring and autumn, the literati climbed high and looked into the distance, chanting and sighing. It inspired Xie Tiao to compose the poem *The Beacon Tower in the Stone City*. Emperor Wu of Qi also climbed this tower and ordered his ministers to write poems. And Xiao Yingzhou was rewarded by him for his excellent poems. Once there was an emergency alarm, the beacon would reach Jiangling from Jiankang to Jiangling in half a day. Until the Song Dynasty, in the eyes of Zhang Shunmin, Lu You, and others, although the Stone City was not high, its cliffs stood tall, and winding, making it a natural fortress.

As time went by, more and more historic legends continued to be made, and the status of Jinling as the state capital was increasingly consolidated. When the Eastern Jin Dynasty first established its foothold in the east of the Yangtze River, a thousand things waited to be done. Allegedly, Wang Dao pointed to Niutou Mountain, facing the south gate of Jiankang, Xuanyang Gate, and said to Emperor Yuan of Jin that it was the chosen spot for a palace. At that time, the city was dilapidated, and Wang Dao called the mountain the future palace probably because he wanted to comfort the emperor.

Even in the late Liu Song Dynasty, bamboo fences were still at the six gates outside the capital. The six gates were built in the second year of the Jianyuan Era (AD 344). Allegedly, at that time, people often found that violet-gold clouds so spectacularly capped the top of Zijin Mountain. Just like the idea of dragons, this mysterious violet-gold cloud color was believed to be the exclusive qi of an emperor. In fact, as Jiang Zanchu pointed out in *Nanjing History*, "It was nothing, but a natural color reflected by the mountain's purplish-red shale under the sunlight." There was nothing miraculous at all. However, common folks would rather believe that there was.

According to the *Folklore of Nanjing*, there was a golden hall that stored treasures on the top of Zijin Mountain, and at the foot of the mountain, there was an old man surnamed Jin, who grew eggplants. The mountain gold gave him a small eggplant as the key to compensate for his loss. But his wife's greed got them nothing. Since then, the treasure box in the mountain has never been opened again, but the qi of the treasure burst out of the ground and turned into a violet-gold cloud capping the mountain. A legend as it is, it shows that Zijin was eager to show its pride and extraordinariness.

Time passed, and Nanjing became more and more confident as an imperial capital. In the Qi and Liang Dynasties, this self-confidence reached its peak. Xie Tiao, one of the most outstanding poets of the fifth century, sang about it:

> The beautiful land in the south of the Yangtze River, Jinling makes the
>   perfect imperial capital.
> As clear rivers ran through it, splendid buildings rose in the mountains.
> An imperial path extends between the buildings, willows shade over
>   the moat.
> Melodies of flute and drum echo as my carriage enters the capital.
> As my advice is accepted in court, fame and wealth are soon to come.
>   —XIE TIAO, *The Song of Entering the Capital*

The poet passed away, but the song has survived in the water of the Qinhuai River, becoming an unforgettable memory of Jinling City.

During the more than 300 years of the Six Dynasties, Jinling's status as the state capital has endured several more tests.

In the 12th year of the Yonghe Period (AD 356), the reign of the Emperor Mu of the Jin Dynasty, Huan Wen led an army to defeat Yao Xiang of the Qiang people and recover the lost Luoyang, so he submitted a memorial to suggest moving the capital back to Luojing. However, the Henan area at the time was dilapidated after a long war. There were insufficient human and material resources to accommodate a state capital. And Huan Wen's proposal to relocate the capital was never to use it as a stronghold to recover the lost Central Plains but to take this opportunity to further control the court and the emperor after dominating the middle and upper reaches of the Yangtze River. Nonetheless, he was not powerful enough to coerce the royal family to move north, so his attempt only lasted a short time and failed. In the middle of the Yuanjia years (AD 424–453), under the reign of the Emperor Wen of the Song Dynasty, there was a rumor that an emperor was going to be born in Qiantang. When Emperor Yongguang was dethroned (AD 465), a rumor that an emperor would be born in Xiangzhou was spread. Both rumors failed to shake Jinling's status as the state capital. Most of the time, the competition was merely between Jinling and Jiangling. In the second year (AD 424) of Jingping's reign, a purple cloud appeared in the city of Jiangling. The qi-tellers called it an omen for a new emperor, but it turned out to be false.

In the third year (AD 501) of the Yongyuan Period of Marquis Donghun of Southern Qi, Xiao Baorong, who became Emperor He of Qi, was only the prime minister then, and his subordinates made a formal appeal to him to mount the throne. Xiao once served as the governor of Jingzhou, so his subordinates imitated the system in Jiankang Palace to build ancestral temples, southern and northern districts, and city gates in Jiangling. In addition, they set up five departments of state affairs, took Shetang in the south of the city as a *lantai* (imperial library), and promoted the southern prefecture chief as *yin* (an ancient official title) to mold public opinion for usurping the throne.

After Yingzhou was stabilized, Xiao Yingzhou proposed to move the capital to Xiakou (an old city on Huanghu Mountain in today's Wuhan), but Liu Chen was dead set against it. Xiao Yingzhou was adamant, and soon, when the soldiers of Badong reached Xiakou, the idea of moving the capital was abolished. Fifty years later, Xiao Yi, Emperor Yuan of Liang, had no idea but made Jiangling the state capital. First, Hou Jing's rebellion hit

Jiankang City, leaving it rather dilapidated; then, his officials, who were Chu locals, wanted to stay in Jiangling and hated to go east. Finally, this was the base before Xiao Yi ascended the throne, which meant a solid foundation. Unfortunately, the good times did not last long. Within three years, this new capital was broken into by the Western Wei army. In its long history, Jiangling served as a state capital so briefly that people soon forgot about it.

On the contrary, people still keep a fresh memory of the favorable geographical position of Jinling. Zijin Mountain, like a coiling dragon, was easy to defend and difficult to attack, and Stone City, both strategically located and difficult to access, controlled the river (Qinhuai River), thus being the favorite spot of military strategists. Since the Three Kingdoms Period and Eastern Jin Dynasty, Stone City has always managed to defend itself in times of crisis. From "Stone City full of chariots" in *A Prose Poem about Wu* by Zuo Si to "a flag of surrender was hoisted in the Stone City" in *Nostalgic on Xisai Mountain* by Liu Yuxi, the stone city has always been associated with battles in literary works. In the first year (AD 322) of the Yongchang Period of Emperor Yuan of the Jin Dynasty, Wang Dun rebelled, and his army invaded Jiankang, and a fierce battle took place in Stone City. There is a colossal stone in the east of the city called Tanggang among the locals. It was where Wang Dun killed Zhou Boren and Dai Ruosi. It is a historic site where people pay homage to the dead. Until the early Tang Dynasty, when Xu Jingye raised his troops against Empress Wu Zetian, he also sent his subordinate Cui Hong to cross the river and repair Stone City to resist the Tang army.

After defeating Xu Jingye, the Tang Dynasty also dispatched 300 soldiers to guard it. Jinling has always been an important place along the river in the Southern Song Dynasty. In the third year of the Jianyan Period (AD 1129), Emperor Gaozong of the Song Dynasty built a palace there, changed its name to Jiankang Prefecture, and established the Jiangnan East Road Anfu Division to manage it. In the first year of the Longxing reign (AD 1163), the Southern Song Dynasty and the Jin Dynasty negotiated a peace, and the poet Lu You submitted a memorial suggesting moving the capital from Lin'an (now Hangzhou) to Jiankang, which was easy to defend, but it was not adopted. Lu You boarded the Appreciation Pavilion west of Jiankang City, looked into the distance, and was washed over by emotions. "Old but still worried for the country, tears ran down my face unnoticed before I even suggested relocating the capital." He was deeply disappointed.

Should Lu You ever have looked, he could easily have found supporters for his proposal to move the capital to Jiankang in the works of the poets of the previous dynasties. In the poem *Move the Capital Back to Sanshan That Overlooks the Stone City* by Bao Zhao, the mountains and river of Stone City radiate royalty. In *Visit the Stone City*, He Xun wrote, "A strategic position of great importance decides the advantageous situation, and it makes a great difference," so straightforward that it leaves readers in awe. Shi Wansui, a general of the Sui Dynasty, led an army to the south, and when they arrived at Stone City, he was immediately in awe of how precipitous the stone city was. Therefore, he wrote a poem:

Whoever made the stone city so precipitous?
Ancient drums sound quieter than the giant rocks
that the wind blows down.
Towering mountains make it impregnable
so that it can guard the southwest.

These are all excellent reasons to build a capital. In the early spring of the second year of the Zhide Period (AD 757) of the Tang Dynasty, amid the turmoil of the Anshi Rebellion, Li Lin, the Prince of Yong, led a fleet eastward to Jinling, and the famous poet Li Bai, who assisted him in the office, composed *Song of the Prince of Yong's Eastern Tour*, confidently demonstrating his military power. In front of this city, Li Bai thought of a coiling dragon and a crouching tiger, which suggests the qi of an emperor, thought of Zhaoyang Hall and Magpie Tower in the Southern Dynasties, thought of the terrain of Yangzhou, where there were abundant rivers and lakes, and thought of the great deeds of Xie An defeating Fu Jian in the battle of Feishui and eliminating Hu Chen. Jinling was perfect to house an emperor. It was meant for greatness to be made—this was the core of Li Bai's imagination.

The Southern Tang and Ming dynasties must have considered its favorable geographical position when it was chosen as the capital. The major power scope of the Southern Tang Dynasty was only in the south of the

Yangtze River, and the foundation of the Ming Dynasty was on both banks of the lower reaches of the Yangtze River. Gao Qi was an essential advisor in the early Ming Dynasty and a master of Ming Dynasty poetry. He had both the vision of a statesman and a writer's sensitivity. In his mind, Jinling was magnificent and extraordinary:

> The roaring Yangtze River runs from the mountain.
> Both the mountain and the river extend from west to east.
> While Zijin Mountain, like a coiling dragon, stretches from east to west as
>   if to defy the river.
> What a spectacle that Yangtze River and Zijin Mountain compete with
>   each other.
> It is said that the first emperor of the Qin Dynasty once buried gold under
>   the mountain to
> suppress the qi of an emperor, but the trees there remain lush.
> —Gao Qi, *Overlooking the River from Yuhua Terrace in Jinling*

It is hilarious that Qin Shi Huang dug the river and buried gold, but in vain, and the qi of an emperor in Jinling was still strong. And the early Ming Dynasty, there was a representative, Zhu Di, the Emperor Chengzu of the Ming Dynasty, who moved the capital to Beijing, making Nanjing the second capital. Still, people could sense the ever-lasting qi of an emperor within the green mountains and hills.

In the mid-19th century, the Taiping Heavenly Kingdom made Jinling its capital and renamed it Tianjing, which sounded fancy and was a sort of self-deification. In their eyes, Jinling has been the home to emperors since ancient times, a famous city where an emperor's qi resided. Second, the south of the Yangtze River was wealthy, had abundant resources, and has been a major financial support for the state since the Tang Dynasty; third, it has a vast territory and high walls. There was a natural barrier of the Yangtze River in the north and the mountains around it. Its advantageous terrain makes it easy to defend it and launch attacks. The first is the historical reason, which is true, but not necessarily reliable, while the third is based on geography.

As early as the Ming Dynasty, in the poem *Climb the Yuejiang Tower*, Wang Shouren wrote, "The way to rule the state is to implement benevolent policies, not with a natural moat and high walls." Later, the more advanced the weaponry, the less they would rely on the natural moat. In December 1937, Nanjing, the capital of the Republic of China, was declared to have fallen amid the gunfire and slaughtering knives of the Japanese invaders and the blood of 300,000 victims in Nanjing. One year later, drowning in unbearable pain, the poet Hu Xiaoshi did not forget to mention Jinling's favorable geographical position:

> Dragon and tiger make it the perfect capital,
> the stone city stands impregnable
>
> —Hu Xiaoshi, *Nanjing Fell and Furious*

Despite all the advantages, it fell. In the end, only the second reason, a strong economy and abundant resources, lasted. More recently, they have become more important.

After the establishment of the Republic of China government, which city was to be the capital was discussed, and the final round was between Beijing and Nanjing. At last, those who voted for Jinling won. They believed that the south was the base for revolution, and making Jinling the capital could wash away the ancient filthy customs of the Qing Dynasty and stay up to date in time. However, Zhang Taiyan, a master of Chinese studies, wrote to the Senate, arguing that there would be five negative consequences in doing so: being in the south of the Yangtze River would prevent the state from exercising its powerful reach beyond the Great Wall; the northern culture has declined, and beyond the Great Wall, national cultivation will be trouble; with the state's center of gravity in the south, the three eastern provinces and the Central Plains have lost their weight, and are faced with Japanese and Russian invasion, and the threat of collapsing; the remaining forces of the Qing Dynasty might have a comeback in the north and having the capital in the south might give them a better chance to retaliate, and it is costly to relocate the capital because the embassies must also be relocated.

To "achieve long-term and far-reaching ruling," Zhang Taiyan even proposed to make Ili in Xinjiang the capital, which he believed was the ideal choice. Loyal as he was, this was an exaggeration. However, as early as in the late Ming and early Qing dynasties, Huang Zongxi had put forward a different view from the perspective of the economy in his book *Interviews with the Ming Barbarians*: during the Qin and Han Dynasties, the fields in the central Shaanxi plain were opened up, and it was populous and abundant in resources, much more prosperous than Wu and Chu, which were newly civilized; in the Ming and Qing Dynasties, the central Shaanxi plain was far inferior to Wu in the southeast in such matters.

A country is like a family, and the wealthy places of Wu are like a warehouse in the house, and the owner must guard it personally; as for other places, which are like the courtyard, the owner can entrust them to servants and concubines. During the Anshi Rebellion and the Huang Chao Uprising, the Tang Dynasty did not collapse at once. The most important reason was that the economic artery of the southeastern region was not completely cut off. When there was less developed transportation, the location of the capital had a very far-reaching impact on the country's development and military defense. However, everything changes as time rolls forward. In modern times, transportation and communication have become increasingly developed. When choosing the capital, the terrain is probably no longer the most critical factor. Instead, it should comprehensively evaluate the environment, resources, national policies, and economic development.

In Li Shangyin's poem *Chanting History*, he wrote:

Xuanwu Lake calms down,
a flag of surrender is hoisted.
Three hundred years feels like a dream.
Where is the coiling dragon on Zijin Mountain?

In the Three Kingdoms Period, when the "coiling dragon and crouching tiger" saying came out, there was no dragon in Zijin Mountain at all. Later, when Sun Quan died, he was buried in the Sun Cemetery at the foot of the Mountain, now called the Wu Tombs. During the reign of Emperor Wu of Qi in the Southern Dynasty, a Shangbiao Pavilion was built there, also known as Jiuri Terrace, where monarchs and ministers often climbed to a height to overlook the scenery, lecture on scriptures, and practice martial arts. In modern times, plum blossoms have been planted all over the Sun Cemetery, making it a favorite tourist attraction among Nanjing citizens, and Plum Blossom Mountain is named after the flowers. Rumor has it that Zhu Yuanzhang chose Wanzhu Mountain of Dulongfu at the southern foot of Zijin Mountain as his tomb, and in this way, he made Sun Quan his tomb guard. According to the old belief, Zhu Yuanzhang can be regarded as the rightful emperor even by the strictest standards. Having soared for decades, this dragon finally coiled at the foot of Zijin Mountain. The idea of "a coiling dragon at Zijin Mountain" seems to be a prophecy that has been waiting for a thousand years. History is so coincidental, so dramatic. Like everybody else, I went out of the city one spring to enjoy plum blossoms. Standing on the top of the Sun Cemetery, overlooking the Ming Tomb Scenic Area in the trees, I could not help but compose the following verse:

> The Dragon rides the clouds in the sunset,
> and the plum fragrance spreads from the old nest.
> The rightful emperor grew old,
> and the lucid water ran cold.
> People pity me as much as they pity themselves,
> and I see them as much as I see flowers.
> The frost falls heavy in the suburbs,
> the sun sets deep in the royal palaces.

Chapter 3

Making a God

I toured around splendid Nanjing,
and the ordinary-looking Concubine Xu was a loose woman.
The Eastern Han Dynasty has been gone for three thousand years,
and Jiang Ziwen was worshiped as a god for twenty years.
My tears ran dry as I had to leave my homeland,
and I suffered bitter days on a ship to London.
The skyscrapers in England were lit at night,
and it pained me to say goodbye to friends and the spring.

—CHEN YINKE, *I Traveled to London for Eye Treatment*
But Ended in Vain and Returned to Jiangning

Chen Yinke composed this poem in 1946, and it is titled as above in the book *Wu Mi and Chen Yinke*. In *Yinke's Poems*, it is titled *Southern Dynasties*. Of the two titles, the former is explicit, highlighting the background and story of the poem; the latter is more euphemistic, quoting history to express his concern about the current situation. Regarding the poem itself, both titles are acceptable. In its fourth line, "Jiang Ziwen was worshiped as a god for twenty years" is not only an allusion to the Southern Dynasties, but also closely associated with Nanjing.

"Making a God" tells the story of Jiang Ziwen. Who? He was from Guangling (now Yangzhou, in Jiangsu Province), alcoholic, and lecherous, and a free spirit. He seemed to be an indulgent individual. Interestingly, he considered himself perfectly faithful and destined to become an immortal after death. However, before he died, he had little luck in job promotion and remained an insignificant county magistrate of Moling (now Nanjing). Although he was a low-ranking official, he was conscientious. One day, to capture some fugitives, he chased them all the way to the foot of Zijin Mountain and finally caught them. Unfortunately, he suffered a severe injury on his forehead during the hunt. He hastily bandaged it, thinking it was nothing serious. Surprisingly, he died soon after. These events happened at the end of the Han Dynasty (202 BC–AD 220).

Soon after that, Sun Quan made Nanjing his capital. A senior subordinate of Jiang Ziwen told the story that he came across Jiang Ziwen's ghost on the road, who was riding a white horse and holding a white fan in his hand, and he and his entourage looked no different from when he was alive. The subordinate turned pale with fright and hurried away. Jiang caught up with him and said: "I have become the God of Land here now, and I can bless the people. Go back and instruct them to build a temple for me; otherwise, a catastrophe shall fall." In the beginning, people did not take it seriously. In the summer of that year, a wide epidemic broke out in Nanjing. People were frightened, and some began to worship him secretly.

Jiang Ziwen also passed his words through those of witchery. "I intend to bless Sun's regime with all my strength, so build a temple for me as soon as possible. Otherwise, there will be a disaster: bugs will creep into people's ears, killing all of them." Soon, a bug-like gadfly flew into people's ears, and even the famous doctors could not cure the disease, and the patients were simply waiting to die. The people were even more panicked.

At this time, Sun Quan still didn't believe it. Jiang Ziwen once again passed words through those of witchery. "Worship me, or worse disasters will fall soon." This year, Jiankang City had frequent fires, sometimes several in one day, and some even threatened the palace. Regarding this matter, all civil and military officials were convinced that once the gods had a temple to reside in, they would stop punishing the mortals, so they must be pacified as soon as possible. Therefore, Sun Quan sent a special envoy to bestow the title Marquis of Zhongdu to Jiang Ziwen and the title Colonel of the Changshui Guard to his second brother, Jiang Zixu. From that day on, the plague and fires in the capital stopped. The people became increasingly convinced that Jiang was indeed a god, and his temple naturally grew more and more prosperous daily. This story was widely circulated and thus compiled into *In Search of the Supernatural* in the Eastern Jin Dynasty.

However, this is not recorded in official histories such as *The Book of the Later Han* and *Records of the Three Kingdoms*. However, I still believe that Jiang Ziwen was real, except for the supernatural coincidences about him. The interests of the people of the Six Dynasties in supernatural tales and how novelists write about legends always tend to embellish the stories with more twists. Historians would document such stories differently. In *Records of the Three Kingdoms*, there is a tale that in the last years of Sun Quan's reign, a god appeared in the coastal area of Zhejiang Province, and he called himself Wang Biao. Wang ate the same food and spoke the same language as the commoners, but he never showed himself to the public, and his message was always passed on through his maid named Fangji. Sun Quan immediately made Wang Biao, the General Who Assists the State and the King of Luoyang, then sent Li Chong, a Gentleman of the Palace Library, to invite Wang Biao to take up the official post. Along the way, Wang Biao instructed his maid from time to time to greet the gods of mountains and rivers. Although it was his first time going on a long trip, he discussed local political affairs with the magistrates in various places with great familiarity. Sun Quan built a house for him outside the Canglong Gate, and the courtiers around Sun Quan did not dare to offend him but were attentive to him. Wang Biao's predictions about floods and droughts were mainly fulfilled. Jiang Ziwen and Wang Biao have bestowed a title about the same time. At first, Wang Biao seemed to be more respected. But later, Jiang Ziwen eclipsed Wang Biao.

The temple for Jiang Ziwen, Marquis of Zhongdu, was built near Sunlinggang, today's famous Meihua (plum blossom) Mountain in the eastern suburbs of Nanjing. During the Three Kingdoms Period, the state of Wei called Chang'an, Luoyang, Xuchang, Ye, and Qiao the "Five Capitals," and the area within the "Five Capitals" was called the Zhongdu. However, Jiang Ziwen being conferred as the Marquis of Zhongdu has nothing to do with the state of Wei. Zhongdu has another meaning, *duzhong* (in the capital), which holds the same meaning as the same word in the *Historical Records: Book of Pingzhun*. In ancient Chinese, there are many examples of prepositional prepositions (prepositions of location being placed before the object instead of behind), from *zhonglu* in *The Book of Songs: Odes of Bei*, and Shiwei to *zhongye* in *To Ying* by Cao Zhi. Jiang Ziwen's title Marquis of Zhongdu is probably the same use of prepositions.

As the capital's deity, Jiang Ziwen was officially revered and worshipped. Zijin Mountain (bell mountain) in the eastern suburbs of Nanjing was initially named because it was shaped like a bell. Unfortunately, Sun Quan's grandfather was named Sun Zhong (bell), so the name Zhong Mountain violated Sun Quan's family taboo. The emperor ordered a renaming of the mountain as Jiang Mountain. In this way, overnight, it seems that this verdant mountain tomb in the eastern suburbs of Nanjing, where the qi of an emperor resides, had become Jiang Ziwen's fief.

Obviously, Jiang Ziwen was a god worshipped only by the locals of Nanjing at the beginning, and maybe such worship did not go with the ritual system. With a bit of knowledge in the Wei, Jin, Southern and Northern Dynasties novels of supernatural mystery, we have an impression that people in the east of Yangtze were superstitious and often held rituals. The lower reaches of the Yangtze River, with Nanjing as the center, were the heart of such an ethos. There is a story in *Novel of Mysteries* by Zu Taizhi that a gold bell was tied to the arm of a sow next to Qu'a Pool. The embarrassed protagonist who fell in love with the sow was a scholar-official of the Kingdom of Wu who had just returned home from Jiankang for a vacation. In another story, Mrs. Lushan, whom Cao Zhu, a junior official in Jiankang, came across, was of unknown origin. She was probably one of the gods illegally worshipped by the commoners. Only Wang Biao and Jiang Ziwen rose among such gods and were bestowed titles. And this would be unimaginable without the political upheaval.

The year AD 252 was an unlucky year for the Kingdom of Wu: Empress Pan died at the beginning of the year, and Sun Quan was critically ill. Hundreds of civil and military officials visited Wang Biao many times, asking him to cast a spell for blessings. Aware of the negative situation, Wang went missing, which was probably authorized or acquiesced by Sun Quan. When commenting on this incident, Eastern Jin historian Sun Sheng wrote: "A state will prosper when its people are heard; a state will fall when only its gods are heard." In fact, Sun Sheng sounded a tad one-sided. The Kingdom of Wu's superstition of Jiang Ziwen was not only longer but earlier. At that time, when it was about to prosper, it needed ideological support. Jiang Ziwen excelled at expanding his influence through political channels. From the temptation of "I am to bless the Sun family" to the warning of "I am to burn to palaces," he played both good cop and bad cop, and it worked remarkably. The elevation of Jiang Ziwen from an unofficial local god in Nanjing to a rightful god identified by the political authority of the Kingdom of Wu was a process of mutual utilization and integration of Nanjing's local culture and the state culture. When Sun Quan died, his tomb was built under Jiang Mountain. And the peace between him and Jiang Ziwen became a perfect symbol of the harmonious combination of monarchy and divinity, politics and religion, official orthodox ideology, and folk beliefs in the Kingdom of Wu.

Before Sun Quan ascended the throne, this relationship had been unharmonious. There was a violent conflict between Sun Ce and the Taoist Yu Ji. The end of the Han Dynasty was an era when Taoism flourished. Zuo Ci from Lujiang and Yu Ji from Langya were both famous Taoists at that time. Yu Ji traveled to and from Wuzhong, set up a school, made *fushui* (Taoist magic figures or incantations), and treated illnesses. This greatly displeased Sun Ce. He believed that Yu Ji's devious tricks would hurt the morale of the army and destroy the etiquette of monarchs and ministers. So, he arrested Yu Ji and ordered him to make rain in times of great drought. Although his spell worked and heavy rain poured down from the sky in time, Yu Ji was finally killed by Sun Ce. After Yu Ji died, every time Sun Ce sat alone, he felt haunted by Yu Ji's apparition. Once he looked at himself in the mirror and saw Yu Ji's face. He looked around, but there was no one. Having repeated that many times, Sun Ce was infuriated, broke the mirror, and blustered, and the wound from an arrow that had just healed burst and it killed him quickly (by the way, this may have inspired the story of Jia Rui looking in the mirror in *Dream of the Red Chamber*).

When Sun Ce was dying, he said to Sun Quan: "I am better at leading the army east of Yangtze to defeat the enemy than you. However, you outperformed me in using talented and capable people so that everyone can do their best and dedicate themselves to ensuring the safety and prosperity of the east of Yangtze." People speak kinder words when they are dying. And Sun Ce's last words were his self-knowledge. Sun Ce was a fiery character. His courage was mostly without discipline, while Sun Quan was more patient, wise, and brave. That Jiang Ziwen was officially recognized and bestowed a title by the Kingdom of Wu, at last, reflects firstly the real political needs of the Wu regime, which newly made Nanjing its capital, and secondly, Sun Quan's flexible and practical political wisdom.

After the Western Jin Dynasty swallowed the Kingdom of Wu, there was no more need to worship Jiang Ziwen, the official Wu god, even if he was not deliberately neglected. However, this did not mean that he was utterly abandoned but only temporarily marginalized, and when the time came, he would return to the center of cultural discourse. It didn't take long for such an opportunity to present itself as the Sima regime crossed the river southwards. Jiang Ziwen not only restored his past glory but was also promoted. His temple was renovated, and his statue was gilded golden. Judging from *In Search of the Supernatural* by Gan Bao in the Eastern Jin Dynasty, Jiang Ziwen had already become a highly authoritative god at that time. Worshipping him was unusually effective, and more legends about him therefore spread.

There was a man named Liu Chifu who dreamed that Jiang Ziwen urgently invited him to be his Chief Clerk. Liu visited Jiang's Temple to account for his refusal, stating that his family depended on him and he could not leave them behind. So he implored Jiang to find somebody else and recommended Wei Guo from Kuaiji, who was talented at religious rituals, to replace himself. Liu knelt on the ground, kowtowed until he bled, and pleaded, but the temple attendant would not take no for an answer, insisting that Jiang only wanted him, not others. Soon, Liu died, and it seemed that he eventually became Jiang's Chief Clerk.

During the reign of Emperor Jianwen of the Eastern Jin Dynasty, the children of three officials traveled to the eastern suburbs together after some drinking. They visited the temple of Jiang Ziwen. There were several statues of beautiful women in the temple. The three drunk young men pointed to the statues and joked that they would marry them. That night, the three of them happened to have the same dream where Jiang Ziwen sent a minion to deliver them a message: "My daughters are no beauties. Since that doesn't bother you, let's set a date for the wedding." The three were frightened and immediately offered cattle, sheep, and pig sacrifices, begging for mercy, but it was too late. The wedding was not to be refused. Soon, all three died.

In these two stories, Jiang Ziwen is a majestic god whose orders are not to be disobeyed. But at other times, he was a rare and affectionate lover. Since the Eastern Jin Dynasty, the Nandu nobles, who were officials in the capital, often owned manors in the Kuaiji area. They introduced Jiankang's beliefs to the eastern Zhejiang area. There was a lovely 16-year-old girl in Kuaiji County (in present-day Yin County, Zhejiang Province) named Wu Wangzi. Once, she followed a fellow villager to a religious ritual. On the way, she encountered a distinguished man sitting in a boat, surrounded by a dozen servants, all dressed up. The noble invited her to board the boat, but she politely declined. Suddenly, the man vanished in front of her. When she paid homage in the temple of Jiang Ziwen, she looked up and saw the distinguished man on the pedestal. He looked at her and asked gently, "What took you so long?" He threw two oranges from the pedestal to her. After that, Jiang revealed himself as mortal many times, and his love for Wangzi deepened. Whatever Wangzi wanted would immediately fall from the sky. Once she wanted to have fish, two carp immediately appeared in front of her. The further her experience of supernatural power spread, the more mysterious she appeared, and people all over the city came to serve her. Walking on air, gradually, she became impatient with Jiang Ziwen and had some unfaithful intentions. Jiang found out and cut off contact with her.

In the eyes of the people of the Eastern Jin Dynasty, Jiang's divine power was never weakened and worshipping him always helped. New stories kept being made, maintaining and even strengthening people's faith in him. A man was paddling a small boat, and when night fell, he was hurrying on his way with his young wife. On landing, his wife was kidnapped by a tiger. This man has always been superstitious of Jiang Ziwen, worshipping him daily. Anxiously, he turned to Jiang for help. Jiang sent someone to guide him so he could quickly rush to the tiger's den and kill the tiger's cub. The tiger returned later and rescued his wife. At night, Jiang appeared in his dream and understood that his god was watching over him. After returning home, he slaughtered pigs as a sacrifice to express his gratitude.

On the other hand, Jiang Ziwen wasted no chance in demonstrating his loyalty to the Eastern Jin regime. Allegedly, when Sun En stirred up a riot, one rebel escaped into the Jiang Temple. The moment he entered the temple, he was shot dead by an arrow from one of the wooden god sculptures. Wang Changyu, the beloved son of Wang Dao, a famous prime minister of the Eastern Jin Dynasty, fell seriously ill and was dying, and Jiang volunteered to treat him. Although he failed, Wang Dao was temporarily consoled. There is another legend: when Su Jun rebelled, Jiang and the mountain gods of Zijin Mountain joined forces to assist the Jin army in defeating Su Jun.

These kinds of stories appear absolutely absurd in front of modern rationality, but back then, people took them as true history, thus their serious attitude. When Sun En's rebel army was approaching Jiankang, the then-ruling King Sima Daozi of Kuaiji was helpless; he did nothing but visit the Jiang Temple every day to pray for god's blessing. Earlier, when he heard that Fu Jian's army of the Former Qin was crushing the border, Sima Daozi also led a guard of honor to bestow Jiang Ziwen, the title of the prime minister at the Jiang Temple. Such an attitude of the rulers describes the political and cultural background where stories such as the arrow killing one rebel were invented.

During the four dynasties of the Southern Dynasties, Jiang Ziwen's prestige rose steadily. In the early years of the Liu Song Dynasty, improper worshipping of immortals was widely banned. All temples less significant than the temple of Jiang Ziwen were demolished, but such suppression was temporary after all. In the first year of the Xiaojian Era of the Song Dynasty (AD 454), Jiang Temple was renovated, and Jiang Ziwen was once again promoted, becoming the Chancellor and Grand Commander of All Military Forces at Home and Abroad. When Emperor Ming of Song ruled the state, Jiuzhou Temple was built on Jilong Mountain to accommodate a large group of gods. War was breaking out everywhere. Jiang Ziwen was successfully ranked up to King Jiang in a tense atmosphere. In the Qi Dynasty, Duke Donghun conducted a wonton slaughter of old officials and generals, provoking the mutiny of veteran Cui Huijing, and the rebels broke into Taicheng from Guangling. Amid the chaos, Duke Donghun hid under the pedestal of Jiang Ziwen and survived. After settling the military mutiny, he promoted Jiang Ziwen to Emperor Jiang. Later, Emperor Gaozu of the Chen Dynasty also personally visited Zijin Mountain, offering sacrifices to the Jiang Temple.

The most dramatic story happened in the Liang Dynasty. In the sixth year of the Tianjian Period (AD 507), the capital suffered a disastrous drought. An imperial edict was issued to pray for rain at the Jiang Temple. But a hundred days later, there was still no rain. Emperor Wu of Liang was so furious that he was ready to burn down the temple. As soon as the fire was lit, Emperor Jiang revealed himself, dark clouds filled the sky, and rain poured down. Since the emperor ascended the throne, he had never been to the Jiang Temple, so he had the religious ritual organized and brought all courtiers to pay homage. After this incident, imperial power and divine power were not only reconciled but also became closer. The emperor's piety earned him the protection of Emperor Jiang. When Yang Dayan, a general of the Northern Wei Dynasty, invaded the border to the south, Emperor Jiang volunteered to help the Liang army in many ways. It didn't rain those days. However, the river flooded for no reason, catching the Wei army off guard. They fled. When the Liang army returned with a triumph, it was found that the feet of statues of gods and horses in the temple were stained with wet mud, which was interpreted as proof that the gods fought beside the army. Afterward, Emperor Wu of Liang further improved the Jiang Temple. The temple gate was called the Gate of Divine Light, the middle gate was called the Gate of Kindness, the outer hall was called the Hall of the Emperor, the inner hall was called the Holy Residence, and the west pavilion was called Spiritual Vulture. The east pavilion was where Jiang Ziwen resided. In terms of the names and system, the temple applied the same as the imperial palace with the highest respect.

Throughout the 200 years and so of the Southern Dynasties, the Jiang Temple witnessed excellent attendance. Every year, a temple fair was held to celebrate the gods. Those of witchery and commoners in the city were attracted. This unprecedented grand occasion is vividly depicted in *Temple Fair in Saijiang Mountain* by Shen Yue. This deity Shen Yue described as "Over two hundred years old and spanning four dynasties," was truly extraordinary. No wonder the poet Zeng Ji of the Southern Song Dynasty wrote with profound envy in *Praise Jinling: Jiang Temple*:

Coffin closed but a god is made,
the cyan-boned ascended to supreme prestige.

People of the Six Dynasties believed that it was destined that Jiang Ziwen would become a god and be titled king and emperor. This is what he called himself "青骨 (qīnggǔ cyan bone)," thus becoming a god when dead. Whether "青骨 qīnggǔ" or "骨清 gǔqīng" (bone is clean), both are ancient Chinese phrenology sayings with a long history. During the Qin and Han dynasties, when he lobbied Han Xin, Kuai Tong, proficient in the art of reading people's facial features, suggested that "nobleness lies in one's bones." Jiang Ziwen's "骨清 gǔqīng" means he was otherworldly. Since the Han and Wei Dynasties, in which appraisal gained popularity, from the appraisal of characters to the appraisal of poetry and art, when "清 qīng" was used, it was taken as "admiration." At the same time, the standard of "清 qīng" and even the character "清 qīng" itself holds a magic breath. The fresh breeze and bright moon make people walk on air; the Palace of the Emperor of Heaven was called *qingdu* (land of purity); the fairyland was called *qingxu* (land of peace); *qingqu* (slim) was used to describe the appearance of immortals; among the Taoist books, there is *Tai Ping Qing Ling Shu (Scripture of the Great Peace)*. One of the sage-like types naturally has a "清 qīng" bone structure. Phrenology was still popular in the post-Han Dynasty and the Three Kingdoms Period. People at that time believed that Sun Quan "had a majestic appearance, extraordinary bones, and was destined to make greatness." Jiang Ziwen's extraordinary bones are an important asset to his becoming a god.

But it remains unknown why, in later literature, regarding this matter, "骨清 gǔqīng" is often written as "骨青 gǔqīng" or "青骨 qīnggǔ." As a descriptive word and literary allusion, "qīnggǔ" exudes the ferocious and mysterious energy of death, heavy, cold, and dark, while "青骨 qīnggǔ" is lighter and brighter. Generally, "骨青 gǔqīng" or "青骨 qīnggǔ" seems to be more specific, more vivid, and easier to understand than "骨清 gǔqīng" or "清骨 qīnggǔ." In several masterpieces in the early Song Dynasty, such as *Overview of Taiping and Chinese Classics & Culture*, "骨清 gǔqīng" was written as "骨青 gǔqīng" or "青骨 qīnggǔ." At first, this might just be an accidental character variant, but later, it was widely spread. Those knowledgeable scholars in the Northern Song Dynasty knew which was correct. *Song of Lotus* by Ouyang Xiu writes, "Either the slim waist of concubine Jiang or the clear bones of Guangling." Slim matches clear, which is just right. Little was aware of the origin of the allusion "青骨 qīnggǔ" between the Song and Yuan Dynasties. Wei Ju'an, who wrote *Meijian Poetry*, confessed that he only came across the word's etymology when he occasionally read the book *Hai Lu Shu Shi*, edited by Ye Tinggui.

From mortal to immortal, from marquis to emperor, Jiang Ziwen's status reached the pinnacle, and his glory lasted for six dynasties. This was a movement of making a god under the watchful eyes of the public. The process of this movement was always accompanied by the process of building Nanjing as the capital of the Six Dynasties. After the Six Dynasties, this movement continued, especially during the dynasties when Nanjing was made the capital: the Southern Tang Dynasty once conferred a posthumous title to Jiang Ziwen as Emperor Zhuangwu, rebuilt his temple, and gilded his statue; in the second year (AD 1035) of the Jingyou Period of Emperor Renzong of Song Dynasty, the imperial court gifted his temple with a plaque that wrote *huilie* (benevolent and glorious). Compared with the Six Dynasties, this was merely an after-effect. This movement has also completed the shaping of Jiang Ziwen's cultural and literary image. In turn, his image reshaped the cultural and literary tradition of the city of Nanjing. From the Tang Dynasty, Jiang broke through with mystery novels, strode into literary circles, and became the muse of poets. In the hearts of poets and writers, he was a cultural symbol, a literary metaphor, a symbol of Jinling, an important witness to the vicissitudes of the Six Dynasties, and a memory that still retains the charm of the past.

In terms of space, the existence of the Jiang Temple first reminds people of his base in Nanjing. In the Song Dynasty, Sima Guang's poem *Farewell To Wu Zhongshu on His Appointment as Governor of Jiangning*, he writes:

The Cyan-bone Temple stands here,
and the qi of an emperor hides.

The Cyan-bone Temple is the symbol of Jiang Ziwen and Nanjing. It matches the qi of an emperor. This verse ignited a spark of literary imagination, reminding people of Jiang Ziwen's former majesty and reminiscing about the prosperity of the east of Yangtze in the past.

In terms of time, the rise and fall of the Jiang Temple also reminds us of the rise and fall of the Six Dynasties (AD 220–589). The rituals to worship immortals used to be associated with an emperor's qi and a nation's destiny.

The temples are kept new when the nation thrives and receive excellent attendance. When the nation declines, the temples are deserted. In the Six Dynasties, Zijin Mountain stands out among all mountains. Every year, on the third day of the third lunar month, the ladies and gentlemen of the capital used to flock there for a tour. However, in the eyes of Wei Zhuang, a poet in the late Tang Dynasty (AD 618–907), there was only desolation:

Few came to the deserted Jiang Temple in the dilapidated Jianye City.

Perhaps, this is some historical illusion, with a socio-political sigh, solemn and serious. At the same time, there are also some lighter, more magnificent, and more personal imaginings, such as *Divine Hymn to Marquis Jiang* by Wen Tingyun:

The armored horses of Jiang Ziwen clang, the dragon in the pond ripples
  the surface.
The Autumn breeze blows the water to announce the arrival of
  Emperor Bai,
and a white snake coils on the ancient tree in front of the temple.
King Wu's red axe slashed the clouds, sharp swords gathered in
  painted halls.
The Goddess Wu conveyed the message of grief, the bell clangs, hair turns
  grey.
Smoke ascends from the lush Xiang Mountain, a holy bird flies as the sun
  rises in the east.
A black dragon soars in the sky, and concubine Pan does not need
  to fret.

It paints a colorful picture in which Jiang Ziwen appears as distinguished as a king, and the autumn breeze, the armored horses, the dragon pond, and the white snake altogether make him more mysterious. He is also a charming god, loved by the beautiful and affectionate Concubine Pan. The poet sounded reserved but firmly pointed out Jiang's charm. There is another poem by Wen Tingjun titled *The Temple in the Bamboo Valley*, in which is written:

Lonely Xiang River tourists,
stare at the Jiang monument.

It seems Jiang's divine power was not only in the south of Sanwu but went westwards streaming to Hubei and Hunan. Combined with the "ancient local custom of wrongful worship of gods" (*Hearing the God Worshipping in the South of the Yangtze River at Night* by Li Jiayou), he gradually gained such popularity that he could be compared with Emperor Shun and Concubine Xiang.

The meaning of a literary image is increasingly enriched by continuous exploration and creation. In modern times, Jiang Ziwen's lordship has been used as a metaphor for the emperors and rulers of all dynasties, especially those related to Nanjing. It seems that Chen Yinke was the first to discover this metaphor and use it explicitly. In his poem *Twenty Years Since Becoming a God*, it was Sun Yat-sen who died twenty-one years before (1925) that he wrote about. Cheng Qianfan also wrote an article titled *Xin Wei Chong Jiu Ri*, which was also known as *Recent Events of Yizhou*:

The cyan-boned became gods sixteen autumns ago, at dusk returns
    the billow.
Wonder who wins the war in the dream, heard about the prisoners of Chu
    State.
After a catastrophe, soldiers find it difficult to unite, deep snow will always
    follow.
Not long to live but sentimental, Sanmei goes for another long trip.

This poem describes the situation in the Taiwan Strait in 1991. The fusion of ancient and modern allusions adds the poem a literary grace. The writing and naming styles of the poetry are obviously influenced by Chen Yinke while using Jiang Ziwen and Sanmei as a clever metaphor to refer to Chiang Kai-shek and Song Meiling as the creation of Cheng Qianfan. Sanmei, nicknamed Damsel Qingxi (lucid creek), was slightly less famous than Jiang Ziwen. In the original story, there was only Jiang Ziwen's second younger brother, Jiang Zixu, and it was not until later that Damsel Qingxi was added. And even later, there was the legend that after Jiang Ziwen was killed, the woman threw herself and her two daughters into the river, and during the Wanli Period of the Ming Dynasty (AD 1572–1620), a martyr's shrine was built for them. Later generations probably made this up by imitating the story of Shun and his second concubine.

There is a story about the monk Zhu Tansui from the Xie family in *In Search of the Supernatural II*. During the Taikang Period of the Western Jin Dynasty (AD 266–316), the young and handsome Zhu Tansui passed by the Damsel Qingxi Temple. Surprisingly, Damsel Qingxi took a fancy to him and invited him to be the temple's male god, proving that Damsel Qingxi was created as early as in the Western Jin Dynasty. She was commonly seen as a lonely, sullen, and worldly goddess. Among the *Eighteen Songs of Holy Strings*, there is the *Song of Damsel Qingxi*:

Water outside the door, and a bridge stands nearby.
Where she lives, there is no man.

In the fifth year of the Yuanjia Period (AD 428), Guan Xie was attending to Zhao Wenshao from Kuaiji in the East Palace of Qingxi Middle Bridge (where the Sixiang Bridge of today is). Under the autumn moonlight, as he strolled, he started to chant to release his homesickness. Unexpectedly, his singing attracted a gorgeous 18-to-19-year-old girl and a 15-to-16-year-old housemaid, who claimed to come from the *shangshu* (a high official in ancient China) Wang Shuqing's house nearby. The girl opened her mouth and sang:

The wind blows at sunset, and the leaves fall on the branches.
My deepest affection, afraid you might now know.

It is genuinely affectionate and moving. They sang a duet to each other, expressing their heartfelt feelings, and the singing together lasted until 4 a.m. When they parted, they gave gifts to each other to pledge their love. The girl took off the golden hairpin on her head and gave it to him, and Zhao Wenshao gave back a silver bowl and a white glazed dagger. That goodbye was the last time he saw her. Later, Zhao Wenshao came by chance to Damsel Qingxi Temple to rest and noticed that his silver bowl was placed on the pedestal and his white glazed dagger was behind the screen. And the statues of Damsel Qingxi and the housemaid looked exactly like the girls he came across that night. It was not until then that he understood that he was in love with the Qingxi goddess, usually called Sanmei.

The temple of Damsel Qingxi Aunt is adjacent to Qingxi Middle Bridge. She used to reveal herself during the Eastern Jin Dynasty (AD 317–420) and the Southern Dynasties (AD 420–789), and her prestige grew. There was a giant tree in her temple with a bird's nest in it, and people were forbidden to touch it because she raised the birds. Legend has it that in the Taiyuan Period of the Eastern Jin Dynasty, Xie Qing of Chen County rode past this Temple and shot a few birds dead with a slingshot. The next day, he was punished and died suddenly at home.

At the end of the Southern Dynasties, the Sui army broke through Taicheng and captured the emperor Chen Shubao, Zhang Lihua, and Noble Consort Kong in a well of the Jingyang Palace. The two concubines were beheaded at the Qingxi Middle Bridge under the order of Yang Guang, Prince of Jin. In the Song Dynasty (AD 960–1279), there were three women statues in the Damsel Qingxi Temple, and two were concubines of the Chen Dynasty (AD 557–589) who were persecuted to death. What is meaningful is that the moral discourse of mainstream society will forever fix them on the pillar of shame in history while folklore and literature attempts to clear their names and liberate them.

Gū 姑 (damsel) refers to young women by the people of the Six Dynasties (AD 220–589) and are often seen in mystery novels. There are Damsel Plum and Damsel Purple in Liu Jingshu's *Mysterious Tales*, Damsel Purple became the concubine of a wealthy family and was envied by his wife. She died on the fifteenth day of the first lunar month, which became the anniversary for people to worship her. There is Damsel Ding in *In Search of the Supernatural*. Allegedly, her mother-in-law killed her with an overload of work on the ninth day of the ninth lunar month. The people mourned her tragic death, worshipped her on this very day, and created a folk custom that women did not have to do any chores on that day. Damsel Hujiu mentioned in Volume 47 of *Yuefu Poems* was a goddess worshipped locally in Nanjing. Time flies, and when Damsel Ding revealed herself, she was already a white-haired hag, but the beautiful and affectionate Damsel Qingxi seemed to be able to remain young forever. Relying on her relationship with Jiang Ziwen, she rose from a young goddess to Lady Qingxi. This title makes people notice that time has also left some imprints on her face.

In the legends of the Tang Dynasty and after, there are too many stories of scholars like Zhao Wenshao encountering beautiful women. Maybe they were too busy; in the writings of the Tang authors, it was still Sanmei, also known as Damsel Qingxi. *Shaoyi Temple Monument on Shaoshi Mountain* by Yang Jiong reads: "Like Sanmei of Jiang Ziwen, the traces of Damsel Qingxi can be found; the stories of the two concubines of the Emperor continue." With Damsel Qingxi, the two concubines, E'huang and Nü'ying, are not alone in literature; with Damsel Qingxi and Damsel Qingxi in Solitude, in the literary language, the unmarried Yun Ying from Luo Yin's *Gift to a Sing-Song Girl in Zhongling* found a match, making an elegant pair; with Damsel Qingxi, those sexually awakened women will have a literary image to turn to; with Damsel Qingxi, the third daughter (Sanmei) has a spokesperson. In one of the Qing Dynasty Li E's poems *Mourning the Deceased Women*:

> The third daughter compares herself to Damsel Qingxi,
> and encounters the white stone immortal.

Isn't it a beautiful metaphor? With Damsel Qingxi, there will be more lightning or rainbows in the literati's fantasy. Huang Zunxian in *You He Shi Fu* wrote:

> The words of the White Stone Immortal on the paper,
> the picture of Damsel on the sleeve.

Isn't it a subtle hint?

Jiang Ziwen and Sanmei, one at the head of Qingxi, and the other at the end of Qingxi, day and night, year after year, watch over it. In the sixth poem of *Qinhuai Miscellaneous Poems*, Qing Dynasty poet Wang Shizhen, wrote:

> Qingxi water and trees are the best,
> praised by nobles and commoners for six dynasties.

Duan Hou's house in the Song Dynasty has disappeared,
let alone the residence of Jiang Zong in the Southern Dynasties.

Jiang Ziwen's magical cyan bone, the supernatural story of his temple, the charming face of Damsel Qingxi, and the beautiful and moving legends of Qingxi Middle Bridge illuminate the Qingxi water and trees, as if every ripple were filled with the purity of literature.

Chapter 4

Old-Time Glory

By the Red Bird Bridge, luxuriant the wild grass and flowers;
Black Gown Lane entrance
stained by the setting Sun at this hour.
O Swallows, in the great halls of the lords
you used to nest,
Into the commoners' homes you've all flown.

—LIU YUXI, *The Black Gown Lane*

Let's start with a story related to this poem.

It is said that during the Tang Dynasty, there was a young man named Wang Xie in Jinling City. The Wang family had been sailing for generations and had accumulated great wealth. Wang Xie inherited his ancestral estate. He sailed a giant ship to Dashi, a caliphate at that time, to do business. The boat had been at sea for over a month, and one day, suddenly, a gale started to howl, and terrifying waves came at it. Everyone on board fought hard together to keep the ship afloat, but the storm was too strong to handle. The vessel capsized, and everyone fell into the water. Only Wang Xie managed to cling to a wooden board and drifted with the waves. There were whales and sharks around that could quickly kill him, but he survived. After three days and three nights of drifting, he finally reached land. Overjoyed, Wang Xie went ashore, and after walking a hundred paces, he came across an old couple in jet-black, about seventy years old.

They were delighted to see Wang Xie and said cheerfully, "Isn't this the son of our master? What has brought you here?" Wang Xie told them what had happened, and the old couple took him home and offered him some sea delicacies. Wang Xie rested for over a month and recovered, and the old man took him to see the king.

After passing through the dense residential areas, the busy streets, and across a long bridge, they reached the palace. All the ministers in the court wore black gowns and black hats. Having received them, the king urged the old man to take good care of Wang Xie and to give him whatever he wanted. Wang Xie was living under the old man's roof. The old man has a gorgeous daughter. The two young people spent every day together and grew fond of each other. The old man intended to marry his daughter to Wang Xie. In a foreign place, lonely and grateful for their hospitality, Wang gladly said yes. On the day of their marriage, Wang Xie observed her closely and noticed that his bride was so charming that he couldn't love her more. Since he drifted to this land, Wang Xie had accumulated numerous questions about what he had seen and heard. His bride explained to him that this was the Black Gown Kingdom.

As for why the old man called him the son of their master, she said that he would understand soon in the future. After the wedding, when the newlywed couple was having a good time, the wife would suddenly get upset, frown, and burst into tears. Wang Xie was puzzled, but she replied gently that she was afraid of saying goodbye soon and that it was destined, and no one could change it.

The king summoned Wang Xie and held a banquet in Baomo Hall. At the banquet, every item, including musical instruments, was black. When the king urged the guests to drink more wine, he said: "Since ancient times, this state has only received two visitors. It is a rare chance. Why not compose a poem, not only as a souvenir but also as a favorite topic for the future?"

Wang Xie improvised, narrating his experience of the sea storm, drifting to this state, and expressing his homesickness:

Homesickness makes my eyes well up,
how I wish I could grow some wings.

The king read it and readily promised to help him return home. But Wang Xie's wife was upset. "If you wish to go home, just say it. There is no need to ridicule us." Wang Xie didn't understand what she meant nor cared to.

Soon, the sea was serene again, and Wang Xie was about to travel far back home. He bid goodbye to his wife in the Black Gown Kingdom. Before he set off, she gave him an elixir of the sea god, saying that it could resurrect someone who had been dead for less than a month. The king's gift was a black bag called the flying cloud. He instructed Wang Xie to crawl in, sprinkled some drops from a pond, and ordered him not to open his eyes. Immediately, the wind howled, but soon, the surroundings calmed down. Wang Xie opened his eyes and realized that he had returned to his home. There was no one in the hall, only two swallows whispering to each other on the beams. He realized that the so-called Black Gown Kingdom was the Swallow Kingdom.

They were surprised and delighted when the family saw him return safe and sound. Wang Xie gave a statement about the incident at sea without mentioning the days in the Black Gown Kingdom. He had a son, who was only three years old when he left home. Half a month before he returned home, the boy had just died. Wang Xie was overwhelmed with grief but suddenly recalled the parting gift from his wife in the Black Gown Kingdom. He fed the elixir to his son. It worked, and the boy was resurrected.

Autumn came, and the two swallows on the beam were to fly away. Before leaving, they hovered over Wang Xie's head with a mournful cry. Wang Xie composed a poem on a small piece of paper and tied it to one swallow's tail. The following spring, the swallows flew back with a small note tied to one's tail, which was also a poem:

Our past encounter was destined,
but now we are separated for life.
Lovesickness will still come the following spring,
but not the swallows.

Wang Xie was immersed in infinite remorse after reading it. After the spring of that year, the swallows never came again. However, the story of

Wang Xie spread, and people named the place where he lived Black Gown Lane.

This story is collected in the extra fourth volume of *Qing Suo Gao Yi* by Liu Fu from the Song Dynasty titled "Wang Xie Drifting into the Black Gown Kingdom." This plot is so mythical, even though the author quoted Liu Yuxi's *Five Songs of Jinling* to corroborate it, that it is estimated that few will buy it. It will be a treat if one takes this story as a symbol and savors it slowly. In the Tang Dynasty, the prosperity of the Six Dynasties family was long gone, just like the Black Gown Kingdom, which was a world away. After enduring a turbulent storm, the nobles like Wang Xie will naturally be lost in melancholy and remorse as they look back at that glorious history at Red Bird Bridge and Black Gown Lane in the setting sun.

History adds imagination to this ordinary lane, romanticizing it. Before Wang Xie settled down there, the name of Black Gown Lane had already existed. Located on the south bank of the Qinhuai River, during the Three Kingdoms Period, it accommodated the imperial guards of the Kingdom Wu. The imperial guards wore black military uniforms, so it was named Black Gown Camp among the commoners. After the Jin family moved to the south, the Wang and Xie families settled there, and their prestige attracted the Black Gown Lane more attention and fame.

Before crossing the river, the Wang family of Langya was already a powerful political force. The filial son Wang Xiang and the famous court officials Wang Rong and Wang Yan all came from the Wang family of Langya. Later, Wang Dao and Wang Dun played pivotal roles in the political arena of the Eastern Jin Dynasty. In the first year of the Yongjia Period (AD 307), the Rebellion of the Eight Kings had just ended, but the Uprising of the Five Barbarians was pressing. The Sima regime, whose vitality was severely sapped, had little chance of surviving. In the same year, Wang Yan, the representative of the Wang family, made a plan with Sima Yue, the king of the Eastern Seas, to send the king of Langya, Sima Rui, to move to Jianye, saving a way out for the Sima regime. This was a long-term plan that affected the survival of the Wang family and even the rise and fall of Chinese culture. Wang Kuang, Wang Dun, and Wang Dao have all actively contributed their wisdom to the plans. The king of Langya, Sima Rui, moved from Xiapi to Jianye, while Wang Dun and Wang Dao also traveled south as planned, becoming Sima Rui's assistants and advisors.

Tian Yuqing analyzed the stakes in detail in *The Politics of the Eastern Jin Dynasty*. The Wang family were the first to cross the river southwards, and they did it with plans and readiness, which was different from other families that moved southwards. When other aristocrats fled south in haste, they had already adapted to life in the south. In terms of continuing the Sima regime and preserving the lifeline of culture east of the Yangtze, the Wang family, especially Wang Dao, had made an outstanding achievement, which could not happen without sufficient mental preparation.

The northern aristocrats traveled thousands of miles, startled, and embarrassed. When they reached Jianye, they were physically and mentally exhausted. There was a psychological gap and various discomforts in their daily life. Even Emperor Yuan of the Jin Dynasty could not help but sigh, as recorded in *A New Account of Tales of the World Speech*, "Depending on others, I always feel ashamed." On fine spring and autumn days, scholars from the north gathered at the new pavilion in the south of the city, having a feast sitting on the grass. Looking at Jinling mountains and rivers, similar to their old capital Luoyang, they were reminded of the sudden vicissitudes of life. They sighed: "Similar scenery, but there are still differences in the mountains and rivers!"

Hearing this, everyone present had mixed feelings, speechless and weeping. Only Wang Dao became serious and shrieked: "This is the moment that we need to work together to take back the land. How can we behave like prisoners with hope?"

Regardless, it was easier said than done to take back the land, which Wang Dao must have been well aware of. He knew even better that if one fails to boost morale and unite the people, it would be in vain to endure present hardship and put in more effort when power dwindles.

While others were still overwhelmed by the miserable drifting, Wang Dao had calmed down and built confidence to take root in the south of Yangtze for "localization." He was a political visionary who saw the big picture. To establish the prestige of Sima Rui, the king of Langya, as soon as possible in the south of the Yangtze River, he took great pains to design a ceremony: March third was made the traditional *xiuqi* (one of the basic ancient rituals in China) day. He, Wang Dun, and other nobles who moved to the south humbly escorted Sima Rui out of the city. The heads of the local southern nobles, commonly known as the Wus, such as Ji Zhan and Gu

Rong, could not help but be awed. Wang Dao persuaded Emperor Yuan of Jin to apply the carrot-and-stick method to the Wu family to win over and use these local forces and lay the foundation for the regime to establish a foothold in the south of Yangtze.

There have been unsolved misunderstandings between the northern and southern clans for a long time. A few decades ago, the North and the South were rival states. After the South was defeated, the southerners were inevitably reduced to second-class citizens, but now the northerners were stranded in the South. The northern aristocrats have always looked down on the southern aristocrats. They openly despised talented scholars like the Lu Ji brothers. In the early relationship between the northern and southern clans, there was a symbol running through it, that is, the cheese of the North. Allegedly, when Lu Ji visited Wang Wuzi for the first time in Luoyang, Wang Wuzi pointed at the goat cheese and said to Lu Ji, "What do you have in the east of the Yangtze that is comparable to this?"

The proud Lu Ji replied without mercy: "There is water shield soup that tastes delicious even without seasonings." The question that Wang Wuzi tossed out was a vivid demonstration of the condescending and arrogant attitude of the northern aristocrats. However, time could change it all. After the northerners had moved south, once, Wang Dao invited Lu Wan, a member of the Lu family in Wujun, to taste goat cheese. As a subordinate, Lu Wan had to give it a bite due to the etiquette of honor and inferiority. After returning home, the more he thought about it, the more foolish he felt.

The next day, he wrote a note to vent his anger: "Yesterday, I had a bit too much of the cheese, and I was uncomfortable all night. I'm a southerner, and this time I was almost killed by a northerner."

Wang Dao was thoughtful. The Wangs were new to the south, so there was no need to be arrogant toward the Lu's. He probably had an innocent intention to simply share the delicacy of goat cheese. Wang Dao knew that at this time, arrogance was no good. When the state was in a survival crisis, he had to keep a good relationship with the Wus, which meant that he should swallow his pride. He took the initiative to propose a political alliance with Lu Wan through the marriage of their children. Unexpectedly, the other party declined decisively, arguing that "The good and the bad shall not mix."

These words sounded harsh and provocative, but Wang Dao did not take it to heart, let alone hold grudges.

At that time, Wang Dao's political reputation was so high that even Emperor Sima Rui respected him as a *zhongfu* (an honorific title of a minister from the emperor) and invited him to sit on the throne as if he were the emperor's equal. There was a famous saying: "Wang and Sima co-rule the world." The Wang family was surprisingly placed ahead of the Sima family. Among the aristocrats, it was also popular to call Wang Dao *jiangzuo guanyiwu* (a talent able to save the state). He was compared to Guan Zhong, who helped Duke Huan of Qi achieve hegemony during the Spring and Autumn Period. Wang Dao was a magnanimous man, or at least in the early days, and he was generous and humble. Some later generations accused him of faking to be lenient, mostly because he killed Zhou Ji by making a third party the instrument of a crime.

However, that was probably false. He was prestigious because he was calm and benevolent in politics, respected nature, and put himself in a humble and open position.

The Eastern Jin Dynasty gradually established its foothold east of the Yangtze River and the Wang family also stood firm in the political arena of Jiankang. Since then, talents have emerged in large numbers in the Wang family, whose glory lasted for five dynasties.

The rise of the Xie family came later than the Wang family but faster. In the Western Jin Dynasty, Xie Heng was just an erudite scholar, serving as a *guozi jijiu* (an official in the imperial college), and his reputation was not high. By the time of the Jin Dynasty, his son Xie Kun was already a well-known minister in the imperial court. Xie Kun appeared unrestrained, but he deeply understood the current situation and was extremely sensitive and cautious politically. He made the Xie family famous and laid a political foundation.

After moving south, Xie Heng's grandsons, Xie Shang, Xie Yi, Xie Ju, Xie An, Xie Wan, Xie Shi, and Xie Tie became a strong force, which won over the people's admiration. Xie An humbly spent years in seclusion on the East Mountain, but he demonstrated great ambition when he returned to the outside world. The result of the Battle of Feishui would decide the survival of the Eastern Jin Dynasty and the fate of the Xie family. No one dared to take it lightly. This was a fight for the monarchy's survival and for the family's honor.

When Xie Xuan dispatched troops, Han Kangbo, who had always been at odds with him, also believed that Xie Xuan would go all out to defeat the enemy. The gods were with Xie An, Xie Xuan, Xie Shi, etc. The victory of this battle not only saved the Eastern Jin Dynasty but also greatly improved the status of the Xie family. After the Feishui triumph, the Xie family entered its heyday. In the Southern Dynasty, Xie Hun, Xie Lingyun, Xie Huilian, Xie Zhuang, and Xie Tiao were consecutively born, expanding the family strength and outshining most common clans.

During the Jin Dynasty, the political situation was turbulent, like the storm in the story at the beginning. The northern families represented by the Wangs and the Xies were like Wang Xie, who survived the storm and settled south of Yangtze. The legend of the Black Gown Kingdom was a vivid metaphor for this period of history. As the stronghold of the Wangs and the Xies in Jianye, Black Gown Lane has gradually become a symbol, and the descendants of the two families were called Black Gown Men. As time passed, this name accumulated richer and richer cultural significance. At the end of the Eastern Jin Dynasty, the Huan Xuan rebels who invaded Jiankang took a fancy to Black Gown Lane and wanted to requisition it as a barracks, but Xie Hun came forward to stop it. As the leader of the Xie family at that time for him, the lane was not a simple ancestral home but a symbol of the glory and tradition of the family.

These aristocratic families gradually merged with their settlements and gave each other meaning. This narrow alley took the Wangs and the Xie's, or in other words, the Wangs and the Xies walked through this narrow alley into the prosperous Tang Dynasty and into history.

Chapter 5

Six Generations of Black Gowns

"The scenery is no different from that of Luoyang, but the state has disintegrated."

That being said, in fact, the scenery of Nanjing differs significantly from that of Luoyang. It is not the scenery and climate of Nanjing that northerners had difficulty adapting to, but the cultural geography and the political scenery.

In this regard, one must admire Wang Dao's long-term vision and extraordinary insight. At the beginning of their move to the south, other northern nobles were weeping at the New Pavilion and taking pity on themselves. They did not take Wu locals seriously, let alone the Wu dialect. But Wang Dao had already begun to learn the Wu dialect and used it. One day in midsummer, the talker Liu Dan paid a home visit to Wang Dao. He saw prime minister Wang placing the chessboard on his belly and mumbling, "何乃渹 *hénǎihōng* (how cold)!" The pronunciation of "渹" is *qìng*, which means cold in the Wu dialect. Later, Liu Dan was asked how he felt when he met the prime minister. Liu Dan replied, "Nothing special except that he could speak the Wu dialect." Liu Dan was not particularly pedantic and stubborn, so he was not surprised, but it must have taken courage for Wang Dao to speak the Wu dialect in front of this northern gentry. As the Wang senior set an example, the young Wang Huizhi and Wang Xianzhi were no longer ashamed to learn the Wu dialect. At the beginning of learning a new dialect, one's expression and tone might sound unnatural and sometimes even funny. So, the dapper Wang Huizhi and Wang Xianzhi appeared clumsy and foolish in the eyes of the eminent monk Zhi Daolin when they spoke the Wu dialect, like "white-necked birds that let out only a hoarse cry." Sounding hilarious is an unavoidable price to pay in language learning. Living in a different place and not learning the native tongue may lead to misunderstanding and friction, and a more significant price may have to be paid. Learning the local language is the first step toward cultural integration.

To use a modern term, many of the descendants of the gentry in the Eastern Jin Dynasty and Southern Dynasty can be regarded as "bilingual" talents. Chen Yinke summarized in his thesis Wu Dialect in the Eastern Jin Dynasty and Southern Dynasty that officials of those periods generally spoke the northern dialect when they received scholars and generally switched to the Wu Dialect when they received the common people. Over time, their original northern pronunciation has undergone interesting changes. This northern accent was initially centered on Luoyang, but after a long time in the south of the Yangtze River, under the influence of the Wu dialect centered on Jiankang, a new mixed accent, which contained both elements of the northern accent and the Wu dialect, came into being as the new Jiankang dialect. As the capital of the Eastern Jin and Southern Dynasties, Jiankang was undoubtedly the primary intersection of the northern and southern cultures at that time. The Nanjing dialect of today still retains the characteristics of both northern and southern accents, which reflects this period of history.

To the northern gentry, the Wu dialect was characterized by sounding light, which they deemed a shortcoming; northern phonetics, including the popular *luoshengyong*, is characterized by stress and voiced sounds, which are also its advantages. *Luoshengyong* was at first an accent of Luoyang scholars when they recited poems. Without the "star effect" of the distinguished and admirable prime minister Xie An, it would not have gained popularity in the south of the Yangtze River. Xie An had suffered from rhinitis since childhood. He used to pinch his nose when speaking. In addition, he had a strong Yangxia of Chenjun (Taikang, Henan Province) accent. When he recited, his pronunciation was unique, especially stress and voiced sounds. Regarding the social influence at that time, Xie An was a "star" in both politics and culture. His fame and unrestrained demeanor made *luoshengyong* all the rage. Celebrities in the south of the Yangtze River followed suit. To sound more alike, some pinched their noses when speaking. It worked, but their posture appeared somewhat awkward. Surprisingly, over a hundred years later in the Southern Qi Dynasty, a literary celebrity with the surname Wu mastered this ancient "fashion." It was more legendary that this "fashion" was said to have saved his life. A few bandits kidnaped Zhang Rong from Wujun in the barren wasteland. On a sudden inspiration, he decided to act like a celebrity speaking in *luoshengyong* calmly. The bandits had never heard such a peculiar tone and were astonished. In the end, they let him go without hurting a single hair on his head. Perhaps this was the charm of being distinguished and admirable.

The power of *fengliu* (distinguished and admirable) is everywhere, which Gu Kaizhi must deeply understand. This outstanding painter from Wuxi—called Jinling* back then—was undoubtedly a sentimental man. He was at the center of fengliu, able to lead it without being affected by it. As a master in chanting, he was invited to perform *luoshengyong*, but he vehemently refused and growled: "Why on earth would I learn to sound like a hag?" In the past, as Huang Jigang explained, in the word *fengliu, feng* was temper, personality, and *liu* was style. A man as famous as Gu Kaizhi would be more temperamental, more pompous, and a little maverick. Most people would tolerate it and see it positively. But this time, Gu Kaizhi did not pretend to be "cool" on purpose, as his words meant more than what they said. It turned out that Huan Wen once highly appreciated him. After Huan Wen died, Xie An, who took over the power, did not put him in an important position. Gu Kaizhi was deeply disappointed. That he jeered at *luoshengyong* was actually to vent his discontent with Xie An. The ancients believed in rejecting an opinion on account of the speaker, while Gu Kaizhi rejected an accent on account of the speaker.

The Eastern Jin Dynasty was the heyday of aristocratic politics in the Six Dynasties. Members of the Wang and Xie families were usually the leaders and spokespersons of that era's romance, and the promotion of many romantic fashions depended on them. This was true in language, life, politics, and in literature. Let's take a look at an example of a fan. Xie An had a fellow countryman who was about to go home. He was impecunious, but he possessed many unsellable cattail leaf fans. Xie An took one and always

---

*The Jinling here is 晋陵 jìnlíng instead of 金陵 jīnlíng. The former was an old county in Jiangsu while the latter refers to the city of Nanjing.

waved it when giving a speech or entertaining guests. Suddenly, scholars in the capital scrambled to follow suit, and the fans were quickly sold out. The second example is about a garment. The government was in financial distress at the beginning of its move southwards. It could not afford to pay the salaries of hundreds of officials, so it decided to pay them with the tens of thousands of pieces of cloth in the warehouse. But this cloth was so coarse that no one wanted it. In the end, Wang Dao took the lead in wearing a garment made of this cloth. After this became a popular trend, this cloth quickly became the rage of the market. Sometimes, it doesn't make sense that fashion works this way.

In politics, Wang and Xie descendants were hot figures. This was manifested in power and position on the one hand and in marriage on the other. In the age of aristocracy, marriage was the biggest focus of political power relations. Allegedly, when Sima Rui was new to ruling Jianye, it was during the Yongjia Rebellion and material conditions were poor. A little pig was obtained. It was a rare delicacy. There was a particularly plump piece of meat on the pig's neck. It was reserved exclusively for Sima Rui. Later, Emperor Xiaowu of Jin asked Wang Xun to find an eligible husband for his daughter, Princess Jinling,* and Wang Xun recommended Xie Hun. At this time, another aristocratic family, the Yuans, also intended to marry their daughter to Xie Hun. The Yuan and Xie families were well-matched, but Wang Xun warned the Yuan family to give up because it was "a chunk of meat for the royal family's exclusive consumption." This analogy may seem vulgar, but it was telling. Being compared to that meant that Xie Hun was no ordinary person. In fact, he was not only the "exclusive chunk of meat to the royal family" but also a core figure of the Xie family after Xie An passed away, and the literary tutor and life coach of Xie Lingyun, a rare talent. It was a pity that he died at the hands of Liu Yu in the bloody political struggle between the Jin and Song Dynasties. Princess Jinling was forced to divorce the Xie family and remarried into the Wang family of Langya, and her two daughters were entrusted to Xie Hongwei. After Liu Yu became Emperor Wu of the Song Dynasty, he allowed Princess Jinling to return to the Xie family. Ironically, when Liu Yu usurped the throne, Xie Dan of the Xie

---

*This Jinling is 晋陵 instead of 金陵, which has the same pinyin as the former. It was an old county in Jiangsu Province.

family passed the seal to him in court. After all, the majesty and legitimacy of imperial power were inseparable from the support of the nobles, so Liu Yu needed the cooperation of the Xie family. The changes of the Six Dynasties were like a multi-act political drama. One scene ends, and at once, another begins. Here, the "glorious" masters of ceremonies were often Wang and Xie descendants: When Huan Xuan usurped the throne, it was Wang Mi, the grandson of Wang Dao, and Xie Dan, the grandson of Xie An, who handed over the imperial seal; when the Southern Qi Dynasty was founded, it was Wang Jian who passed the seal. Since they were popular characters, they were naturally the target of public criticism. And many had a similarly tragic ending like Xie Hun.

The Wangs and Xies were both political stars and experts in literature. It was difficult to tell in which aspect they were professionals or amateurs. In literary circles, sometimes their opinion could magically make a less interesting idea go viral. During the Eastern Jin Dynasty, Yu Chan, a young writer from the Yu family in Yingchuan, wrote the *Prose Poem of Yangdu* and presented it to Yu Liang, a prominent figure in his clan. On the surface, it revolved around the construction of the capital city Jiankang, but the actual theme was to praise and advocate the resurgence of the Eastern Jin Dynasty. It was as courageous and commendable as the *Prose Poem of Resurgence* by Wang Yu. Perhaps Yu Liang had long realized that although this prose poem was politically correct, it had few artistic novelties. Still, for fear of hurting the feelings of his relatives, he spared no effort to boast about it, claiming that it was as good as *Two Capitals* by Zhang Heng and *Three Capitals* by Zuo Si. He also predicted that people would scramble to copy and read it and that the price of paper in the capital would rise as a result. This was undoubtedly an exaggeration and suspicious of favoritism, so it was no wonder that Xie An sang a discordant tune. Xie An criticized this prose poem as "a parody" that lacked novelty, thus unlikely to cause a sensation, and impossible to raise the price of paper in Jiankang. He was right.

This example is not given to show that Xie An never practiced favoritism but that important figures like him were too influential, and their opinion should never be underestimated. Yuan Hong wrote *The Legends of Scholars*, but it was much less influential because he did not get Xie An's support. Some parts of this book were stories of Xie An, so after it was finished, Yuan Hong presented it to Xie An to read. Xie An taunted him for being so pedantic that he seriously took all the jokes he made back then. As soon as this comment spread, the reputation of *The Legends of Scholars* plummeted. Coincidentally, Pei Qi wrote *Yulin*, which was similar to *The Legends of Scholars*. Xie An was told of the two paragraphs that were written about him in *Yulin*, and he called it an absolute fabrication by Pei Qi. Also, Xie An recited *Jing Jiu Lu Xia Fu* by Wang Xun mentioned in the book, and he didn't even bother to comment. After that, although *Yulin* did not disappear, it was no longer one of the central topics for the nobles to discuss and was gradually forgotten. Yin Zhongkan had a similar experience with Wang Gong. He had a friend who excelled at writing prose poems in the style of *Shu Xi*, and Yin Zhongkan admired those prose poems. He gladly shared them with Wang Gong. While he was overjoyed reading them, Wang Gong remained silent from beginning to end, making Yin Zhongkan both disappointed and embarrassed. Had Wang Gong shown a different attitude, these works might have been handed down.

Xie An paid no heed to *Yulin* and *Jing Jiu Lu Xia Fu* by Wang Xun, probably because he held a grudge against Wang Xun. The Wangs and the Xies had the highest status, and while they looked down upon other clans, they never ceased to praise the descendants of their own family without humility to elevate their fame. It was so common that uncles praised their nephews and nieces in these two families, and elder brothers complimented younger siblings. Other families were no exception, either. In the beginning, the Wang family was so arrogant that they despised the Xie family and regarded them as nothing but new money. Xie Wan once visited Wang Tian, but the arrogant Wang Tian gave him the cold shoulder. After the status of the Xie family rose, Wang and Xie families often lent each other a hand and flattered one another.

When Wang Huzhi lived in seclusion in East Mountain, he was so poor that he could hardly afford food. Tao Fan was the magistrate of Wucheng at the time, and he gifted him with a boatload of rice. Wang Huzhi resolutely declined the help. He proudly stated that even if he were dying of starvation, he would only beg the Xies for food, and not deign himself to receive assistance from the ordinary Tao Fan. Wang Xizhi and Xie An had close contacts, traveling together and discussing various topics. When they were alive, it was probably the "honeymoon period" for the two families.

Wang Xizhi and his son kept a close friendship with the Xie family, so good that his wife was jealous of the fact that they were closer to them than to her family. She was so angry that she told her younger brother not to visit her again because the Wang family was enthusiastic when they received the Xies, but much colder when they received her brother. From the Eastern Jin Dynasty to the Southern Dynasty, the Wang and Xie families had the strongest alliance. It was inevitable that they had quarrels and split, and held grudges for a long time. The marriage of Wang Ningzhi and Xie Daoyun was somewhat discordant. The hostility between Wang Xun and Xie An may have stemmed from the marriage of their children, which ended in divorce. With that being said, the title Past Glory has fallen naturally from the romantic cloud of history, getting closer to the real world and adding a slight coldness to it.

The Qing Dynasty poet Wang Shizhen wrote in *Qinhuai Miscellaneous Poems*:

There is the most lucid water in Qingxi,
and the Wangs and Xies have been praised for six generations.

The story told in the last paragraph begs to differ. There are more stories like that to be told, but they stain the romantic image of the Wangs and Xies, and it is best that we stop.

Chapter 6

Death of the Concubine

The dark clouds cast a shade upon the stairs,
The icy frost chills the hall.

—QIU LINGJU, *Dirge of the Concubine*

The concubine was dead.

She was the most-loved concubine of Emperor Xiaowu of the Liu Song Dynasty. This was definitely explosive news in Jiankang early in the fourth lunar month of the sixth year of the Daming Era (AD 462). Inside and outside Taicheng, in the streets and alleys of the capital, everybody was gossiping about her sudden death. They became both curious and anxious: how would the death of this beautiful and mysterious woman affect the political situation of the state? This was by no means an unnecessary concern nor unfounded speculation. It was well-remembered that eight years before, the Prime Minister, the Governor of Jingzhou, and the Prince of Nanjun Liu Yixuan staged the rebellion that shook the whole state all because of her. After the war ended, this woman entered the harem and became the concubine of Liu Jun, Emperor Xiaowu of the Song Dynasty. It was well-known that she held a special spot in his heart as the emperor's favorite concubine. In the past eight years, various secrets and gossip about her had been circulated among the people, attracting their endless curiosity. These rumors were usually groundless; they still spread like wildfire without an origin.

It was believed she was surnamed Yin and was the daughter of Yin Yan of Chenjun. At least, this was what the imperial court announced to the public. At first, living under the roof of Liu Yixuan, she was either his concubine, the Prince of Nanjun, or his son. After Liu Yixuan's rebellion was suppressed, she was taken into the harem by Emperor Xiaowu. The winner takes it all as usual, and history is the witness. However, most people did not believe the official statement. Simply, the bad luck of Yin Yan was the evidence.

Yin Yan came from Changping, Chenjun (now northeast of Xihua County, Henan Province). Indeed, this refers to his ancestral home. He was a member of the northern gentry who moved to the south. Yin Yan was highly appreciated by Emperor Wen of the Song Dynasty in his early years. During the Yuanjia Period, he had already been a government official who was appointed to the princes' palaces and local prefectures. In the first year of the Xiaojian Era (AD 454), when Liu Yixuan started the rebellion, he was the Interior Minister of Luling. When the rebels stormed the city, he fled. If his daughter were Liu Yixuan's concubine or his son's concubine, he would not need to escape. After the rebellion was stopped, he was caught and imprisoned but was soon released, and the case was closed. It remains unknown what happened exactly, but it doesn't seem that Concubine Yin was pulling the strings from behind. Otherwise, her status as a favorite concubine would help her father rapidly advance his career in the following years. In fact, he had little luck in being promoted the next year. It was a flat career.

After Emperor Xiaowu passed away, his son, who was stripped of the title of the crown prince, ascended to the throne and began to comprehensively straighten out the debts with her and others. A legion of people was involved, but oddly, Yin Yan was not one of them. This only proves that the concubine was not Yin Yan's daughter, and even if there was a father-daughter relationship between them, it was never biological. There might have been a political transaction behind Emperor Xiaowu's forgiveness of Yin Yan: Yin Yan recognized her as his daughter under the imperial edict so that she would have a legal origin; the emperor forgave him for everything and allowed him to redeem himself by good service as an official again. It was easy to pretend for a short time but challenging to keep it up for years. After her death, Yin Yan had to express his grief to make the story believable. As expected, he wrote *The Eulogy of a Concubine*, and today there are still four sentences of this lost article recorded in Volume 385 of the *Taiping Imperial Encyclopedia*—in my opinion, this eulogy must have been written under the imperial order or by a ghostwriter, and it was a necessary step of the deception.

In the eyes of the people at that time, this eulogy was self-deceiving. The more it tried to hide, the more the falseness was exposed. They believed that behind the lie was the truth: the concubine was not surnamed Yin but Liu, and she was the daughter of the prime minister, the feudal prefectural governor of Jingzhou, and the Prince of Nanjun, Liu Yixuan. From *The Book of Songs* and *The History of the Southern Dynasty* to *The Comprehensive Mirror in Aid of Governance*, orthodox historians leaned towards the view that from that time to the Tang and Song dynasties. Emperor Xiaowu of the Song Dynasty Liu Jun was notorious for his lechery. No matter the occasion or the object, he could not care less about ethics. He put up women from outside the palace in the residence of his mother, the empress dowager, for the night. And there was the gossip that he committed incest with the empress dowager. This scandal spread outside the palace and to the Northern Dynasty. Yan Zhitui pointed out in the *Motto of the Yan Family: Articles* that Emperor Xiaowu had a notorious reputation, suggesting that it might not be a false accusation.

Regarding exposing the emperor's secrets, *The Book of the Song Dynasty*, which was based on the national history of the Liu Song Dynasty, was less aggressive in general. Still, *The Book of the Song Dynasty: Biography of Liu Yixuan* bluntly accused him: "Emperor Shizu (the temple name of Emperor Xiaowu) was promiscuous, toying with Yixuan's daughters. Yixuan was infuriated and plotted to rebel against him." In fact, Liu Yixuan was the uncle of Emperor Xiaowu, and his daughters were the emperor's cousins. That the emperor committed incest with several of them went beyond Liu Yixuan's tolerance and most directly provoked him to rebel. Once upon a time, in the battle against Liu Shao in the last years of the Yuanjia Period of the Liu Song Dynasty (AD 424–453), Liu Yixuan fought side by side with Emperor Xiaowu and made outstanding contributions.

After Emperor Xiaowu ascended the throne, Liu Yixuan was appointed the prime minister, and *The Book of the Southern Qi Dynasty: Records of Officials* writes that he was also the premier. Whether prime minister or premier, he was the second most powerful person in the country. Since the Wei and Jin Dynasties, the premier position has only been used as a conferred title, not as a real post with power. In the Eastern Jin Dynasty, only a few powerful officials, such as Wang Dao, Wang Dun, and Huan Wen, had served as prime ministers, while only Liu Yu, who usurped the throne, served as premier. A mediocre talent held the second most powerful position. What more could a man ask for? Of course, the real reason why Liu Yixuan rebelled was that Zang Zhi, Inspector of Jiangzhou, had ulterior motives and did his best to provoke him. However, had Liu Yixuan not suffered the scandal of the incest between his daughters and the emperor, however, eloquent Zang Zhi was, would not have ignited the fire of rebellion within Liu.

The family drama escalated into a national matter and, at last, into domestic turmoil. As the center of this domestic turmoil, the concubine was held accountable. *The Book of the Song Dynasty: Biography of Liu Yixuan* documents that at first, he planned to instigate a rebellion in the winter of the first year of the Xiaojian Period (AD 454), but as confidential information was leaked, he started the rebellion in February of that year, which was less than a year after Emperor Xiaowu ascended the throne. Specifically, it was only ten months. The adultery between Emperor Xiaowu and Liu Yixuan's daughters must have occurred within these ten months. The Qing Dynasty historian Zhao Yi wrote in his *Notes on the Twenty-Two Histories* that the Song palace witnessed great lechery, and there were countless scandals between the emperor, empress, concubines, princes, and princesses. The incest between Emperor Xiaowu and Liu Yixuan's daughters was just one of them.

Liu Yixuan's rebellion started in a great hurry and lasted only four months before it was suppressed. Liu Yixuan was sentenced to death in Jiangling. And one of his daughters was secretly taken into the palace by Emperor Xiaowu and became a *shuyi* (one of the concubine titles). She, falsely surnamed Yin, pretended to be the daughter of the Yin family. Later, the dethroned Crown Prince Liu Ziye took his aunt, Princess Xincai, the daughter of Emperor Wen of the Song Dynasty, as his concubine, changed her surname to Xie, thus the name Empress Xie in the palace. To deceive the public, Liu Ziye killed a palace maid and declared that the princess was dead. He pulled the same trick as his father, Emperor Xiaowu. Like father, like son.

She was probably not always passive in the relationship between Emperor Xiaowu and his concubines. Naturally, even if she couldn't avenge her father's death, she could still commit suicide to keep a clean name, but she gladly accepted the position of Emperor Xiaowu's favorite concubine. In the next seven or eight years, she gave birth to five sons and a daughter for him. After that, when Liu Yixuan's other daughters were forgotten in history, she alone stayed in the historical spotlight as the favorite in the harem. In AD 462, when this love was still burning, she passed away. Perhaps she knew that her death would bring great sorrow to her children, endless grief for Emperor Xiaowu, and change the fate of many people, but she never expected that it would bring disaster to the country.

When she was alive, people used to call her Yin Shuyi, but soon after her death, she was renamed Concubine Yin or Concubine Xuan. Not calling her by this name might irritate Emperor Xiaowu, who was still immersed in grief, and get themselves beheaded. In the harem system of the Liu Song Dynasty, under the empress, there were three *furens* (the higher ranking of a concubine) and nine *pins* (the lower ranking of a concubine). Shuyi was only one of the nine *pins*, while *guifei* (the highest ranking of a concubine)) ranked first among the three *furens*, meaning that she was second only to the empress. It was believed her status was as high as a premier. There was no *guifei* in the harem titles of the Song Dynasty. Emperor Xiaowu added it in the third year of the Xiaojian Period (AD 456). It might have been tailored for Yin Shuyi, but it remains unknown if the title was ever bestowed on her. Perhaps, he was waiting for the best timing. Unexpectedly, Yin Shuyi died so suddenly that Emperor Xiaowu was caught off guard, and it had to be conferred as a posthumous gift to her. For the deceased, the gift could not mean less, but for the living, it was meaningful. For Emperor Xiaowu, this late gift was his memorial and compensation for her; for her two sons and one daughter, it sufficed to consolidate and even elevate their status; for the crown prince, it appeared as an aggressive threat.

No one has raised any doubts about the posthumous title of Concubine Yin. Why bother? The emperor's mind was made up so firmly that challenging it would not change it. And it was nothing more than a posthumous gift, after all. What's more, there was a more substantive problem: the posthumous title, which was an evaluation of a person's whole life, so it had to be discussed carefully to present the emperor with a satisfying result.

At this time, Jiang Zhiyuan couldn't wait to share his idea, which proved a reckless move. Jiang Zhiyuan had been by Emperor Xiaowu's side for a long time and was always appreciated by him.

Not long before, he had offended Emperor Xiaowu and was transferred to serve as the chief of staff for Liu Ziluan, the Prince of Xin'an, who was Yin Shuyi's son. The emperor wanted him to ponder over his mistakes behind closed doors and to reflect on himself thoroughly so that he could appoint him to more important positions in the future. Jiang Zhiyuan, confident and quick-witted, was eager to make up for his previous mistakes, so he proposed to use the character "怀 huái." According to the Law of Posthumous Matters, it means both benevolence and short-lived death. The former sounds great, but the latter not so, even though it was true that she died young. In all fairness, this posthumous title itself was not derogatory at all. On the contrary, it signified sadness and sympathy.

However, Emperor Xiaowu decided it sounded unpleasant and didn't look like a proper title. He even suspected that Jiang Zhiyuan messed with him on purpose and held grudges. One day, the emperor led an entourage, including Jiang Zhiyuan, on horseback to the tomb of Concubine Yin, which was under construction. He pointed a horsewhip at the stone pillar in front of her tomb. He snarled to Jiang Zhiyuan: "I shall never see the character '怀 huái' on it." Poor Jiang Zhiyuan, who had always been cautious, was deeply frightened, fell ill, and soon died. The ministers understood what the emperor wanted, and someone proposed to use "宣 xuān," which means understanding and sincere, as the posthumous title. It sounded much more musical to the emperor's ears than "怀 huái." So, he accepted it. Since then, Concubine Xuan has become her standard title, and it was commonly used in poetry about her at that time.

The tomb of Concubine Yin rests in the south of Jiankang, forty-five li southwest of Jiangning District in Nanjing. Emperor Xiaowu personally selected the tomb site. It was said that the cliffs and rocks there were dangerous, so it was called Rock Mountain; the mountain resembled a dragon, so Emperor Xiaowu changed its name to Dragon Mountain. Two years later, Emperor Xiaowu's Jingning Mausoleum was built there before he passed away. Concubine Yin's tomb project was so huge that it took at least half a year, unprecedented since the moving southwards in the Eastern Jin Dynasty. Plenty of stonemasons were hired to cut into the mountain and build cemetery roads that extended dozens of *li*, and many of them were injured during the construction. Without *The Comprehensive Mirror in Aid of Governance*, we could hardly believe that there was such a luxurious tomb in Jiankang City in the Middle Ages. Before the mausoleum's completion, Emperor Xiaowu personally visited the site to supervise the construction; after its completion, he often led a group of ministers to the mausoleum to pay tribute to Concubine Yin. It was a pity that the tomb was removed soon after the dethroned crown prince took the throne.

To commemorate the concubine, Emperor Xiaowu made two other significant moves. One was that a Buddhist temple was built in Jiankang City. Because her son was titled Prince of Xin'an, the temple was named Xin'an Temple. He invited the eminent monks Shi Daoyou and Shi Fayao to be stationed in Xin'an Temple. He appointed Shi Daoyou, who advocated the theory of enlightenment, to be the master of the temple. The entire city knew about the unusual background of Xin'an Temple. For a time, monks gathered there, making it a rising star of all Jiankang Buddhist temples. The other move was that he built a temple in the name of the concubine in Jiankang City. It was a well-known fact that this move was not allowed. According to the ancient ancestral temple system, concubines were not qualified to enter the ancestral temples. Even Empress Dowager Bo, who gave birth to Emperor Wen of the Han Dynasty, and Madame Gouyi, who gave birth to Emperor Zhao of the Han Dynasty, only had a bedroom temple in their cemetery. There has never been a case where a temple was built for the concubine alone. However, since the emperor ordered it, the relevant departments naturally did not disobey it. They called it rightful even if it was not: now that "the concubine was so distinguished," of course, "a new temple should rise." Historians, including the scholar Hu Sanxing who annotated *The Comprehensive Mirror in Aid of Governance*, scolded Emperor Xiaowu for his infatuation with lust and failure to follow an ancient rule. Obviously, he failed to follow the rules, but there was some love involved, which made it somewhat acceptable.

It remains a mystery whether people at that time realized that from the day when the woman he loved died in the fourth lunar month in AD 462, Emperor Xiaowu changed, becoming moody, and even those who knew him best believed that he held a deep grudge against Jiang Zhiyuan. He often got irritated for no reason and became more and more greedy for money and alcohol. In the beginning, he was spotted walking to Yin's bier every night before going to bed. He poured out the wine for offering to drink, talked to himself as if he were talking to Concubine Yin, and burst into tears as he finished the wine. At her burial, he had a special coffin customized. The upper cover of this coffin could be easily pulled open like a drawer. When he missed her dearly, he opened it to gaze upon her. After several days, her face remained intact, which was a miracle. After the burial, Emperor Xiaowu was still in deep grief. He showed less interest in handling political affairs. He drank almost every day and night and fell into bed when he was drunk. He spent the last two years of his life deeply muddled. Occasionally, when an urgent matter from the court was reported to him, he could pull himself together immediately, looking sharp. At this moment, people could see the "witty and courageous" emperor again. However, when the urgency was addressed, he sank back into listlessness and a mental trance. Overeating and swilling alcohol were his most accustomed self-distractions in his last years.

The 25th day of the tenth lunar month in the sixth year of the Daming Period of the Liu Song Dynasty (AD 463) was the day when Concubine Yin was buried. The emperor authorized the use of the *wenliang* cart (an ancient hearse), *huben* (one of the imperial rewards), patterned swords, imperial chariots, imperial flags, and imperial drums and pipes. Such a grand ceremony was almost comparable to that of the emperor and the empress. Civil and military officials, concubines, and maids all attended her funeral. It was a crowded funeral procession, winding south through the cold wind of early winter. On this day, Emperor Xiaowu visited the Nanye Gate of Jiankang Palace and shed his tears of grief. When he walked past the hearse for the last time, he was overwhelmed with grief, and the people next to him couldn't help but shed tears. It was a sad moment.

It seems that Emperor Xiaowu was indeed an affectionate person. Indeed, he had many shortcomings: lecherous, wasteful, greedy, brutal ... He had 28 sons and an unknown number of daughters, the most among the emperors of the Liu Song Dynasty. Over a dozen of his concubines are listed in *The Book of the Song Dynasty*, and probably countless are not listed. However, he only loved Concubine Yin. For a dictatorial monarch, this was extremely rare. In the fifth month of the eighth year of the Daming Period of the Liu Song Dynasty (AD 464), the 35-year-old Emperor Xiaowu died. He lived for only two years after Concubine Yin was gone. Yi Shunding, a modern poet, once wrote a poem about Nanjing:

> In the other world, as a ghost,
> she was still beautiful and lustful,
> while the talented emperor
> south of the Yangtze River was still infatuated.

Yi Shunding believed Concubine Yin became a lustful ghost even if she had died, and Emperor Xiaowu, who loved her more than his state and power showed his true colors.

> The law has an end, but deep love never rests.
> The clouds, the sun, and the moon, everything makes me lovesick.
> I miss your strolls, your voice. It saddens me to think of you.
> I weep and weep.
> Drowning in grief, without you, I cannot live.
> When the grief is over, what can I do to love you more?

These were the verses he wrote to mourn his Concubine Yin, which sounded deeply sincere. The historical records label him "a well-rounded scholar, with talent for writing." The *Shi Pin* (*Comments on Poems*) calls him an excellent poet who could compose the finest verses effortlessly, and it was no exaggeration.

The concubine was dead. This passionate love that happened in Jiankang City as the fifth century ended while the turmoil of the Liu Song regime had just begun.

Chapter 7

Cold Up High

Gorgeous outfits were forgotten, yet an extravagant feast was held.

The pines absorb the moist from mist,

and the grass has grown into a plain.

—JIANG ZHIYUAN, *Elegy of Concubine Xuan*

The concubine was dead.

In Jiankang in early April of the sixth year (462) of the Daming Period of the Liu Song Dynasty, people exhibited different reactions to this news: some people were grieving; some were celebrating; some were relieved that the nightmare came to an end; some were worried what the future would be like. More people realized right away that it was too rare opportunity to be wasted, and they couldn't wait to make a move. Henceforth, many people in Jiankang City started to dash about, racking their brains out for their own interests. Around this woman's death, political shows and contests were unfolding one after another in Jiankang City.

The imperial concubine died on the second of April that year. She had given birth to five sons and one daughter to Emperor Xiaowu. Liu Ziwen, the fourth eldest, died the youngest, Liu Zhiyu, the second eldest son and Prince Jing of Qi, died at the age of two, and Liu Ziyun, the third eldest son and Prince of Jinling (晋陵, not 金陵, as explained on Page 65) only lived to be four years old. Two sons and one daughter survived. Liu Ziluan, the eldest son and Prince of Xin'an, was only eight years old at the time, and Liu

Zishi, the youngest and Prince of Nanhai, was just three.

Looking at their children, Emperor Xiaowu was lost in tremendous grief. "Drowning in grief, without you, I cannot live. When the grief is over, what can I do to love you more?" The few verses he composed in the prose poem are his truest affection. Perhaps, he had already made up his mind at this time to take the best care of their children so that she could rest in peace in heaven.

His love for her extended to everything about her. In fact, it was well-known in Jiankang City that before she died, Emperor Xiaowu had doted on her children. Her two sons were crowned kings at the age of four, and no prince born by other concubines had enjoyed such preferential treatment. Emperor Xiaowu had a total of 28 children. Liu Ziluan, the son of Concubine Yin, was eighth eldest, but his favorite. In the fourth year (460) of the Daming Period of the Liu Song Dynasty, Liu Ziluan, who was only five years old, was bestowed the title Prince of Xiangyang, who could levy a tax on 2,000 households there, and he also served as the General of the Household Who Pacifies the East and the Prefect of Wujun. In the second year, he was promoted to the General of the Household Who Pacifies the North, Inspector of Southern Xuzhou, concurrently appointed as Administrator of Nanlangya Commandery. Southern Xuzhou was a prefecture established for those who had lost their home in the war. From the eighth year (AD 431) of the Yuanjia Period, its governance started in Jingkou (now Zhenjiang, Jiangsu Province). As the eastern gateway to the capital Jiankang, it was highly important. After Liu Ziluan became the Inspector of Southern Xuzhou, Emperor Xiaowu specially assigned Wujun to Southern Xuzhou, thus further expanding its territory.

Wujun has always been a prosperous zone in the south of the Yangtze River. With the tax revenue from it, the economic strength of Southern Xuzhou has immediately improved. Such favor was granted to him one after another, and other princes were deeply jealous, including even Liu Ziye, the crown prince, and Liu Zishang, the second prince, the children of Empress He. Liu Zishang used to be the favorite of Emperor Xiaowu, but since Liu Ziluan was born, he lost the emperor's exclusive love. Naturally, he was frustrated.

Liu Ziye was a bookworm since he was a child, and he was gifted and a quick learner. He was made the crown prince at the age of six. However, he was reckless and stubborn, which Emperor Xiaowu often reprimanded him for. After Liu Ziluan was born, the crown prince noticed that the emperor was nitpicking at him in everything. Once, when his handwriting was sloppy, he was scolded, so he rewrote the memorial to the throne again, and was reprimanded again. He knew what the real problem was, certainly. Deep in his heart, the seeds of resentment had been sown and grew bigger daily.

In the following days, bad news continued to go to the crown prince, making him fidget more and more. There were rumors that Emperor Xiaowu was deeply disappointed at the crown prince's recent mistakes, and intended to make Liu Ziluan, the Prince of Xin'an, the new crown prince, and that some ministers seconded this motion but Emperor Xiaowu dropped it for the time being because *shizhong* (an official title) Yuan Yi kept speaking up for him, strenuously praising his academic diligence.

In fact, Emperor Xiaowu did not completely drop the idea, but simply believed it was not the best timing. After all, Liu Ziluan was too young, and he urgently needed a right-hand man by his side to teach him, assist him, and help him build a good reputation in intellectual circles. Therefore, Emperor Xiaowu first deployed the talents he appreciated and valued to Liu Ziluan's mansion to help him grow. Almost all of China's most famous literary talents were dispatched to the palace of Xin'an. Most of them were descendants of prestigious families at that time, with good reputations, including Wang Sengqian of the Wang family of Langya, Xie Zhuang and Xie Chaozong of the Xie family of Chenjun, Zhang Yong, Zhang Dai, and Zhang Rong of the Zhang family of Wujun, and Shen Wenji and Shen Faxi of the Shen family of Wuxing, and Gu Chen of the Gu family in Wujun. Wang Sengqian first served as *fujun zhangshi* (an official title, chief of staff) in the residence of Liu Zishang, the Prince of Yuzhang, and then he was transferred to be the *beizhonglang zhangshi* (an official title, chief of staff) for the Prince of Xin'an, Liu Ziluan. The two princes happened to be the emperor's favorites.

The most intriguing was what Emperor Xiaowu said to Zhang Dai. He asked Zhang Dai to serve as Liu Ziluan's *biejia* (an official title, assisting minister), while in fact, he acted as the Inspector of Southern Xuzhou in Liu Ziluan's stead. The emperor comforted Zhang Dai, promising that this was just temporary and that he would be given the chance to make great achievements in the future. The implication was also intriguing. Shen Wenji was the son of Shen Qingzhi, an important minister of the Emperor Xiaowu during the founding of that dynasty. In the fifth year of the Daming Period, he was transferred from being the henchman of the crown prince to the Chief Clerk of Liu Ziluan. This connection between him and Liu Ziluan was particularly eye-catching. Most of these personnel were arranged by the emperor himself, and it did not require much political acumen to see the real intention. The smart crown prince certainly saw it through. He was anxious to make it stop. Just as he was caught up with apprehension, something major happened.

For the politics of Emperor Xiaowu, the second day of April in the sixth year of the Daming Period was an ordinary day, but the death of Concubine Yin made it a turning point. Both Liu Ziluan's Xin'an Palace and the Crown Prince's East Palace tried to make this turn in their favor. The Xin'an Palace seemed more active, with more frequent moves, for obvious reasons.

On April 8, six days after Concubine Yin's death, it was believed to be the birthday of Siddhartha Gautama. A grand ceremony was held in Jiankang City to expiate the sins of the dead Concubine Yin, and to raise funds for the construction of Xin'an Temple. The officers and assistants of the Xin'an Palace have made generous donation. Everybody seized this rare opportunity to put on a show, donating thousands and tens of thousands. Zhang Rong came from a poor family and only donated one hundred.

At first, Emperor Xiaowu appreciated Zhang Rong's capability, and promoted him as *jiangfu canjun* (military officer) of Liu Ziluan. After this tiny donation, Emperor Xiaowu and Liu Ziluan decided that Zhang Rong did not behave well, and exiled him to Fengxi County, Jiaozhou, somewhere extremely desolate. Not to mention that he went through great hardships on the way to his new post, more importantly, he was never put in an important position again before the death of Emperor Xiaowu. Zhang Rong donated little not only because of poverty, but also because of his lofty character and pride. He paid a high political cost for it. After all, there are only a handful of people like him, while most will suck up to the superiors.

For example, Qiu Lingju was one of them. He was the father of Qiu Chi, the author of *Letter to Chen Bozhi*. It may be unfair to accuse Qiu Lingju of this. After all, he was listed in *The Book of Southern Qi: Biography of Literature* and a well-known scholar at the time. He was merely an insignificant official in the sixth year of the Daming Period. After Concubine

Yin died, he composed three elegy poems that resonated with Emperor Xiaowu.

> The dark clouds cast a shade upon the stairs.
> The icy frost chills the hall.

The murk set off the sullen mood. Emperor Xiaowu recited it over and over again and had a deep impression on the name Qiu Lingju. It didn't take long for Qiu Lingju to become a new military advisor of Liu Ziluan. Maybe, he was recruited to replace Zhang Rong.

Jiang Zhiyuan was another example. At that time, he was already the Chief Clerk of Liu Ziluan. Not long ago, he had just offended Emperor Xiaowu and was demoted from assisting the emperor to assisting the Prince of Xin'an. There was still tension between him and the emperor. The death of Concubine Yin gave him the chance opportunity to repair his relationship with the emperor. He presented an *Elegy of Concubine Xuan*. Judging from the remaining verses of this poem, it seems not as good as that of Qiu Lingju. At least, the relationship between Jiang Zhiyuan and Emperor Xiaowu did not improve. On the contrary, by proposing to use the word "怀" as the posthumous title of Concubine Yin, he irritated Emperor Xiaowu again. Had Jiang Zhiyuan's elegy been composed after he proposed the posthumous title, it would have been useless no matter how good it was.

Xie Chaozong was the grandson of Xie Lingyun, who returned to the capital from the Lingnan exile a few years ago. Like his grandfather, he had outstanding literary talent, and just as rebellious. In the sixth year of the Daming Period, he was serving as a Palace Attendant in the residence of Liu Ziluan, the Prince of Xin'an. He wrote a eulogy to Concubine Yin, and after reading it, Emperor Xiaowu greatly praised him as talented as Xie Lingyun. This eulogy won him the Emperor Xiaowu's appreciation and trust, and helped his family reconcile with the imperial power. Xie Chaozong was immediately transferred to serve as the Aide-de-Camp to the Pacifying Army General for Liu Ziluan, occupying a more favorable position. Therefore, the political gain of this eulogy was rather satisfying.

Xie Zhuang worked the hardest and was most adventurous in this aspect. He had already built a high reputation before being appointed as Chief

Clerk of Liu Ziluan. This was precisely what Emperor Xiaowu planned for Liu Ziluan: the prestige of Xie Zhuang could help the young Prince of Xin'an build his authority. Naturally, Xie Zhuang was not indifferent to this. After the death of Concubine Yin, he elaborately wrote *Prayer for Concubine Xuan of Emperor Xiaowu*. The most noteworthy verse in the prayer was:

> Educated the children as well as née Tushan,
> assisted the Yaos to ascend the throne.

The first part quoted the allusions in the *Biography of Women in Ancient China* and compared Concubine Yin to the daughter of née Tushan. Dayu married her daughter as his concubine and she gave birth to Qi, and née Tushan alone assumed the responsibility of educating Qi. Qi succeeded Dayu to the throne, but there was no monarchy at that time, so it was not perfectly ideal to quote this allusion. The latter was based on the allusions of *The Book of Han*, the Yaos included Yao's mother, whose pregnancy lasted 14 months before Yao was born, and Zhao Jieyu, Lady Gouyi, the love of Emperor Wu of Han, gave birth to Emperor Zhao of Han also after fourteen months of pregnancy. Therefore, Emperor Wu of Han called the residence of Zhao Jieyu as "Yao's mother's."

"Assisted the Yaos to ascend the throne," obviously compared Concubine Yin to Zhao Jieyu. These two women were not the wives, but they were the husband's favorites for a while, and their status were similar. From this point of view, the quote was spot-on. The son of Lady Gouyi was not the first-born son of Emperor Wu of the Han Dynasty. So, would Concubine Yin's son be made the heir of Emperor Xiaowu as well? It was such a sensitive matter that pointing it out would be unwise. So, Xie Zhuang beat around the bush in the prayer, but the sophisticated Emperor Xiaowu must have figure out what he meant, and so would the crown prince who was knowledgeable with the ancient facts.

The best part is that Xie Zhuang might have taken advantage of the Emperor Xiaowu's admiration for the eloquent and talented Emperor Wu of the Han Dynasty. After the death of Concubine Yin, Emperor Xiaowu played the role of Emperor Wu of Han twice. Once, he summoned a wizard to cast a spell (hypnosis), and through a veil, he saw the dead Concubine Yin again. She was as stunningly beautiful as when she was alive, and Emperor

Xiaowu was so excited that he was speechless. He wanted to step forward and hold her hand, but instantly, she vanished. Emperor Xiaowu was so regretful that he started to sob.

This experience was the same as that between Emperor Wu of the Han Dynasty and his late Concubine Li, and it happened earlier than that between Concubine Yang for Emperor Ming of Tang, who ordered a Taoist priest to conjure the ghost of Concubine Yang. The other time, he imitated Emperor Wu of Han, who composed *Prose Poem of Li*, and wrote a prose poem to mourn his Concubine Yin. He applied the same writing style and tone. The death of the imperial concubine made Emperor Xiaowu consciously or unconsciously strengthen his identification with Emperor Wu of the Han Dynasty. At this time, it would be a natural choice to take advantage of his love for Concubine Yin and persuade him to dethrone the crown prince, and make Liu Ziluan, the son of Concubine Yin, the new crown prince, as Emperor Wu of the Han Dynasty did before.

Clearly, the literary creation theme with Concubine Yin was not merely a literary performance, nor just to appeal to Emperor Xiaowu and attract his attention. Of course, different works have different political sensitivities, some less sensitive, while some are aggressive, such as this prayer by Xie Zhuang. Was this action instructed by the Prince of Xin'an, or did he actively seek to conform to the wishes of His Majesty? Or was it a combination of both? One must know that Emperor Xiaowu was an expert on literature. In front of him, no ambiguity between the words could escape his eyes. He knew perfectly well what message Qiu Lingju and Xie Chaozong were trying to convey. Interestingly, Emperor Xiaowu did not punish Xie Zhuang, but instead praised his writing, which naturally makes us wonder more.

On the first lunar month of the seventh year (AD 463) of the Daming Period of the Liu Song Dynasty, the relevant departments proposed to build a temple for Concubine Yin so that she could be worshipped all year around. This was against the tradition, but it was passed when the court discussed it. The key was with Xu Yuan and Yu He, both of whom were etiquette experts. Xu Xuan was the Left Minister. Observant and quick to switch sides, the emperor regarded him highly. Yu He was a learned scholar at the Imperial College at the time. They quoted *The Spring and Autumn Annals*, and cleverly justified the building of the temple. In the Spring and Autumn Period, after the death of Zhong Zi, the second wife of Duke Hui of Lu, the state of Lu built a temple for her. Since Concubine Yin ranked first among the three *furens*, she was surely qualified to have a temple built in her name. This argument omitted the fact that the first wife of Duke Hui of Lu died early and had no children, and that Zhong Zi was the second wife and her son had long before been made the crown prince. It was raised merely to elevate the status of Concubine Yin so as to please Emperor Xiaowu and the Prince of Xin'an. It demonstrated perfectly what flattery is. With the strong support of Emperor Xiaowu, the less than ten-year-old Prince of Xin'an has changed drastically. According to *The Book of the Song Dynasty: The Biography of the Fourteen Princes of Xiaowu*, after Concubine Yin was buried, Liu Ziluan, the Prince of Xin'an, was immediately promoted, and his elevation continued to happen. His status skyrocketed to be almost the second most powerful person in the state. Had Emperor Xiaowu not died suddenly in the fifth month of the eighth year (AD 464) of the Daming Period of the Liu Song Dynasty, the subsequent history might have been completely different.

To build a temple for Concubine Yin, the old minister Zhang Yong was ordered to contribute. As the general construction designer of Jiankang City in the Song Dynasty, he had served as Chief Architect for many times. In the seventh year (AD 463) of the Daming Period, Zhang Yong, who had been promoted to be the crown prince's right guard, once again served as the Chief Architect responsible for the construction of the Concubine Xuan Temple. This was a major political project that would tolerate no mistakes. After successfully completing the project as scheduled, Zhang Yong was promoted Right Guard General, which was his reward for the success.

After Concubine Yin was buried, Emperor Xiaowu used to lead his ministers to the cemetery to pay respects. Once, he told Liu Deyuan, the Prefect of Qinjun next him, that if he could wail for Concubine Yin, he would reward him generously. Liu Deyuan immediately burst into tears as if he were really overcome with grief. Emperor Xiaowu was satisfied and promoted him to be the Inspector of Yuzhou at once. Emperor Xiaowu also ordered Yang Zhi, the imperial physician present, wail for Concubine Yin. Yang Zhi first whimpered, and then tears rolled down his face. A few days later, when asked how the tears came so fast, he revealed that his concubine had just passed away in those days, and those tears were not for Concubine Yin but his dead concubine. It seems that after the death of Concubine Yin,

Emperor Xiaowu became a little obsessed. Since it was an order, the tears were not real, but only for this political task. These two had to shed tears. They fulfilled the task well, and if lucky, they could expect greater rewards.

However, in less than two years after Concubine Yin died, the sullen Emperor Xiaowu passed away. It was such a sudden death that Prince of Xin'an was obviously caught off-guard. The Crown Prince Liu Ziye ascended the throne at once, and the suspense was unexpectedly gone. The long-suppressed rage in Liu Ziye's heart erupted. The first step, naturally, was to wreak vengeance on Concubine Yin. Liu Ziye sent people to excavate her tomb to vent his grievances that he had accumulated for years. He intended to have the Jingning Mausoleum of Emperor Xiaowu dug as well, but the ministers tried persuaded him out of it. Instead, he had feces dumped there. He ordered the brand-new Xin'an Temple to be demolished, the monks to be dismissed, and he threatened to kill the monks and nuns in the vicinity, probably because he held the grudge over their being timeservers in the past. The second step was to take down Liu Ziluan, the pain in his ass. Liu Ziluan was removed from important positions and sentenced to die. His half-brother, the 22nd prince, Liu Zishi, and the second princess of Emperor Xiaowu were given the same result. He had the remaining three children of Concubine Yin killed, too. The third step was torturing the people who sided with the Prince of Xin'an. The first to bear the brunt was Xie Zhuang, whose dirty deeds were no secrets to Liu Ziye. His flattery to Emperor Xiaowu and Prince of Xin'an was terribly disrespectful to the crown prince Liu Ziye. He wanted to kill Xie Zhuang, but the people around him kept imploring him for mercy, and his anger faded and let Xie Zhuang live. But Xie Zhuang failed to escape a few months of imprisonment. Had Liu Ziye been a more merciful emperor and ruled longer, Xie Zhuang might not have lived to the day of his release.

This was the retaliation after long-term pressure, and a perverted counterattack. Without Concubine Yin, Emperor Xiaowu might not have treated the crown prince so terribly; if Concubine Yin had lived, Emperor Xiaowu might have lived a few years longer, Liu Ziye might have been dethroned as crown prince and Liu Ziluan been made the new crown prince. Their tomorrow would have been different. However, the concubine died.

Only a few words are available in *History of the Southern Dynasty: Biography of Yin Shuyi*, "beautiful and with a charming smile." It is a formal historical description, but unfortunately not specific enough. Cai Dongfan portrayed her look in *History of Romance in the Northern and Southern Dynasties*. It was quite vivid, but unfortunately fictional. After entering the palace, she quickly elevated herself to Concubine Yin, and whoever dared to reveal the truth of her rise would be killed. "Beautiful women are like flowers blooming on the clouds," her image became more and more mysterious, her stories more vague, and it was difficult to tell the truth. She died 300 years earlier than Emperor Xuanzong of Tang Dynasty and 294 years earlier than his Concubine Yang. This Jiangnan beauty in the Middle Ages, the concubine of the Jinling emperor, might have had a life with less twists and turns than Concubine Yang, but it never lacked in drama; her influence on the current situation may not be as earth-shattering as Concubine Yang, but still tremendous. "After the death of Concubine Yang, Emperor Xuanzong returns to the capital, and he misses her more each day." The Tang Dynasty didn't mind the history of failure. From ancient poetry, novels, operas to modern novels and films, Concubine Yang has been brought back to life again and again. However, what packs the story of Concubine Yin was just a dynasty with incomplete territory, a history of decline, and a messy memory with an unclear theme. "The old stories of the Six Dynasties are gone with time, but the grass turns green again and again." She was long forgotten. Over a thousand years have passed, how many people still remember this woman who was once pampered in Jiankang Palace?

Concubine Yang lives, but Concubine Yin died.

Chapter 8

The Qixia Mountain

Among the temples in Nanjing, Qixia Temple is a late comer. It was not built until the Southern Qi Dynasty. However, it surpassed the earlier temples and became more and more influential. Today, it still boasts good attendance. Every autumn, when the frost and dewfall and the leaves turn red, tourists flock there. After worshipping the Buddha and admiring the statues in the grottoes, they climb the mountain to appreciate the red maples. The mountain is filled with laughter when it is the peak tourist month. It is impossible to fathom that this secluded place used to be so quiet.

Qixia Mountain was originally called She Mountain, and no temple was on it. Regarding the story of the famous temple on this mountain, let's start with Ming Zhengjun, whose real name was Ming Sengshao, an erudite scholar in about the second half of the fifth century between the Liu Song Dynasty and Qi Dynasty. The Ming family was an influential and privileged family of scholar-officials of Qijun. It was not until the end of the Song Dynasty that they moved southward. They were one of the few families that moved to the south late.

Today, the Ming Zhengjun Stele, an antique made over 1300 years ago in the third year (AD 676) of the Shangyuan Period of Emperor Gaozong of the Tang Dynasty, still stands on the right side of the gate of Qixia Temple. The stele pavilion is sealed with glass walls and closed with iron locks all year round. Even antiquity-lovers are prevented from reading the stele closely. It can only be appreciated from a distance. The inscription on the stele was written by Li Zhi, Emperor Gaozong of the Tang Dynasty. It is a rhythmical prose characterized by parallelism and ornateness, a style that was popular back then. And the calligraphy of the inscription was done by Gao Zhengchen, a famous calligrapher at that time. The script style of this stele is close to that of the *Preface of Holy Doctrine* in the Huairen Collection, and it was prevalent back then. The tremendous fame of its writer and calligrapher was undoubtedly a favor to the Qixia Temple and to Ming Sengshao, who had been dead for over a hundred years. This favor could happen because of Ming Chongyan, the six-generation grandson of Ming Sengshao. Ming Chongyan was proficient in sayings about spirits and deities and fortune and disaster. Emperor Gaozong particularly favored and trusted his purposely making a mystery of simple things and exorcism. In 677, he was hired as one of the cabinet members of the emperor. And Emperor Gaozong approved his request and wrote this inscription for the Ming Sengshao. The inscription is so long that most people need more patience to read it all carefully. Therefore, in the *Biography of Ming Chongyan* in the *Old Book of Tang*, the protagonist in the stele was mistaken for Ming Shanbin, the son of Ming Sengshao. Even in the epigraphy masterpieces, from *Jinshilu* by Zhao Mingcheng in the Song Dynasty to *Baoshuting Jinshi Wenzi Bawei* by Zhu Yizun in the Qing Dynasty, the mistake continued. Ming Shanbin served in the Qi and Liang dynasties. He was one of the favorite officials of crown prince Zhaoming and not the stele inscription's protagonist.

Ming Sengshao was a native of Pingyuan, Qijun (now Shandong Province). According to legend, the ancestor of the Ming family was Meng Ming, the son of Bailixi, a *dafu* (senior state official in feudal China) of the Qin State in the Spring and Autumn Period. And Ming Sengshao was born in this family, and his ancestors served in the Jin and Song dynasties. Probably because of his personality, Ming Sengshao showed a strong interest in Buddhism and had a precocious understanding of it since he was a child. However, he had no desire for fame and fortune throughout his life. The Song and Qi dynasties offered him some high positions at least six times, but he politely declined using various excuses. In this way, his reputation grew higher and higher, becoming the most famous hermit at that time.

Many hermits in the Southern Dynasties particularly liked mountains, waters, springs, and rocks. This preference was their style of life. Ming Sengshao is no exception. The places he chose to live in seclusion and practice were all scenic spots with springs and rocks. At first, he resided in

Lao Mountain in Qingdao, Shandong Province, hid in Yanyu Mountain in Lianyungang, Jiangsu Province, and finally moved to She Mountain. The scenery on these mountains is beautiful, and commonly they are characterized by lucid water and rare rocks. Ming Sengshao climbed them, strolled among the trees, listened to the birds chirping, and watched the sunsets. Wherever he traveled, his knowledge and good deeds earned him numerous followers. Regarding his charisma, several anecdotes are recorded in the inscription, all of which are quite legendary. For example, when he was reclusive in Lao Mountain, he gathered his disciples to lecture: "Thousands of people attended his lectures."

And it even moved the local bandits, who decided to "show kindness, and make a pact that they will not invade where Zhengjun lectures." In the second year of Taishi (466) of the Liu Song Dynasty, Qingzhou and Jizhou were occupied by the Northern Wei army, and Sengshao was forced to move south. At the time, his younger brother Ming Qingfu was the governor of Qingzhou, which was actually a county established by the war refugees during the Eastern Jin Dynasty and the Southern Dynasty. Today, it is located in the area of Dongyuntai Mountain, Lianyungang City. For the lack of food, Sengshao had to follow Qingfu to Lianyungang, where he built an abode called Qiyun (on the clouds) for his monastic cultivation on the top of Yanyu Mountain. He stayed on the mountain without entering the city once, keeping a distance from reality and politics on purpose. It was at the end of the Liu Song Dynasty, specifically on the eve of the usurpation of the throne by Emperor Gao of the Qi Dynasty, Xiao Daocheng. Xiao Daocheng invited Sengshao twice to win over the Ming family to work for him. When Cui Zusi went to replace Ming Qingfu as the Prefect of Qingzhou, Xiao Daocheng wrote a letter to Cui Zusi, asking him to suggest that Ming Qingfu bring Sengshao to the capital with him when Qingfu left office, and both of them would be placed in high positions.

Among the northern aristocrats, although the Ming family moved to the south quite late, they quickly earned a seat in the politics of the Southern Dynasty. Six Ming people became prefects from Song Dynasty to Qi Dynasty, obviously a political power worthy of attention. When the new dynasty was established, Emperor Gao of Qi urgently needed a scholar like Ming Sengshao, who had both an aristocratic background and a reputation of a respectful hermit, to make his cabinet look good. As the autumn came and the weather cooled, he wanted to hold a lecture and specially invited the Ming Sengshao to attend it. The presence of such a highly respected hermit in such a political event would naturally cheer up the public. Emperor Gao of Qi showered him with gifts such as bamboo-root-like wish-fulfilling scepter and a bamboo crown. He was sincere and courteous to the wise. However, he still received a rejection. In this case, there was no need to force it. He laughed it off and said he respected his decision not to attend it. This further elevated the status of Ming Sengshao.

In the second year (480) of the Jianyuan Period, the reign title of Emperor Gao of Qi, Ming Sengshao at last followed his younger brother to Jiankang, the capital of the Southern Dynasty. The emperor was delighted, except it was a pity that the hermit was just passing by and his actual destination was She Mountain in the northeast of the capital. The mountain is shaped like an umbrella, so the locals call it Umbrella Mountain. The mountain also had an abundance of medicinal herbs, thus beneficial to health care (*shesheng* in Chinese), hence the name She Mountain. Before the Eastern Jin Dynasty, little of She Mountain had been developed. During the Three Kingdoms Period, there used to be a Defense Camp where Gu Ti, General of the Kingdom of Wu, was stationed. Since the Eastern Jin Dynasty, more and more refugees from the north have moved to the south. Therefore, in Jiangcheng County, a county was set up to accommodate the refugees, called Linyi County of Langyajun.

At the end of the Eastern Jin Dynasty, Hu Qian, an alchemist, who claimed to be able to tell one's luck, once set up his residence there, making it a stronghold for the development of Taoism. Unfortunately, an epidemic completely destroyed it and eradicated Taoism from this mountain. When Ming Sengshao arrived, She Mountain was still desolate. He had to cut through thorns, remove weeds, and dredge ditches to build his residence and resume his lectures. Soon, it gained popularity in the local area. She Mountain was densely forested during the Southern Dynasties, and ferocious tigers were lurking around. After Ming Sengshao came, more people visited the mountain, and the tigers were kept away. In the inscription's narrative, this is labeled as a miracle of Ming Zhengjun's "fearless heart get him through it all." Of course, it can also be spread as the victory of Buddhism.

One day, Ming Sengshao made a special trip to Dinglin Temple in Zijin Mountain to visit the eminent monk Shi Sengyuan in the temple. It was a normal exchange between monks in the mountain. Unexpectedly, Xiao Daocheng happened to be in the temple, but Ming Sengshao still avoided meeting him, which was embarrassing for both of them. After that, the number of times Ming Sengshao entered the city was less and less. With the same idea of his Qiyun abode, he named his residence in She Mountain Qixia (in the sunset) Abode. This abode with a poetic name laid the foundation for the Qixia Temple in terms of both fame and strength. A master named Seng Bian came to the mountain to pay his respect. He lived next door to Ming Sengshao, and the two gradually built a close friendship. Originally, Ming Sengshao had a deep connection with Buddhism. He came from a Buddhist family. His name Sengshao had long been associated with Buddhists. On the surface, he also claimed to "practice both Confucianism and Buddhism and include Taoism as well." He deliberately combined the three beliefs of Confucianism, Taoism, and Buddhism, which was the common ideological tendency of many scholars in the Southern Dynasties. He compared Buddhism and Taoism and believed that the former "conceals" while the latter "opens." Therefore, his mind actually leaned more towards Buddhism.

Unfortunately, Master Seng Bian passed away in a sitting posture in the newly built temple. He wished to build a Buddha statue on Qixia Rock during his lifetime, but it was not realized. Ming Sengshao missed his friend so much that he dreamt of the Buddha statue sitting on a high mountain rock. As he strolled in the forest on the mountains, he seemed to hear "an echoing call in the sky," smell "a charming scent from the peak," and see the Buddha statue "coming to life" on the rocks. These kinds of omens convinced him more and more that this was the will of the Buddha and the will of heaven. It was time that he took over the unfinished business of his late friend. At this time, in northern China, the Yungang Grottoes had already taken shape, and the Luoyang Longmen Grottoes had not yet been excavated. Therefore, the north influenced the Buddha statue Seng Bian and Ming Sengshao wanted to chisel. Since there are boulders on Qixia Mountain, it was a perfect spot to make that happen.

In the second year (484) of the Yongming reign, Ming Sengshao, who had just started preparing "building a great Buddha on the cliff," also passed away. His son Ming Zhongzhang, who missed his late father dearly, respected the old man's last wish and turned his former residence into a Buddhist temple, so the size of the temple was expanded for the first time.

Back then, the nobles, including crown prince Wenhui of Qi, Prince of Jingling Xiao Ziliang, went into action without delay, "donating generous sums of money to the cause," and fought for the chance to finance the carving of the Buddha statue on the cliff. There was one code for Buddhist monks: "on the old foundation, a new system is built, and over ten niches for statues, too." The Thousand Buddha Rock in Qixia Temple, which rose to fame nationwide, began to attract attention. In the Liang Dynasty, Emperor Wu of Liang took the lead in worshipping the Buddha and set the popular trend of Buddhism in the vicinity of Jiankang. Jiming Temple was only a few steps away from the palace, earning it the most royal favor. Qixia Temple was also a hot spot among Buddhist temples. When Xiao Hong, the Prince of Linchuan, was appointed as the Prefect of Yangzhou, he "on the 15th year of the Tianjian Period, built a Buddha statue that had a height of five zhang." It was the most magnificent sculpture in the temple and still exists today. After the Liang Dynasty, new sculptures were made, and later generations carved new inscriptions in the caves dug in the previous generation. Therefore, the Thousand Buddha Rock became the most concentrated, dense, and important Buddhist sculpture group in the south of the Yangtze River.

In the Chen Dynasty, Qixia Temple had already grown to a considerable scale. In the first year (587) and the second year (588) of the Zhenming Period, Emperor Chen Shubao and his ministers, Jiang Zong and Xu Xiaoke, went into the mountain twice to visit Master Huibu and stayed overnight in the guest house of Qixia Temple. He wrote some of the earliest chants about Qixia Mountain. Jiang Zong also inscribed the famous Qixia Temple Stele of She Mountain. Later, the literati visited there, seeking seclusion and exploring the beautiful nature, gossiping about the mysteries, or making poems and inscriptions. These have expanded the popularity of this mountain and this temple and added their cultural weight in history.

In the early Tang Dynasty, Qixia Temple was expanded on a large scale and gradually became the largest Buddhist temple south of the Yangtze River and one of the "Four Great Temples." The establishment of the Ming Zhengjun Stele has made it more important. Southern Tang rulers also energetically promoted Buddhism and rebuilt a beautifully carved stone stupa based on the ruined Sui Dynasty wooden stupa. On the cliff next to this stone stupa, the inscriptions by Xu Xuan and Xu Kai, the famous scholars and calligraphers of the Southern Tang Dynasty, are still vaguely visible. The temporary imperial abode for Emperor Qianlong was built on the waist of Qixia Mountain. He stayed there five times during Emperor Qianlong's tour to the south of the Yangtze River. He admired the scenery of this mountain deeply and called it "the number one most beautiful mountain in Jinling." Qixia Temple kept a proper distance from the political center from the Southern Tang Dynasty to the Qing Dynasty.

Let's make a comparison. Jiming Temple, which was called Tongtai Temple in Liang Dynasty, was built when Emperor Wu of Liang changed the reign title to Datong. Emperor Wu of Liang visited the Tongtai Temple every year and made generous donations multiple times to pray for blessings from the Buddha. At first, Tongtai Temple rose to fame through political authority. Although Emperor Wu of Liang's favor was helpful for a while, it lacked eminent monks and supernatural miracles. In addition, it stood too close to the political center, and almost every time there was a war, it suffered damages, and the recovery was long. Some notes in the Ming Dynasty record that Zhu Yuanzhang, the first emperor of the Ming Dynasty, visited Jiming Temple and believed it was overlooking the palace. He saw it as a threat and intended to demolish it. Fortunately, a Taoist read his mind and informed the temple in advance so the monks could make a compelling speech to persuade Zhu Yuanzhang to drop the idea. The Qixia Temple, which is located in the remote suburbs and far from the political center, has recorded more cultural information after each dynasty change, and at last defeated Jiming Temple and many others of the Southern Dynasty that had long disappeared, becoming the most important Buddhist temple in Nanjing and a stronghold for Buddhism in the city. In this way, in addition to Ming Sengshao, Ming Chongyan, a master of sayings about spirits and deities and fortune and disaster, also deserves to be mentioned in the history of Qixia Temple and Nanjing.

There is a popular saying that famous mountains are home to most Buddhist temples, and monks are what make them famous. What is the subtext of this saying? What is the attitude of the people towards these monks? Envious or discontent? From the perspective of cultural geography, many famous mountains worldwide are renowned for their prestigious monks. The height of a mountain contributes less than a monk to its fame. We should thank them, and so should Qixia Mountain.

Chapter 9

A Girl Named Mochou

The Yellow River runs eastward,
and there was a girl from Luoyang named Mochou.
When she was thirteen, she could weave the most beautiful silk;
when she was fourteen, she could harvest mulberry leaves in the field.
When she was fifteen, she was married into the Lu family;
when she was sixteen, she gave birth to her son named Ahou.
The Lu residence was sumptuous,
the beam was made of expensive wood,
and every room had a floral fragrance.
On her head, a dozen golden hairpins shone bright,
and on her feet, patterned silk shoes looked exquisite.
On the coral shelf, mirrors reflected light,
and the help in plain cloth carried her luggage.
Where is wealth to be found?
How I wish I could into the family of money named Wang.

—*Song of the River Water*

This woman has a weird but well-known name. If she were a citizen today, she would probably become a media favorite. It is a pity that there were no newspapers, no radio, no television, and no electronic networks in those times. There were only business trips, official journeys, gossip, and hearsay, that were made into poems and spread all over the state. Over a thousand years ago, this damsel paddled a boat and berthed it by chance on the river bank of the ancient capital. At that time, maybe no one expected that she and city would become inseparable ever since.

Back then, folk songs and dance music were popular in Jing, Ying, Fan, and Deng (Lianghu and Jiangxi of today) in the middle reaches of the Yangtze River. There are 34 songs and dance music genres mentioned in *Gu Jin Yue Lu* (*Records of Ancient Music*), among which the more famous ones are *Music of Shicheng (stone city)*, *Song of Dark Night*, *Song of Mochou*, and *Music of the Merchants*. *Music of Stone City* and *Song of Mochou* are both dance songs, and it was believed they came from foreign music. Little do we know what this dance looks like, but it is certain that 16 dancers were required at first, and the number was reduced to eight in the Liang Dynasty. And it is with the rhythm of this dance that Mochou comes to our knowledge:

Where is Mochou? In the west of the Shicheng.
The boatman paddles the boat, urging Mochou to come.
Having heard that he is leaving for Yangzhou,
she'll see him off in Chu Mountain.
Arms around each other's waist,
they see no longer to the east does the river flow.

This dance music came from Shicheng. Shicheng is located in Yingzhong Town of Zhongxiang City in Hubei Province. When the Western Jin Dynasty *taifu* (an ancient official in charge of rules of etiquette) Yang Hu was guarding Jingzhou, he built a city there. Emperor Hui of Jin set up Jingling County in the ninth year of the Yuankang Period (AD 299). And the government office of Jingling happened to be in Shicheng. In the Jin and Southern Dynasties, it was well-known. The local folks loved music, and everyone could sing and dance. One day in the fifth century, Zang Zhi, the local prefect, noticed from the city tower a group of beautiful young boys in the distance singing melodiously. Their youthful vitality and the beautiful melody of the songs inspired him to compose these lyrics of the *Music of Shicheng*:

She grew up in Shicheng, from a family in downtown.
She fancied a boy in the city, and bravely confessed her love.
Flowers bloomed in the spring, and she wore one pedal on her ear.
All scruples were forgotten as she walked alongside him,
and together they vowed to be together forever.
Among the hundreds of merchants ships, her man's was about to leave.
Tears rolled down her face as they held hands,
when would she see him again?
Three thousand people were on the ship, but the river was flooding.
The ship had to stay longer,
and being able to spend more time with him made them much happier.
She heard he was traveling far, so she saw him off at Fangshan Pavilion.
The wind howled, and she hated the sound of saying goodbye.

The song sings of passionate love, as does *Song of Mochou*. Like other youths in Shicheng, Mochou could also sing and dance. According to *Old Book of Tang: Musical Records*, there was a kind of sound called "forget the scruples" in the harmony of Shicheng music. As most of the lyrics at that time were lost, it remains unclear what happened exactly. In the *Music of Shicheng*,

All scruples were forgotten as she walked alongside him,
and together they vowed to be together forever,

perhaps refers to the kind of sound called "forget the scruples." Joy was sought in the music while scruples were left behind. The sound was added to the harmony as a result. Mochou means "to forget scruples." At the beginning, this might not be a person's name, but the harmony in the song, or a woman good at this kind of singing. Over time, it became a proper noun, and the music name became a person's name.

Mochou was a native of Shicheng in Hubei Province, instead of the Stone City of Nanjing. This was a true fact that could not be more certain. However, as her stories spread, there were more and more versions, and her birthplace was described as being in Hubei, Luoyang, Jinling, and other places. Today, besides scholars specializing in history and the Zhongxiang locals, most people probably know the Mochou Lake in Nanjing, but few people know the Mochou Village in Zhongxiang City.

Song of Mochou belonged to the folk music bureau in the early stage of the Southern Dynasty. In essence, it was produced in the city. Not only the common citizens liked it, but also the aristocratic literati enjoyed chanting it. Its tunes, lyrics, and characters have all been inspirations to the literati. As an ancient poem, *Song of the River Water* must be the creation of the literati. Some believed that it was Xiao Yan, Emperor Wu of the Liang Dynasty (AD 464–549), who composed it. And this is possible. If that is the case, the absolute influence of Emperor Wu of Liang would have definitely helped the song spread farther and attract more attention.

This four-line-seven-character song changes its rhyme once in the middle.

"When she was thirteen, she could weave the most beautiful silk" and "when she was fifteen, she was married into the Lu family" do not rhyme, unlike the early four-line-seven-character poems that must rhyme in every line. It cannot be earlier than Bao Zhao. Some of the lines have done well in terms of harmony in the tonal pattern, such as "the Yellow River runs eastward," "when she was fourteen, she could harvest mulberry leaves in the field," "when she was sixteen, she gave birth to her son named Ahou," "the Lu residence was sumptuous, the beam was made of expensive wood, and every room had a floral fragrance," and "on the coral shelf, mirrors reflected light." This kind of phonological awareness and level did not appear until the later period of the Southern Dynasties, that is, the Liang and Chen dynasties. Before that, the *Music of Mochou* had been introduced to Jiankang along with businessmen or officials traveling between the middle and lower reaches of the Yangtze River. During its dissemination, the storyline changed a lot. Only the core characters remain, and they are not what they used to be.

Compared with *Music of Mochou*, Mochou in *The Song of the River Water* is much wealthier: Her family moved from the remote Shicheng to the bustling city, Luoyang, which is the ancient capital of the previous dynasties; Her activities took place on the land instead of around the water; Her identity is no longer a singing-girl, but a capable and distinguished housewife of a wealthy family. Her image was obviously inspired by Luo Fu in *The Music Bureau* of the Han Dynasty. Luo Fu "harvested mulberry leaves in the south of the city," while Mochou "harvested mulberry leaves on the southern street;" Luo Fu praised her husband as, "a junior local officer at the age of fifteen, a senior state officer at the age of twenty, a chief imperial commander at the age of thirty, and a state governor at the age of forty," while Mochou also praised herself according to her age. Certainly, on the other hand, this is also because of the commonality of folk songs. *Song of the Mulberries* does not clearly state where Luo Fu lived, but later literati often specified her background when they recreated it. This is a process from vagueness to clarity, transitioning from a small place to a big place, and from a peripheral township to a central city. Maybe because Luo Fu was a Qin Dynasty woman, and *Song of the Mulberries* was collected by the Han Dynasty *Music Bureau*, Wu Jun and Li Bai chose Chang'an and Weiqiao respectively as the background of the story. For example, *Song of the Mulberries* by Li Bai sings:

The beauty from the east of Weiqiao
deals with silkworms when spring returns.

Chang'an was the capital of the Han and Tang dynasties and the center of politics and culture at that time. In retrospect, it is no coincidence that the story background of *The Song of the River Water* was set in Luoyang.

Luoyang was the capital of both the Eastern Han Dynasty and the Western Jin Dynasty. For the people of the Eastern Jin and Southern Dynasties, it had been a political and cultural center. It was not the present tense for them. However, they remembered it the best because it was the closest to them in terms of time. The inheritance of history and culture is linked and difficult to break. The descendants are often involuntarily shrouded by the previous generation. Many literary images of the people of the Six Dynasties have always lingered in the imagination of the people of the Han Dynasty. They were the shadow of the past.

In this way, it is understandable why people in the Southern Dynasties still liked to write about Luoyang, even though the city was no longer in the territory of the Qi and Liang. Especially from the 17th Year of the Taihe Era of Emperor Xiaowen (479), Luoyang was made the capital of the Northern Wei Dynasty. Emperor Jianwen of Liang, Emperor Yuan of Liang, Emperor Chen Shubao, Shen Yue, Xu Ling, Zhang Zhengjian, Chen Xuan, and

Jiang Zong did not have to rhapsodize about it in poetry and prose. They lavished their words to praise how prosperous the city was, how wide its streets were, how beautiful the local girls were, and how open and civilized the local culture was. There are a number of such works in Volume 23 of *Yuefu (Music Bureau) Poems*, and many of them share the same title *The Luoyang Roads*. To sound serious, isn't this propaganda for political rivals? During the confrontation between the Southern and Northern Dynasties, the struggle for the official culture was extremely fierce, and no concessions were allowed. However foolish the emperor and ministers of the Southern Dynasties were, they didn't have to seek trouble for themselves.

It must be remembered that the Luoyang in the poems is no real Luoyang, but the traditional Luoyang; the Luoyang streets in the poems are not real, but an imagination of the literati; they reminisce in their imagination, creating an artistic charm, and obtain some nostalgic satisfaction. However, it would be incorrect to call these descriptions completely false and without basis. The real prototype of these poems is actually the city where they lived, that is, the Jiankang City they were so familiar with. Jiankang hides behind the linguistic curtain, while a replaced character appears on stage. Luoyang in poetry is a literary metaphor for Jiankang. The most self-evident example is the four lines by Fan Yun in the poem co-composed by He Xun and Fan Yun:

We both live in the Luoyang City, east and west,
yet every time we are apart, it is seasons long.
When we parted, the snow fell like confetti.
When we meet again, colorful flowers will be blooming.

Fan Yun resided in the east of Jiankang while He Xun lived in the west of the city. However, it took seasons for the old friends to reunite. It was a common trick of the poets to use Luoyang instead of Jiankang for the sake of quaintness. Meanwhile, the gap in aesthetics creates a nostalgic atmosphere between the lines.

Both *The Luoyang Roads* and *The Song of the River Water* pulled the same trick. Since this city was no longer under the rule of Emperor Wu of Liang, Luoyang in *The Song of the River Water* may simply be pure imagination; since *The Song of Mochou* was spread to Jiankang, the fact might be that it was Jiankang City in *The Song of the River Water*. There was a stone city (Shitoucheng) in Jiankang in ancient times, the name of which was only one character different from Shicheng. And some simply called the stone city by the name of Shicheng. In the natural space, from Shicheng to the Stone City, the Yangtze River that flows down the east connected them; in the imaginary space, it was only one syllable away. In the Qing Dynasty, the Nanjing poet Yao Xihua wrote *Mochou Lake*. He joked: "The river runs eastward from Shicheng. Stories of Mochou were told in both Wu and Chu. It was likely that she paddled the boat and followed her man to Yangzhou." Since Mochou had already sailed eastward along the river, it makes sense to use Luoyang as a metaphor for the Stone City of Jiankang.

Over the years, this metaphor became a literary tradition of the Southern Dynasties, and inertia has carried it forward. As the territory of the Chen Dynasty further shrank, Luoyang was farther and farther away from the Chen territory, to which the poets turned a blind eye. They kept composing poems similar to the *Luoyang Roads*. The most interesting one is the Mochou in the *Luoyang Roads* by Cen Zhijing of the Chen Dynasty:

The lively river in Luoyang, the prosperous pier of Pinjin.
Appreciate peach blooms on the road,
harvest mulberry leaves by the street.
Carts gather to look at Wei Jie, hands are held to look at An Ren.
Whoever stays, Mochou looks even more charming.

Pan Anren (Pan Yue) and Wei Jie were both celebrities in the Western Jin Dynasty. The time of the poem was the Western Jin Dynasty and the location thereof was Luoyang, but the actual background of the story was Jiankang in the Chen Dynasty. By this time, Mochou has become a literary image that belonged to both the Southern Dynasty and Jiankang. Therefore, in the poem *The Newly-Weds* by Zhou Hongzheng of the Chen Dynasty, Mochou is a symbol of a beautiful and happy bride:

At the age of fifteen years old, Mochou got married.
The bridegroom was handsome, and the bride gorgeous.
Their parents cried as loud as the night rain,
they smiled as charming as the morning sun.

The shy bride politely refused the fan gifted by the groom,
the groom was stunned by her beauty.

From an innocent singing-girl in the songs to a happy bride in the poetry, Mochou, who moved to the capital in the east, has been given a different face. Jiankang, as the center of politics and culture back then, was also the center of the right of speech, which attracted Mochou to move from Jingling County to the capital, and gave her a new image as pleased: she was gradually assimilated by the Southern Dynasties, becoming a noble character and a true southern dynasties citizen. She blended into the literary atmosphere of the Southern Dynasties, but more charming, and more easily accepted by the literary traditions of the time and the future. Zhang Tongzhi of the Republic of China put it nicely in *Song of the Forty-Eight Scenes of Jinling: An Overview of Mochou*: "Because of the importance of the Southern Dynasties, the story of the wench that married into the Lu family was widely passed on."

Chapter 10

A Thousand Faces of Mochou

Mochou had a thousand faces.

In the hands of the Tang Dynasty people who enjoyed versifying, Mochou has been given a thousand faces. Let's start with an example of being more faithful to the real person. *The Song of Mochou* by Zhang Hu chants:

> I live in Shicheng.
> You came to Shicheng.
> Since you left Shicheng.
> I am always waiting in Shicheng.

Some ideas in this poem came from the classic *Song of Mochou*, but her image was given a new connotation. The heroine in the classic *Song of Mochou* is carefree, young, and happy, as her name suggests, while the girl in Zhang Hu's poems stares at the gate of Shicheng all day long, like a statue lost in sorrow. Over time, maybe she will turn into a husband-waiting rock. Her sorrow becomes heavier in the eternity of waiting, and so does her image.

For the literary tradition of later generations, the aristocratic *The Song of the River Water* obviously wields a greater influence than the *Song of Mochou*. There is a trace of *The Song of the River Water* in *Journey of a Luoyang Girl* by Wang Wei. The Luoyang girl in this poem is not Mochou, but more. She also came from a wealthy family. When she was at her prime as a teen, she inhabited a splendid mansion, had luxurious furniture, took the most advanced vehicle, had the most delicious and rarest dishes, and befriended the wealthiest families. She lived an extravagant life. Luoyang, the eastern capital of the powerful Tang Empire, had long been accustomed to such lavishness. Perhaps Wang Wei intended to borrow Mochou's glory from the south of Yangtze and return it to this city in the Central Plains.

The Song of Mochou by Li He was developed entirely based on *The Song of the River Water*:

> Weeds grow wild on the hill. Crows caw on the city parapet.
> Who in this city plants pomegranates in the corners of the city?
> Reins on five horses and halters on two cattle.
> Paddle a canoe like a fish for ten *li* at night.
> As we return, the night is so deep
> that no one is there to disturb us.
> We climb the wooden tower.
> A guqin stands next to the bed
> as the moon casts light onto the window.
> Today the flowers bloom. Tomorrow, autumn comes.
> Not to waste this life, why is your name Mochou?

Not only Mochou's living environment and lifestyle are aristocratic, but also her behavior. However, no matter how much wealth there was, she was not happy but sullen. A soulmate is hard to find, and her youth was wasted. Until the end, she was immersed in melancholy. This is the despondent Mochou and also the despondent Li He. Can't we hear the sadness?

What is the identity of this Mochou? The poem has a blank space, but we can imagine: Is she a young unmarried maiden? Is she a wife that misses her husband? Is she another victim of a fickle man? Over a hundred years before Li He, in the early Tang Dynasty, a poet named Shen Qiqi once pictured Mochou as a lovesick wife or put Mochou in the frame of a lovesick wife. Here is his famous poem *Lovesick*:

> The young housewife of the Lu family lives in a mansion with tulip-
>   scented halls.

The petrels come and reside in pairs on the gorgeous roof beams.
In September, as the cold wind comes, the leaves fall one after another
amid the urgent sound of pounding laundry.
Her husband has been on an expedition to Liaoyang for over ten years,
and she misses him dearly.
There is no message from the Liaoyang area
north of the White Wolf River.
The young wife living alone in the south of Chang'an suffers
particularly long and lonely autumn nights.
She lamented: How I miss my man?
Why let the bright moonlight shine on the curtains?

This young housewife of the Lu family was, of course, Mochou. From
the Wei and Jin Dynasties to the Southern and Northern Dynasties, the
Lu family was always a great family in the north, and it did not move
southward with the Sima family. Therefore, in *The Song of the River Water*,
the metaphor of the Lu family obviously contains a nostalgic meaning. In
the Tang Dynasty, Cui, Lu, Li, and Zheng were first-class families, and the
metaphor of the young wife of the Lu family obviously had a real meaning.
In the description of Mochou's living environment, Shen Quanqi both
imitated and created. Borrowing the idea of tulip, he created the tulip-
scented hall: he decorated it with gorgeous beams and had petrels perch
there. The temporal and spatial background of this story was unclear. Those
who have not read *The Song of the River Water* in advance may be misled
by the sentence "the young wife living alone in the south of Chang'an
suffer the particularly long and lonely autumn nights," and mistakenly think
that this young woman came from Chang'an. When the original color of
the story began to fade, its specific time and space began to blur, and the
classicality of the literary image began to surface, Mochou joined the ranks
of classic literary characters.

Mochou was assimilated by the trend of frontier poetry in the Tang
Dynasty. *Lovesick* is an example of the early Tang Dynasty, while *The Song of
Mochou* by Xu Ning is one of the middle Tang Dynasty. Xu Ning must have
been a poet who deeply fancied the sentiments of the Six Dynasties. He did
not write many poems but often quoted Six Dynasties' history. *Reminiscing*

Yangzhou is his most famous work:

> The beautiful face of Xiao Niang
> could not hide the tears of parting,
> and the little sadness between the eyebrow of Tao Ye
> was easily detected.
> There are three signs of the brilliance
> of the bright moon in the world.
> Lovely Yangzhou, you have taken two.

The second half of this seven-line poem is the most famous about the scenery of Yangzhou. Unfortunately, this is Guangling City north of the Yangtze River, not Jiankang City in the south. However, it is Xiao Niang and Tao Ye who contributed most to the beautiful yet sorrowful atmosphere of the poem. They were two beautiful and passionate women related to the Southern Dynasties and Jinling. Mochou in *The Song of Mochou* was also a beautiful girl, a typical young wife who missed her husband at war. Shen Quanqi must have influenced this image, but she was more lonely than Shen Quanqi (a famous Tang Dynasty poet), pictured, like a dream in the freezing wind:

> The battle dress was made by the bed,
> while the leaves rustled outside the window.
> As she dreamed of her man fighting in the west of Liaoning,
> the moonlight was as cold as needles and the wind cut like knives.

And *Spring Resentment* by Jin Changxu had an equally satisfactory result regarding a lovesick wife:

> I beat the branches to scare
> the warbler away from the tree.
> Its clear cry awakened my dream:
> I went to western Liaoning
> and met my man guarding the border.

In fact, Mochou in *The Song of the River Water* was sullen, too.

Where is wealth to be found?
How I wish I could marry into the rich Wang family.

What is the story of the wealthy Wangs mentioned in the poem? Most people in the Tang Dynasty believed it was Wang Chang. Shangguan Yi stated in the poem *To the Duke of Gaoyang*:

The nature of the south is great,
and Wang Chang of the rich family is missed.

According to *The Old Biography of Xiangyang Elders*, Wang Chang was styled Gongbo, and was a *sanqi* (an ancient official title) in Dongping. He was Mochou's true love, as described in *Zheng* by Yuan Zhen: *Mochou loves Wang Chang secretly*. However, due to various reasons, they did not end up together.

The red wall, like the galaxy, separates the two love birds.
Who reported the news to Wang Chang? The lovebirds married at last.

This is Li Shangyin's poem *Reply on Her Behalf*. The obstacles to their love frustrated them terribly. Tang people seem to know the story better, and today we know little about it. However, despite the hardship, this poem has a happy ending. The poet was willing to honor true love, so Mochou became the embodiment of happiness. Therefore, he wrote in *The Young Marquis of Fuping*:

In the morning of the marquis residence,
the gatekeeper no longer announces the visitors as usual,
because the young marquis is newly wed to a beauty named Mochou.
Under these circumstances, he dares not disturb him.

And in *Ma Wei*, he wrote:

Having ascended to the throne,
the emperor was still not as happy
as the Lu son, who married Mochou.

The former Mochou was a beautiful bride, while the latter was a carefree young wife.

Yuan Zhen wrote a poem called *Moqiu*. I believe this is probably his typo. The poem says:

> She watches the sun sink in the west
> and misses her man in the military.
> Crows caw on the trees outside.
> She rests alone on her jade bed.

Indeed, rich as she was, she was no happy woman. Certainly, sometimes, Li Shangyin couldn't help but make her sullen again, such as his Mochou:

> If there are no boats in Shicheng,
> Mochou will still have her own sorrows.

In the words of the same poet, Mochou has successfully changed her face more than once.

The geographical background of Mochou helps her to put on a thousand faces. Poets have always paid close attention to it. In Wei Zhuang's *Reminiscence of the Past*, he writes:

> At the table, the handsome young man from the west is called Wuji,
> while the beautiful lady from the south is called Mochou.

He emphasized that Mochou was a beautiful lady from the south, not from the north or the west. When addressing her, the poet liked to style her Mochou. Li Shangyin might have been the one who started this trend. Between men and women, calling each other by their style names shows equality, appreciation, intimacy, and warmth. Ouyang Xiu seemed to disagree with Wei Zhuang, so in his *A Gift Poem* he writes:

> Mochou lives near Luochuan, and her slender waist is famous.

He regarded her as the beauty of Luoyang. Whether she came from the south or Luoyang, it made sense. It was just that before the Song Dynasty,

Mochou was seldom associated with Jinling. *West River (Jinling Nostalgia)* by Zhou Bangyan might be the first:

> Looking at the thriving and beautiful Jinling,
> who can remember the prosperity of the Southern Dynasty?
> The old capital is full of vitality and surrounded
> by green mountains and winding lucid water.
> Mountains peaks face each other, forming a ring.
> The raging waves beat the lonely city bank,
> and the boats sail away quietly.
> The old tree on the cliff still hangs upside down.
> Who tied the boat in Mochou Lake to the shore?
> Today, only the relics of the past and the green trees remain,
> and the thick fog shrouds half of the city wall.
> Late at night, the moon rises above the parapet at the city gate
> and shines into Jinling City.
> The poet gazes sullenly at the Qinhuai River in the east.

Where is the bustling market with flying flags at pubs and noisy gongs and drums? In retrospect, the two families of Wang and Xie once lived there. The swallows don't know what year it is. They fly to the alley and nest in ordinary people's homes. In the afterglow of the sunset, they chirp while they fly, as if telling the story of the rise and fall of this place over thousands of years.

Like a collage, this poem cut out several predecessors' poems and recombined them, including *The Song of Mochou*. Since *The Song of Mochou* gives the answer, "Where is Mochou? In the west of Shicheng," it is often quoted: "Mochou lives in the west of Shicheng" (*Thoughts with Friends* by Wu Rong). Until the late Tang Dynasty, many poets still remembered that she lived in Shicheng of Jinling. Hu Zeng wrote in *Song of the Epic Shicheng*:

> Dark clouds disperse over the Snow Tower
> in the ancient capital, and the Han River still runs around Shicheng.
> Who knows that the moon in the broad sky
> once sent Mochou to the wealthy families?

Luo Qiu explicitly pointed out that fact in *To Compare with Hong'er*:

The roads extend long in the West of Jingling,
paddle the oars to greet Mochou without reason.

However, Zhou Bangyan openly regarded Mochou as a historical site of Jinling and further specified its location as the west of Jinling City. His *Looking at the Huai River in the East* was inspired by this idea, too. Some people criticized Zhou Bangyan for making a mistake. Is it possible that the knowledgeable Zhou Bangyan would not know that Mochou in the poem came from Shicheng rather than the Stone City of Jinling? His poetry is so particular about rhetoric, how could he be so careless? In Zhou Bangyan's time, Mochou lived in the Stone City and had become a piece of common knowledge. Perhaps, Zhou Bangyan was following the public recognition.

This Mochou puts on a new look: she is the singing girl living west of the city in *The Song of Mochou*, and the young wife of the Lu family in *The Song of the River Water*. That she officially "settles down" outside the Shuixi Gate of Nanjing means the birth of Mochou Lake in human geography. Its humanistic life began in the early Song Dynasty at the latest.

Mochou Lake was still part of the Yangtze River during the Six Dynasties. When Li Bai traveled to Jinling, the area around Jiangdongmen today is still *"The river divided into two branches by Egret Island."*

Later, as stated in *Nanjing's History*, as the main waterway of the Yangtze River gradually migrated to the northwest, the sandbars were connected with the land. Those wide and deep-water channels became the waterway for the Qinhuai River to join the Yangtze River. In contrast, other river branches of different depths gradually became lakes or ponds, including today's Mochou Lake, which did not rise to fame until after the Song and Ming Dynasties.

In the Ming Dynasty, Xuanwu Lake was a royal lake, and ordinary people were not allowed to enter without authorization; Zijin Mountain is where the Ming Xiaoling Mausoleum stands, and the commoners dared not set foot in it, while Mochou Lake is located in the west of the city. Its beautiful scenery attracted more and more literati to visit, quickly becoming a scenic spot in the city. After the middle of the Ming Dynasty, more and more literati flocked there. Old-schooled inscriptions were like embroidery. The more work done, the more beautiful the lake became. In the Jiajing reign (AD 1522–1566), the poem *Mochou Lake* by Huang Shangshi from Nanjing was one of the earlier poems with this theme:

Search for the truth in the mist;
beautiful people of the Six Dynasties are affectionate.
Thousands of flowers surround the lotus pavilion,
and the boat with blue oars floats as light as a leaf.
The egret flies low and ripples the lake's surface,
and the reflection of the green hills is broken.
Sing even though drunk,
and enter the city while it is still dark.

During the Wanli Period of the Ming Dynasty (1573–1619), Gu Qiyuan had already used Taoye Pier and Mochou Lake as pairing material in Volume 10 of *Ke Zuo Zhui Yu* (a book of historical records). In this context, the story of the Shengqi Building came into being, which has made Mochou Lake even more famous. Allegedly, Zhu Yuanzhang (the first emperor of the Ming Dynasty) and Xu Da (his marshal and hero in the founding of the Ming Dynasty) once played Chinese chess by the lake. Xu Da was a chess master, but he knew Zhu Yuanzhang hated to lose. Every time he played against Zhu Yuanzhang, he always lost to the emperor on purpose.

One time, Zhu Yuanzhang asked Xu Da to set aside all scruples and show his true skills. At the end of the game, Zhu Yuanzhang found that he had defeated Xu Da again and was about to accuse him of losing on purpose, but Xu Da calmly suggested the emperor take a closer look at the chessboard. It turned out that the pieces on it had already been put into the word "long live." The emperor was delighted and gifted the lake building to Xu Da, thus the Shengqi (chess victory) Building. This lake building has therefore been associated with "the *qi* of an emperor" and "the *qi* of a hero."

The beauty of legend is that it is both true and false. The details are fictional, while the spirit is real. To understand the relationship between Zhu Yuanzhang and Xu Da, there is nothing better than this story. Some scholars have verified that this fiction came from the descendants of Xu Da. The origin of this story is the chess gambling of Xie An of the Eastern Jin Dynasty (AD 317–420) in a villa, which also took place in Nanjing. Scholars must have some basis for their statement, but in the eyes of the ordinary, such textual research may be troublesome, even a bit unpleasant. More legends are being made, and there are always people keen to make up stories and spread them widely. With these legends and storytellers, our dull life will have a different taste.

There is a legend that Mochou was a daughter of a poor family in Luoyang between the Liu Song Dynasty (AD 420–479) and the Southern Qi Dynasty (AD 479–505). When she was fifteen, her father died of illness. To bury him, she sold herself to the Lu family in Shicheng as a daughter-in-law and gave birth to a son A'hou. Later, her husband joined the army to guard the border, and for ten years, she heard nothing from him. Mochou was devoted to helping the poor and the weak, thus deeply loved by her neighbors. Her father-in-law strongly opposed her and even framed and humiliated her. Mochou could not bear it any longer, so she threw herself into Shicheng Lake and died. To commemorate her, people renamed it Mochou Lake.

Another recent legend has another twist. Mochou's real name was Qiu'nü (autumn girl) because she was born in Luoyang in autumn. After her mother died, her father raised the family by selling herbs collected in the mountains. She followed her father up the mountain to gather herbs and tulips. Unfortunately, her father fell off a cliff and died. She cried on the street about her bitter life.

Overwhelmed with grief, she changed her name to Chou'nü. In order to bury her father, she sold herself to a Jiankang businessman surnamed Lu to be his daughter-in-law. She and the Lu son were in love and raised a son. The Lu family built a Tulip Hall for her. Her husband changed her name to Mochou. One day, Emperor Wu of Liang came to the Lu residence, and when he saw Mochou, he wanted her for himself. So, he schemed to have her husband enlisted as a soldier, and her father-in-law killed and summoned her to court. Mochou had no choice but to escape by boat. Before she left, she couldn't bear to leave the villagers. As the boat was lingering around, Mochou Lake came into being. The villagers lied to Emperor Wu of Liang that Mochou threw herself into the river and died. The emperor was ashamed and composed *The Song of the River Water*.

When the revolution was associated with the makeover of Mochou, the core of the 20th-century version of her story underwent drastic changes.

Without a doubt, these stories are strongly political. Class, conflict, suffering, hatred, and death are all typical rhetorical devices of revolutionary discourse. The old faces of Mochou are nowhere to be found. This seems to be an exclusive special interest in revolutionary times. The ancient literati were still fascinated by her elegance and relished writing about her beauty and passion. Wang Xiangqi wrote the *Mochou Lake Couplet* and praised her:

> The beauty of Mochou from the north
> eclipses the shine of women from the south.

Zhang Tongzhi during the time of the Republic of China wrote *Tour Around Mochou Lake in Poems to Entertain*:

> In her boudoir near the lake,
> her man seeks nothing more than her.
> When they cross the river in a canoe,
> he calls her name Mochou loud and clear.

This is a much happier Mochou, unlike the lovesick lonely wife mentioned before.

Mochou and Emperor Wu of Liang, a hero and a beauty, Shengqi Building and Tulip Hall, Mochou and King of Zhongshan, Xu Da and Zhu Yuanzhang, about Mochou Lake, there are so many suitable pairing materials that are enough to embellish the beauty of the lake, to express the elegance of the poet and, to compose beautiful landscape poems. These realities, the spirit of the Six Dynasties, and the emotions of the vicissitudes of life caused by the stories are also suitable materials for pairing. For example:

> Over five hundred years of ruling, heroism still lives in Mochou Lake;
> During the two months of spring, the soul of beauty lies in the blooms.
> For another example:

> The current situation is like a chess game,
> and I envy the heroes who win it all;
> A good name is passed down in anecdotes,
> and the beauty looks more attractive in front of the scenery.

Time goes by, but heroes and beauties are always side by side. He Shaoji, a calligrapher in the Qing Dynasty, wrote a couplet for West Lake in Hangzhou by quoting from *Pi Pa Xian* by Jiang Kui of the Song Dynasty and *Feng Ru Song* by Yu Guobao of the Song Dynasty:

> When the boat comes,
> the passenger looks like peach root and peach leaf;
> When the boat leaves,
> the love lingers in the lake water and lake mist.

The words are light but carry the history of the six dynasties. If Mochou could see from above, she would definitely protest: the couplet above should be inscribed on the pillars of the small pavilion by Mochou Lake, so why are they at the West Lake?

Chapter 11

In the Misty Drizzle

In the vast south of the Yangtze River,
there are birds chanting and swallows dancing everywhere,
and colorful flowers dotted around the green trees.
Wine flags wave in the city, on the waterside,
at the foot of the mountains, and in the villages.
Many ancient temples left by the Southern Dynasties
are now shrouded in a misty drizzle.

—Du Mu, *Spring in the South of Yangtze*

The poet did not exaggerate at all, except that time has erased the traces of the temples, leaving people in doubt of their actual existence.

Back then, melodious morning bells and drums used to echo in famous mountain resorts such as Zijin Mountain, Fuzhou Mountain, Qixia Mountain, and Terrace of the Raining Flowers; on both sides of the Qinhuai River, among the densely populated streets, the smoke of incense burnt to worship Buddha lingered. As recorded in *Biographies of Eminent Monks*, Jiankang housed the most temples, including Jianchu Temple, Anle Temple, Changgan Temple, Wuyi Temple, Xie Temple, Shangdinglin Temple, Xiadinglin Temple, Waguan Temple, Daochang Temple, Qixia Temple, Kaishan Temple, Yecheng Temple, Heyuan Temple, Songxi Temple, etc. As for eminent monks, the list was even longer. In the deep meditation room, literary celebrities talked eloquently; eminent monks spoke with fervor and assurance in the towering temple.

How unprecedentedly grand! If Jiankang, Jiangxi, and East Zhejiang were titled the three major centers of Buddhism in the south of the Yangtze River at that time, Jiankang must have been the center of the centers. The eminent monk Huiyuan came from Jiangxi, which was centered on the Donglin Temple in Mount Lu; eastern Zhejiang also had eminent monks such as Zhidun, Zhu Faqian, Huijiao, and others; inside and outside Jiankang City, eminent monks could be seen everywhere.

Jianchu Temple in the south of the city is one of the earliest strongholds of Buddhism in Nanjing. In the tenth year (AD 247) of the Chiwu Era of the Kingdom of Wu, when Kang Senghui set foot on this land, the city was still almost a virgin land for Buddhism to be opened up. Kang Senghui, a newcomer with fancy clothes and self-proclaimed Sramana with exaggerated speeches, surprised and delighted people and left them in doubt about Buddhism. In the early years, Sun Quan, the King of Wu, had met Zhi Qian, a monk who came to Wu to avoid chaos. It was a brief encounter, and he only absorbed a little knowledge of Buddhism from the monk. When the monk Kang boasted about the efficacy of the Dharma and the holy light of the Buddhist relics, he sounded doubtful yet kept spouting.

To Sun Quan's ears, it was almost a fantasy. Empty talk was useless. Kang Senghui had no choice but to devoutly invite him for a seeing. After 21 days, at 5:00 a.m., there was a sudden clanging sound in the serene night sky. Following the sound, a relic had already fallen into a copper vase. This relic was genuinely magical. Its colorful light illuminated the copper vase. Its texture was hard, like a diamond. An iron hammer failed to smash it into pieces, but a gentle touch with the copper plate broke it immediately. This extraordinary effect shocked the court, the public, and Sun Quan, the ruler of the Kingdom of Wu. He kept his promise and allowed Kang Senghui to build a temple in Jiankang. This unprecedented temple was named Jianchu Temple, and the place where it was built was called Fotuoli (within the Buddha). Buddhism conquered the first city in the south of the Yangtze River, and the curling smoke of incense burnt at Jianchu Temple was its banner of victory.

Probably, thanks to the blessing of Kang Senghui, Jianchu Temple, after hundreds of years of thick and thin, still retains its spiritual light. During

Sun Hao's reign, Buddhism was once banned, but its position was never shaken. When Su Jun rebelled, this Buddhist temple was burnt down but rebuilt not long after. After that, the temple was repeatedly renamed. It was renamed Baita (white pagoda) Temple in the Southern Qi Dynasty. In the early Tang Dynasty, the old name of Jianchu was restored. Fa Rong of the Niutou School was once in charge of the Jianchu Temple, and he made it shine bright in the history of Zen Buddhism. After that, it was renamed Changqing Temple in the middle of the Kaiyuan years (AD 713–741), Fengxian Temple in Southern Tang Dynasty, and Baoning Temple in the early Northern Song Dynasty. The plaque on the temple gate was changed repeatedly, but it has always been an important temple in Jiankang as Buddhism's first stronghold in this city.

In the last years of the Western Jin Dynasty, the Central Plains were chaotic and turbulent. Like those carp crossing the river, the monks who traveled south from Chang'an and Luoyang reached their first foothold in the south, Jiankang. After a long time, along the Qinhuai River, at the Terrace of Raining Flowers in the south of the city, at Zijin Mountain in the east of the city, at Qixia Mountain in the northeastern suburbs, and at Niushou Mountain in the southern suburbs, the sound of the temples' *yugu* (a percussion instrument made of bamboo) was heard. From the Eastern Jin Dynasty to the Southern Dynasties, the emperors showed great respect to the eminent monks. The nobles and the famous of the vassal family used to pander to them, gifting them with houses, land, money, and help. It was common that they funded the construction of the temples. In the early years of the Liu Song Dynasty, Xu Sang, the magistrate of Pinglu County, donated a piece of his land to build Pinglu Temple. Fan Tai not only built Qihuan Temple but also donated 60 acres of fruit and bamboo orchards to the temple. In the history of Buddhism, this was the "honeymoon period" of the relationship between scholar-officials and monks.

The city of Jiankang gathered countless monks. The eminent monk Xuanchang was initially stationed in Guangyang County, Minshan Prefecture. When Xiao Yi, King Yuzhang of the Qi Dynasty, was guarding Jingxia, he invited the monk to Jiangling. In the early years of the Yongming Period of the Qi Dynasty (479–502), the crown prince Wenhui brought Xuanchang back to Jiankang and housed him in Linggen Temple. After the death of this eminent monk who came from afar, he was buried in front of

Dragon Hill on Zijin Mountain, where the Ming Xiaoling Mausoleum was located. Also, Xiao Ying, the king of Linchuan, erected a monument for him, and Zhou Yong inscribed it. The monk was respected both before and after his death.

It is said that monks are usually frugal. From another angle, these monks were also a group of luxury consumers—they consumed the kingly spirit of the city, the excellent attendance of the temples in the mountains, the piety and obsession of believers, and the lucid water of the Qinghuai River and Qingxi Creek. At the same time, let's not forget that they were also a special group of creators—they created the story of the city, created the legend of the world, and their names embellished the history of the ancient capital. Their glory deserves to be remembered, and the memory lingers in our minds. The time that has silently passed by, therefore radiates a rhythmic charm. Sometimes, their consumption pattern itself was a kind of creation. Moreover, consumption is short-lived, while creation is eternal. Zhu Fati, who promoted Buddhism at Waguan Temple, Zhu Daosheng, who first advocated the theory of enlightenment at Qingyuan Temple, and Shi Sengyou and Monk Huidi (Liu Xie), who wrote books and established theories at Dinglin Temple, and monk Huidi (Liu Xie), and monk Baozhi, whose whereabouts were uncertain but left a great number of magical stories, have had their names shine in the history of Buddhism, and illuminate the history of the city.

Zhu Daosheng came from the north and stood out for his talent in understanding Buddhism in his early years. He lived a hermitic life on Mount Lu for seven years and then traveled to Chang'an with Huirui, Huiyan, and others to study under Kumarajiva. In Jiankang, he stayed at Qingyuan Temple and quietly studied Buddhism. One day, Zhu Daosheng, who was meditating, had a sudden awakening: all sentient beings have a Buddha nature and can get enlightened. He was so excited that he preached this idea everywhere, shocking both the Taoist circle and the commoners in Jiankang City. Conservatives who clung to the old doctrine deemed it heresy and fiercely attacked it. Daosheng remained unrelenting, insisting on his theory, and sometimes vowed solemnly to be pious. Years later, the Nirvana Sutra was spread to Jinling, which coincided with what Zhu Daosheng preached. The public sighed and admired his lonely understanding and foresight. Zhu Daosheng, with this scripture, naturally gained more confidence when preaching this theory. Unfortunately, he had already left Qingyuan Temple by then.

The Qingyuan Temple, where Daosheng resided, was prestigious in Jiankang City at that time. It had a strong backing, being founded by the last empress of the Eastern Jin Dynasty, Empress Gongsi, née Chu. Legend has it that soon after Daosheng arrived in Jiankang, he was invited by Empress Chu to be the head of the temple. Once, Daosheng entered the palace to elaborate on the Nirvana Sutra for the empress. His explanation and analysis were easy to understand. Not only were the empress and her maids fascinated, even a stone next to them nodded in approval. Certainly, this is merely a legend, but it shows at that time, people's admiration and praise for Daosheng's Buddhism were obvious. It was such a high commendation that flowers and applause were overshadowed.

Flowers and applause are not easily expected, especially for pioneers. In fact, loneliness is often the fate of pioneers. If Daosheng could read *On Climbing the Tower At Youzhou* by Chen Ziang, "Where are the great men of the past? Where are those of future years? The sky and earth forever last; Here and now I alone shed tears," he would be moved to tears. In classical literature, there is another version of the legend of the stone that nodded, which might have been more widely circulated than the previous one. Daosheng gathered stones from his disciples in Huqiu Mountain in Suzhou and explained the scriptures to them, and the stones nodded in agreement. There was no audience and no applause. Humans rejected him, keeping a polite distance, but only the cold and lifeless stones nodded silently. There was nothing more embarrassing and bleaker than this for a speaker. A slight change of the story background, and the story is rewritten completely, shocking. People only remember the flowers and applause in front of the successful. Who dares to say that the early days of Daosheng in Jiankang were not awfully quiet?

For monks, it might be that nothing stays unheard, and Daosheng found unbearable the suspicion and exclusion of other monks. In a rage, he walked away and started anew with his promotion of Buddhism on Huqiu Mountain in Suzhou. One day in summer that year, a lightning bolt struck the hall of Qingyuan Temple in Jiankang. Through the dazzling ray of lightning, people saw a glowing dragon soaring into the sky. Everyone in Qingyuan Temple believed it was a rare auspicious omen and agreed to change the temple's name to Longguang (dragon light) Temple to commemorate this supernatural occurrence. However, the soaring dragon also meant that Daosheng had to move to another temple. As expected, it didn't take long for him to leave for Mount Lu, farther and farther from the capital.

Naturally, a few people in the capital got Daosheng, but fewer could accept new ideas all at once. It took some wisdom to embrace new ideas. And the wise are hard to come by. Back then, famous literati of aristocratic families, such as Wang Hong of Langya, Fan Tai of Shunyang, Yan Yanzhi of Langya, and Xie Lingyun of Chenjun, all admired Daosheng and kept close contact with him. Xie Lingyun was most faithful to Daosheng's theory of epiphany. He once wrote an article *Distinguishing Sects*, which aimed to give full play to the meaning of Daosheng's theory of enlightenment. Xie Lingyun once confidently said to Meng Yi: "What is required to attain the Way is wisdom and good deeds. You may ascend to heaven before me, but surely you will attain Buddhahood after me." In Jiankang City, at the beginning of the Song Dynasty, many people were involved in this dispute between epiphany and gradual enlightenment, including the emperor. Emperor Wen of Song, leaned towards epiphany, but he was powerless to end this debate. Faced with the doubts of dissenters, he couldn't help missing Zhu Daosheng, who had gone to heaven. Daosheng had two disciples, Daoyou and Fayuan, who abided by their teacher's teachings. Emperor Wen invited them into the capital and provided them with a forum so that Daosheng's epiphany theory could be carried forward. In the history of Buddhism, Zhu Daosheng advocated epiphany, abandoned the old ideas, and opened up the line of Zen after the Tang Dynasty. He was as important as Wang Bi, who broke away from the Han Dynasty Yi studies, which focused on the study of image-numerology and opened up the dark learning of the Wei and Jin Dynasties. And it was from Jiankang that his career took off.

Huirui of Wuyi Temple was also a famous monk in Jiankang. He was a classmate of Daosheng and deeply understood the sounds of scriptures. Wuyi Temple was close to the residence of the Wangs and the Xies, so the children of the two families often visited the temple. Xie Lingyun, a fan of Buddhism, showed great interest in studying Sanskrit phonology. He used to learn modestly from Huirui about the Buddhism scripture and its sounds. The king of Pengcheng, Liu Yikang, also highly respected Huirui. As they recited the scriptures often, many monks were proficient in the sounds of the scriptures, and many were good at chanting sutras. One of them was Shi Tanzhi of Jiankang Dong'an Temple, who passed away in the fifth year of the Yongming Period (486–493). At that time, there were a few more sutra teachers, each with expertise in sutra chanting. In Volume 13 of *Biographies of Eminent Monks* it is written:

> "Daolang excels at a slow tone, Faren is good at a drumming sound, Zhixin is good at *cetiao* (one tone of the ancient Chinese music), and Huiguang likes the flying sound."

These sounds are like the cadence of the Chinese language. And these eminent monks showed their own characteristics. With the dissemination of this knowledge to the secular world, and the literati's recitation of the Sanskrit and their understanding of the sounds, the theory of "four tones" officially appeared in Chinese in the next year of the Southern Qi Dynasty and the rules of "eight rhythms" also came into being. The history of Chinese poetry had since opened a new page. And it started in the west residence under Jilong Mountain (in the area of today's North Pole Pavilion), that is, the residence of Xiao Ziliang, King of Jingling, an urban forest.

There is no clear boundary between the city and the mountains. Power, fame, and fortune, the hustle and bustle, elements of the mortal life drifted into the mountains and forests with the wind, but the temples were generally quiet. And celebrities and scholars usually dare not act rashly when they go there. The article *Bei Shan Yi Wen*, which Kong Zhigui wrote to tease Zhou Yong, hid this reality behind the jokes. Mountains and forests were the paradise of learned people with noble interests and character and the domain of monks. Eminent monks and hermits used to sympathize with each other and see each other as soul mates. And the grand ceremonial chariots and horses of the powerful and the wealthy had no use there. They became accustomed to slowing down and lightening their paces, temporarily purifying their dusty hearts, setting aside the secular fatigue, and allowing their minds to focus on their spirits and wander in the realm of nothingness.

The mountains and forests were the ideal places to decipher Buddhist scriptures, read, and write. There was a sufficient number of listeners, soulmates, wise minds for advice, and even confrontational opponents. Temples in Jiankang were the birthplace of many new teachings, and many young diamonds in the rough lived there, honing, sleeping, thinking, and lecturing. It was not uncommon for people to study the sutras intensively and understand Confucianism simultaneously; there were also people with free minds and literary talents. In *Biographies of the Eminent Monks*, Huilin, a disciple of Daoyuan in Pengcheng Temple, was a monk witty in conversation. Like other famous scholars, he was adept at writing and proud of his talent. Shi Sengyuan of Shangdinglin Temple was a monk who "could not care less about wealth." He once declined the invitation of Emperor Ming of the Song Dynasty but actively befriended the hermits who shared his opinion about wealth. And more with the same pursuit flocked to the temple to pay their respects to him.

Shangdinglin Temple also gathered a sea of talents, including Sengyou and his disciple Liu Xie. Sengyou read extensively, researched widely, and wrote many works, among which *Hongming Collection* and *Chu Sang Zang Ji Collection* are particularly famous. The former is of great documentary value for the study of Buddhist history, while the latter is an ingenious and distinctive bibliography of Buddhist scriptures, which holds a paramount position in academic history. Sengyou was an artist who carved statues and a collector of classics. He established scripture collections in Jianchu Temple and Shangdinglin Temple, and his disciple Liu Xie helped him categorize and catalog them.

Liu Xie, talented in literature, having studied with Sengyou for over a decade, mastered the classics. Back then, he inscribed almost all the steles in new temples, pagodas, and famous monks' statues in Jiankang City. Unfortunately, most of them are lost today. But fortunately, his *Wen Xin Diao Long* (the literary mind and the carving of dragons) has been passed down. The emergence of this masterpiece of literary theory criticism of the Six Dynasties is inseparable from Liu Xie's Buddhist experience and the intellectual training he received from it. He lived a torturous life. In his early years, he was alone and poor, so he was not husband material, and seeking a way out in Dinglin Temple seemed an inevitable choice. He became an official in his middle age and was highly regarded by Xiao Hong, King of Linchuang, and Xiao Tong, Crown Prince of Zhaoming.

In his later years, under an imperial edict, he co-wrote scriptures at Dinglin Temple with the monk Huizhen, and eventually became a monk and changed his name to Huidi. From the East Palace to the North

Mountain, his footprints were left inside and outside Jiankang City. He switched between a monk's life and a commoner's life, which was a life trajectory with apparent characteristics of the Six Dynasties.

However, the stories of Liu Xie were much less dramatic than those of the crazy and weird monk Shi Baozhi (Baozhi). Baozhi was said to be the prototype of the mad monk Jigong. Since the Southern Dynasties, his story has spread more and more mythically among the people. Nobody knows how many years he actually lived. People vaguely remember that when he first arrived in the capital, he stayed at Daolin Temple before the Emperor Ming of the Song Dynasty. Nobody knows when he acted strange and talked crazy. He had uncertain conduct and an irregular diet. Sometimes he did not eat for days and felt no hunger. He walked among the streets and alleys of the capital, barefoot in the cold winter, but he sensed no cold. He often held a tin staff, on whose end hung scissors, a ruler, a whisk, and a mirror, which were believed to be a metaphor for the four dynasties of Qi, Liang, Chen, and Ming. He could not care less about people's ridicule.

He used to talk nonsense that nobody understood, but later they knew they were prophecies, and each of them came true, so they looked at this mad monk with admiration and dared not underestimate him. Legend has it that he wielded magic, made three clones of himself in three places, spit out a swallowed fish back to the basin alive and was able to control the weather. This reputation of wizardry gradually spread into the palace, arousing the emperor's vigilance. From Emperor Wu of Qi to Emperor Wu of Liang, the emperors thought of various ways to frame him, imprison him, restrict his access, etc.

All were in vain, and the emperors were fearful. In the end, they caved and granted him absolute freedom. As a result, nothing evil happened. In the thirteenth year (514) of the Tianjian Period, Baozhi died without a disease and was buried in Dragon Hill on Zijin Mountain, occupying a spot with excellent *fengshui*. Next to his tomb, the emperor ordered the building of Kaishan Temple and Baogong Pagoda. The famous Lu Chui carved his tomb, and Wang Yun wrote him an inscription. His death marked the end of his playful confrontation with imperial power. Unfortunately, a few hundred years later, he suffered from an emperor who was more authoritarian and violent. Zhu Yuanzhang took a fancy to the spot where his tomb was and expelled him. His name was erased from this land, and Kaishan Temple and

Baogong Pagoda were relocated to where Linggu Temple is today. Only the cryptic prophecy on his staff still ridicules the secular power and maintains a spiritual victory.

Mountains are famous for the temples instead of height, and temples are famous for the monks instead of a number. Of course, we are talking about eminent monks and famous temples. The magical experience made the monk famous, and the temples and the mountains where they are located. Waguan Temple, Kaishan Temple, and the Terrace of Raining Flowers are examples of this theory. Terrace of Raining Flowers used to be named Stone Ridge. During the Southern Dynasties, it was already an area with numerous temples, whose attendance was excellent, and many monks. Faxian, a great traveler of the Eastern Jin Dynasty that wrote *Records of the Buddha Kingdom*, once translated six Buddhist scriptures in ancient India at the Daochang Temple there. The Ganlu Temple, also known as the Gaozuo Temple, is where eminent monks used to elaborate the scriptures.

The most shocking story is that during the reign of Emperor Wu of Liang, when Master Yunguang was teaching the Lotus Sutra, his eloquent speech moved the heaven, and flowers rained down and turned into cobblestones, hence the name Terrace of Raining Flowers. In fact, this beautiful legend was originally a pirated copy of the Buddhist scriptures, where the Buddha's teachings moved the gods, and fragrant flowers rained down from above. This legend seems to have been made up by some of the Tang people. As a result, Stone Ridge, a dull place, was given a literary and poetic name. Terrace of Raining Flowers became famous, and the city added one more place of interest. It makes us wonder: are there still people like them? Can there be such a good thing?

Everything has passed, Six Dynasties of misty drizzles, the temples, and the pagodas.

Chapter 12

Riding a Crane in Yangzhou

In every city of every era, some places can particularly inspire the poetic and literary ideas of the poets. In other words, these places have the most fertile literary soil and the most literary significance, such as the Qinhuai River and Confucius Temple. People love to linger on the banks of the Qinhuai River and the Confucius Temple, and the past seems to be within reach, right in front of us. Only a few places, like the Confucius Temple, used to be thriving and still are today. As time rolls forward, more places that used to be popular have been abandoned by future generations and by living individuals. Only their names that are difficult to be erased become the carrier of history, recording the collective memory of the past. From today's standpoint, as we try to restore the urban scenes in the hearts of the people of the Six Dynasties through some place names, which stimulated the most emotions and best had poets and scholars linger on?

As the capital, a transportation hub between east, west, north, and south at that time, and an important base for travel, the places in Jiankang City that witnessed coming and going are poetic. Back then, it was in Square Mountain that people saw off passengers who traveled south. From the city center there, it took one day by boat, and before the final departure, they shook hands and said goodbye. Inside the minds of literati of the Six Dynasties, Square Mountain was like the Baling (the tomb of Liu Heng, Emperor Wen of the Han Dynasty) in the eyes of the Han Dynasty people. It inspired many poets. Xie Lingyun, Wang Biaozhi, and He Xun wrote farewell verses as they saw their guests off to Square Mountain. Travelers going west used to set off from Xinlinpu or take a break in Xintingzhu (both were old places in Nanjing that no longer exist). He Xun wrote two poems called *Setting Off from Xinlin*, and Xie Yu wrote *To Xuancheng County from Banqiao of Xinlinpu*. Both were based on journeys. Xie Tiao saw off Fan Yun, who took a new post in Lingling in Hunan Province, all the way to Xintingzhu. Over a thousand years have passed, the past roads have long been desolated, and the ruts have long been buried under the ground. Only these place names still exude the scent of vicissitudes.

Zijin Mountain and Qixia Mountain were popular travel destinations for literati and scholars. Zijin in the eastern suburbs at first had few trees. Since the Eastern Jin Dynasty, it was stipulated that whoever left the capital to serve a new post or was dismissed and returned to court plant 50 to 100 trees in Zijin Mountain before leaving the capital. As time went by, a lush forest rose in Zijin Mountain. A tree-lined city is loveable. In this matter, Nanjing citizens have a long tradition of environmental protection and cherishing greenery.

After the Qi and Liang dynasties, Zijin Mountain was filled with thatched cottages for hermits, viharas (a kind of Buddhist monastery) for religious cultivation, and temples for worshipping Buddha. Zhou Yong, who Kong Zhigui joked about in *Beishan Yiwen*, once lived in seclusion on Zijin Mountain. And Shen Yue and Fan Yun had villas there. Shen Yue's villa was in Dongtian below the mountain, and he once depicted the scenery there in *Prose Poem of Suburban Residences*. Today, the eastern suburbs are full of lush greenery. It is an urban forest that Nanjing citizens are proud of. However, no debris from the temples and cottages of the Six Dynasties can be seen there.

It was an elegant game for ancient literati to climb high, gaze far, and chant poems. The Stone City, which stood on the riverside, was a fortress guarded by Nanjing City and also a frequent travel destination for literati. The high point Yecheng, located in the present Chaotian Palace, was also a popular place where people from the Six Dynasties climbed in spring and autumn. Even in the times of war, when people climbed high and gazed far, as depicted in *A New Account of the Tales of the World: Languages*, they would leisurely daydream of staying away from the mundane world. Today's Stone City remains a popular spot where tourists climb during the peak season. It reminds us of its strategic importance for being at such a height back then, while Yecheng was submerged in rows of buildings, losing its open view of the landscape. Fuzhou Mountain by Xuanwu Lake is another good place to climb high.

Gazing north, we see the sky still vast and the water still green, but it has long been renamed Jiuhua Mountain. During the Six Dynasties Period, imperial gardens and palaces scattered around Fuzhou Mountain, such as Leyou Garden, Hualin Garden, Hualin Qingshu Palace, Jingyang Tower, and others. These names can now only be seen on the scrolls. From the names, one can vaguely picture the splendor of the past. Emperor Xiaowu of the Song Dynasty depicted what he saw on his visit in *The Poetry of Visiting Fuzhou Mountain*:

Temples stand tall in the highland,
and palaces rise on the platform.

It has become a distant, vague memory. Originally, Fuzhou (a capsized boat) Mountain was so named because it was shaped like a boat lying quiet on the south bank of the North Lake and the north of Taicheng. While water can carry a boat, it can also overturn it. The boat and the water were connected, and the mountains and the lake were integrated, complementing each other. Did the person who named the mountain in the first place intentionally choose this name as a warning to the rulers at that time? Did those who changed its name neglect its political and historical meaning? When Nanjing was made the capital in the Ming Dynasty, the city rose by Fuzhou Mountain, which sacrificed itself to be the new city wall. Its glorious history was stored in every brick of the city wall.

The place name Yangzhou entered Nanjing but eventually left, leaving behind a memory in the history of the city.

Yangzhou is an ancient place name. In the *Book of Documents: Tribute of Yu*, Yangzhou is one of the Nine Provinces. In *The Rites of Zhou: Zhi Fang* is written: "the southeast of China is Yangzhou." *Er Ya* (a lexicon of ancient Chinese): *Shi Di* says: "the south of Yangtze is Yangzhou." These are obviously a name for a wider region. During the reign of Emperor Wu of the Han Dynasty, the Thirteen Feudal Provinces were established, including Yangzhou. Later, it evolved into a first-level administrative establishment, and the territory under its jurisdiction was still vast.

During the Eastern Han Dynasty, the Yangzhou government moved many times, but it was within the present-day Anhui Province each time. During the Three Kingdoms Period, Yangzhou was set up by both the Wei and Wu Kingdoms. The Yangzhou administration of the Wei Kingdom stood in Shou County, Anhui, while the Yangzhou administration of the Wu state sat in Jianye, the Nanjing of today.

The name Yangzhou was used to refer to Nanjing roughly throughout the Six Dynasties. Since the Yangzhou feudal governor's office was in Nanjing, Jiankang, the capital of the Six Dynasties, was named Yangzhou again. The city was a military center, a political center, and a place of prosperity. Liu Muzhi commented that it was the heart of Yangzhou and must remain exclusive. It was the absolute truth. Except for the imperial family and their henchmen, nobody else could take the important position of Yangzhou's feudal governor. As the political and cultural center of the Six Dynasties, Yangzhou, having undergone over 300 years of development, held an unshakeable and irreplaceable position. However, when the dynasties changed, the Rebellion of Hou Jing inflicted great damage on the capital.

There was a story during the Six Dynasties that four people once got together to discuss their ideals. A said that he dreamed of being the feudal governor of Yangzhou, B said he wanted to be rich, and C said he would like to ride a crane to become immortal. D ended the discussion by combing their dreams. He said that he wished to make a fortune and ride a crane to become the feudal governor of Yangzhou. Needless to say, this was pure wishful thinking. He longed for money, power, and immortality altogether. Being the Yangzhou feudal governor undoubtedly meant power and status. Even if he was not appointed the position, riding a crane to tour around it was definitely pleasant enough. The Yangzhou in the story obviously refers to today's Nanjing, but today's Yangzhou locals are happy to tell this story as they introduce their hometown's glorious history.

In the ninth year (AD 589) of the Kaihuang Era, Emperor Wen of Sui's reign, the Chen Dynasty was perished, and all the palaces in Jiankang were destroyed. In Sui Dynasty, Jiangzhou was set up in Stone City, while Danyang County was canceled, and Moling, Jiankang, and Tongxia were merged into Jiangning. In the same year, Wuzhou was renamed Yangzhou, and its government was located in Jiangdu (Yangzhou of today). After that, the name of Yangzhou no longer belonged to Nanjing. With the excavation of the Beijing-Hangzhou Grand Canal, there was one more important channel for north-south traffic in the Sui and Tang dynasties. It bypassed Nanjing and took Yangzhou as the center instead.

Located at the intersection of the Yangtze River and the Grand Canal, Yangzhou held a natural advantage and became an important port for foreign trade in the Tang Dynasty. It evolved from Wucheng, a city that was lamented by the poets of the Six Dynasties, into a city with a prosperous economy and culture, even better than Nanjing. According to the records in *Rong Zhai Sui Bi* by the Song Dynasty scholar Hong Mai, there was already the common belief of "Yang first and Yi second" at that time. In terms of prosperity, Yangzhou ranked first, and Yizhou (now Chengdu, Sichuan Province) second. We have fully appreciated the passion and charm of this city in Du Mu's passionate poems. Zhang Hu, a poet in the middle Tang Dynasty, wrote in *Journey to Huainan*:

The ten-*li* long street markets are connected.
On a moonlit night, people stand on the bridge
to watch the moving, singing, and dancing girls.
Yangzhou is the best place to die.
The beautiful Chanzhi Mountain is the best spot to be buried.

Xu Ning wrote in *Remembering Yangzhou*:

The splendor of the bright moon in the world has three parts.
The lovely Yangzhou holds two.

They sounded sensational. Yangzhou was shining brighter than Nanjing with great momentum.

Nanjing first lost its status as a political and cultural center, and then as a north-south transportation hub. After the Sui Dynasty, it was gradually marginalized. It used to have the power of cultural attraction and assimilation, thus being able to absorb cultural elements that did not belong to itself, but now, even it failed to preserve what it had. In Tang poetry, we often hear the nostalgic sigh of history. The prosperity of reality can be restored, while the sadness of the past cannot be erased, not to mention the endless chanting of poets from generation to generation deepens the pain.

It was a process.

At the beginning of the Sui Dynasty, Sun Wanshou was exiled to guard the south of Yangtze for being disheveled. In his frustration, he composed a poem *Early Departure to Yangzhou and Already Homesick*:

Farewell to my hometown, it was a sullen morning.
The fog shrouds the mountain, the mist covers the river.
It is cold in the middle of the river,
even though spring flowers have bloomed.
I have no wings to fly back, and the sandy wind saddens me.

Undoubtedly, Yangzhou at this time was still Nanjing, which was no longer the splendid capital of the six dynasties, but only part of the south of Yangtze River. No matter in the poet's eyes or his heart, the color of this city had already faded, and in the cold wind, waves of nostalgia hit him, making him shiver. For the time being, Nanjing could still share the name of Yangzhou with other cities, but it was no longer as splendid and majestic as it used to be. In the eyes of the more politically authoritative Emperor Yang of the Sui Dynasty, Yangzhou clearly did not belong to Nanjing but Jiangdu. In *Song of the Jiangdu Palace*, he wrote:

I linger on the old runs of Yangzhou
and long to revisit its beautiful towers and pavilions.
The pavilions and fine trees greet the early summer,
while the golden wheat sees off the late autumn.

Pavilions and fine trees were popular sites that Xu Zhanzhi made in Yangzhou during the Liu Song Dynasty. Emperor Yang of the Sui Dynasty had another poem, *On the Dragon Boat*:

It was a fleet of boats that sailed back home,
triumphantly down to Yangzhou.
It was asked where Yangzhou is,
the north of the Huainan River and the west of the North Sea.

. . .

The city is as big as a palm in the east of Yangtze,
I talk to myself, praising the trip.

The key question here is: "Where is Yangzhou?" And Emperor Yang of the Sui Dynasty had already given an authoritative answer.

In the second year of the Wude Period (AD 619), that is, the second year of the establishment of the Tang regime, the Xingtai Department of State Affairs in the southeast of Yangzhou was established; in the third year, Jiangning County and Lishui County were included in Yangzhou, and the name Jiangning was changed to Guihua; in the sixth year, Yangzhou was restored as it was; in the seventh year, Yangzhou was renamed Jiangzhou, and Guihua County was renamed Jinling County; in the eighth year, the Xingtai Department of State Affairs was canceled while the governor's office was set up in Yangzhou; in the ninth year, the governor's office was removed, and Yangzhou Prefecture was moved to Jiangdu. From Guihua to Jinling, the politically high-profile demeaning movement gradually calmed down; from Nanjing to Jiangdu, the history and reality of Yangzhou's name have diverged and drifted away, so far that most people can no longer see the connection between them, except a few poets mentioned this origin in their nostalgic chants. For example, Li Bai wrote in *To Entertain Court Attendant Cui*:

Yan Ziling was unwilling to follow Emperor Guangwu of the Han
    Dynasty,
so he returned to the Fuchun River, got drunk in the mountain,
and fished in the green stream.
Like Yan Ziling, I had to leave my position in court
and live a hermit life.
I am no Immortal Taibai who visited Yangzhou while drunk.

In the hearts of poets who cared much about history, time froze, and Yangzhou was still the Yangzhou of the Six Dynasties. However, most later generations have forgotten that there was such a name in the history of Nanjing, and they seem to have forgotten this prosperous history of Nanjing, intentionally or unintentionally.

An American student who had just started to learn Chinese asked his teacher where Nanjing is located in China. Except for the general location of Beijing and Shanghai, the student knew almost nothing about other Chinese cities. To make it easy for him to understand, the teacher explained that Nanjing stands in the vicinity of Shanghai in the northwest, about 300 kilometers apart. I felt lost and helpless when I first heard this story a few years ago. Foreigners don't know ancient China or don't know much, and the history of China is almost non-existent. I felt lost and helpless when I first heard this story a few years ago. They might ask where Shanghai is if we go back a hundred years. The answer is that it stands in the vicinity of Nanjing in the southeast, about 300 kilometers away.

Wang Bo sighed in *A Tribute to King Teng's Tower*:

Ah! A beautiful scenic spot is rarely seen,
and a sumptuous banquet like this one
is even less likely to be held again.
The grand gathering at the Orchid Pavilion is historical,
and the famous Jinggu Garden is now in ruins.

Parties end, and few cities thrive forever in history. Old cities are destroyed, and new ones are built. After all, only a few can attract the attention of history for a long time. Among these few, Nanjing is one.

The prosperity of the past is elusive, like floating clouds. Will the glory of the past come back riding a crane?

High Pavilion Facing the River

People say that Heng River is good, but I say that it is bad.
The gale is so strong that it tears down a mountain in three days,
and the white waves rage higher than the Waguan Pavilion.

—Li Bai, *The Heng River*

Li Gongzuo, a native of Longxi, stood on the Waguan Pavilion, leaning on the railing and overlooking the surging river. The green willows wave in the sunshine, and the river breeze blows, cooling the air.

It was the spring of the eighth year of the Yuanhe Period (AD 813). Li Gongzuo, who had just been dismissed from his position in Jiangxi, was relieved. He sailed east along the river, moored on the bank of the Qinhuai River, and visited some old sites and old friends in Jinling for a few days. In the Waguan Temple, where the Waguan Pavilion was located, a monk whose Buddhist name was Qiwu was a friend of Li Gongzuo. He told Li about a strange thing: recently, a woman named Xie Xiao'e came to the temple often and asked him to explain the meaning of two sentences. This woman came from Nanchang, Jiangxi. She went out to do business with her father and husband. Unfortunately, they encountered robbers, and both her father and husband were killed. She fell into the water after being injured by the robbers but was luckily rescued. She went begging in order to survive in Nanjing, a kind Buddhist nun, Jingwu of Miaoguo Temple, took her in. The survivor dreamed that her father sends a message to her: "My murderer is a monkey in a cart, and grass at the east of the door." Her husband also sent a message in her dream: "My killer walks in a field and is a one-day man." She believed the murderer's name was hidden in these two sentences, but she still couldn't understand it even though she had racked her brains out. She spent several years seeking the answer, but nobody could solve it.

Having heard Qiwu out, Li Gongzuo was interested. He leaned against the railings, pondering in silence. It didn't take long for him to figure it out. These were obviously cryptic words, a riddle of characters, and the names hidden behind were Shen Lan and Shen Chun. Monkey in the cart (車) is the word 申 shen (申): removing the two strokes up and down leaves shen (申) in the middle. Among the twelve Earthly Branches, shen (申) also corresponds to the zodiac of monkey. And when the three parts of grass (艹), door (門) and east (東) are combined, it is the traditional Chinese character *lan* (蘭). Walking in the field (田) means to extend the character into shen (申). And to combine three parts of one (一) day (日) man (夫) makes the character *chun* (春). Li Gongzuo asked Qiwu to call the widow over, and having collected the details from her in person, Li revealed the answer to the puzzle that he had solved: the murderers of her father and husband were Shen Lan and Shen Chun. Xie Xiao'e burst into tears, thanked him and left. With this crucial clue, she scoured everywhere and finally found the murderers. Four years later, she captured and killed Shen Lan and Shen Chun, and took down their fellow robbers in one sweep, avenging her family.

This was an amazing true story that happened in the middle Tang Dynasty. Xie Xiao'e was stoic and smart. She was aware that it was only possible to find help in a metropolis like Nanjing in a place like Waguan Temple, where all walks of life converged. This Waguan Temple was located on the Phoenix Terrace in Jinling. It was built in the Six Dynasties. Every spring and autumn, pilgrims and tourists flocked there. It was a rare "public space" in this city. Since the founding of the Southern Dynasties, the Waguan Pavilion has always been a "landmark building" in that area. Standing high, it faced the river and overlooked the city. It was a favorite spot for the literati to climb high and chant poems. In terms of the history, it had no less legendary mysteries and stories than that of Xie Xiao'e.

It was said that making pottery used to thrive in the area of the Waguan Temple. Before the second year of the Xingning Era (AD 364) of Emperor

Ai of the Eastern Jin Dynasty, a pottery officer was responsible for firing pottery utensils. That was where the name of Waguan (pottery officer) came from. Until the Qing Dynasty, when Nanjing citizens built houses, they often went here to collect soil so as to burn bricks and make tiles. Over the years, the hills in the vicinity were full of potholes, and some families' tombs had suffered. At first, this was the cemetery of Monk Zhu Fatai. In the second year of the Xingning era, monk Huili obtained this land, built a temple there, and named it Waguan Temple. But there was another version of the story later: during the Western Jin Dynasty, two green lotuses suddenly grew on the ground there, and the government sent people to dig deep and excavate a tile coffin. Inside the coffin was a monk, who looked rather alive, and it was from the root of his tongue that the lotus grew. Locals said a monk nearby, whose name was unknown, spent his life studying the Lotus Sutra. He recited it over ten thousand times, and his dying wish was to be buried there in a tile coffin. Probably, the locals failed to understand the meaning of "pottery officer" (瓦官 *wǎ guān*), and mistook it as "tile coffin" (瓦棺 *wǎ guān*), which matched the myth of lotus growing on his tongue in Buddhism. This story was probably fabricated to promote this religion. It sounds absurd, but without this odd story, the origin of the Waguan Temple would seem bland, and poets would not remember this name after hundreds of years.

When Waguan Temple was first built, it was simple and crude. According to legend, when the foundation of the pagoda was laid, the first pillar that was erected moved a dozen feet to the east at night. People were puzzled. It was later found that this was the will of God, implying the best location of the foundation. Since the eminent monk Zhu Fatai resided in Waguan Temple, he further expanded its scale. Depending on the terrain, he built more temple halls. Well-educated in Buddhism, Zhu Fatai was highly respected by the Emperor Jianwen of the Jin Dynasty, who invited him to lecture on the scriptures, and even attended his lectures at the temple in person. Also, the nobles flocked to his lectures. As a result, his reputation grew higher.

Every time he gave a lecture, ladies and gentlemen from far and near, old and young, attended it in groups. It was a spectacular scene, and Waguan Temple rose to fame. Zhu Fatai kept a good relationship with the celebrities and the royals, including Wang Qia, Wang Xun, Xie An, Sun Chuo, and others. His management made Waguan Temple stand out among the scattered Buddhist temples in Jiankang City, occupying a commanding height not only geographically but also politically.

What impressed the Taoists and the commoners the most, and left an unforgettable footprint in history, were the three specialties of the Waguan Temple. The first specialty was a four-foot-two-inch jade Buddha, which was a gift to Emperor Xiaowu of the Jin Dynasty from the king of the Lion Kingdom (now Sri Lanka). It took monk Tan Moyi over ten years to deliver it. It was a precious treasure and a symbol of close friendship. The second was the Zhangliu bronze Buddha designed and sculpted by the famous painter Dai Kui. It was a first-class size at that time and breathtaking. The third was the Vimalakirti Portrait painted by the famous painter Gu Kaizhi. He was styled Hutou (tiger head) and known at that time as a genius, excellent painter, and perfectionist. He was unique and different. In order to build the Waguan Temple, the abbot raised funds from the scholar-officials in the capital, and most donated at most 100,000 ancient coins.

One day, this young painter who lived nearby, came to the temple and pledged to donate one million ancient coins, shocking everyone. Some believed that he was bluffing, trying to steal the thunder, and would never be able to give such a large sum. Gu Kaizhi asked the abbot to give him a freshly painted white wall to paint a picture. It took him a month to paint a portrait of Vimalakirti on that. The Buddha looked energetic and lifelike. It was so radiant and refreshed that everyone in the temple was in awe. The news spread like wildfire, and people from far and near flocked to see it. Gu Kaizhi told to the abbot: "Those who come to see it on the first day will donate 100,000 ancient coins; those who come on the second will donate 50,000 ancient coins; those who come on the third can donate whichever amount."

The "ticket" revenue has exceeded one million ancient coins in a few days. The miraculous Vimalakirti portrait he painted was also known as the golden Buddha. It was a sensation in Jiankang at the time, and after hundreds of years, people still remember it. When the poet Du Fu visited Jinling, he made a special trip to the temple to see the painting, and even asked a friend to get a copy of it. A few years later, he still clearly remembered the eagerness to see it: "The Vimalakirti portrait by Gu Hutou, so amazing that I cannot forget."

Waguan Temple was the activity center of Taoists and the Six Dynasties' common people. Eminent monks and scholars gathered there to conduct an ideological confrontation. According to *The History of the Southern Dynasties: Biography of Lu Jue*, there was a monk named Wang Bin, who later returned to a secular life. He came to Waguan Temple to listen to Master Yun's lecture on *Satyasiddhi Shastra* (Proof of Reality). The temple hall was so crowded that only one seat was available next to monk Huichao. When Wang Bin took the seat. Huichao reprimanded him sharply for not asking for it politely. Wang Bin fought back and started a debate with Huichao. It was such an interesting clash that Wang Bin suddenly became famous in Jiankang City. In *A New Account of the Tales of the World*, we can see that Liu Yin, Wang Meng, Huan Yi and other literary celebrities gathered in Waguan Temple to discuss the great figures of the Western Jin Dynasty and in the east of the Yangtze River. The conversation between literary celebrities and eminent monks was usually a confrontation of agility and wit. One day, Wang Xiuzhi, a literary celebrity whose nickname was Wang Gouzi, came to the Waguan Temple and had a word with the monk Yi, discussing names and theories. The monk asked, "Does a saint have feelings?"

Wang Xiuzhi replied, "No."

The monk asked again, "In your eyes, is a saint no different from the pillars in this temple?"

Wang Xiuzhi replied, "A saint, like an abacus, has no feelings, but the person who controls the saint does."

The monk continued, "Who can control the saint?"

Wang Xiuyi was at a loss for words and could not answer. There must have been plenty of conversations of this kind at that time, but little was documented in the literature.

In the Liang Dynasty, the Waguan Temple built a 240-chi (about 60 meters) Waguan Pavilion, an impressive height even by present standards. There was no better spot than the Waguan Pavilion to climb high and gaze far. During Li Bai's days in Jinling, the southwest area of the city, from Phoenix Terrace to Waguan Pavilion, was where he lingered on. He once "Climbed the Waguan Pavilion in the morning and overlooked the Jinling City."

What he saw was:

To the north is the towering Zijin Mountain,
and to the south the pavilion eaves face the vast Huai River.
The chanting of sutras from the temple sounds holy,
and the ensemble is heavenly music.
Drums rumble on both sides of the temple corridors,
and the iron horse pieces at the four corners
of the cornices tinkle in the wind.
The pavilion towers into the sky,
as if we could easily reach for the sun and the moon.
The autumn scenery of Zijin Mountain is depressing,
and the qi of an emperor is exhausted;
How many sad stories accumulated in the long history?
The sea of clouds is boundless in the night,
and the lofty palace is as high as the clouds.
Only the word "Palace" written on the door plaque
and the word "Phoenix" on the building plaque
are still vaguely recognizable.
The thunder rumbles, the mountain shivers,
the houses are about to fall, and the gods come to help.
How precious is the Holy Light Hall?
It can bless Jinling City safe for a long time.

In Li Bai's eyes, this place had both geographical openness and historical depth, although most people tended to focus only on the former. Kang Renjie, a man of the Five Dynasties, had this verse:

After the dark clouds have dispersed,
I stand on the pavilion and gaze into the distance
to have a panoramic view of the mountains and rivers.
As the evening sun sets in the west, the afterglow shines over the city,
half the city is golden and the other half is dark.

It also depicted the height of Waguan Pavilion and a stunning view from there. The high pavilion faced the river, and the wind and waves were strong, leaving the building in jeopardy. It was no wonder that the Waguan Pavilion leaned to the southwest not long after it was built. Li Bai wrote in *The Heng River*:

> The gale is so strong that it tears down a mountain in three days,
> and the white waves rage higher than the Waguan Pavilion.

This was of course the poet's exaggeration, but there was some factual basis. In the ninth year of the Kaiyuan Era (AD 721) of Emperor Xuanzong of Tang, a gust of gale blew it straight again. The magic of nature never ceases to amaze and make a miracle.

After the Six Dynasties, Waguan Temple was renamed a few times, from Shengyuan Temple in the Southern Tang Dynasty to Baoning Temple in the Northern Song Dynasty, and then to the Chongsheng Jietan Temple in the Southern Song Dynasty. In the Southern Tang Dynasty, it was briefly named Shengyuan Pavilion, as a symbol of the capital of the Southern Tang Dynasty. In the eighth year of the Kaibao Era (AD 975), when the Song army attacked south, thousands of scholar-officials, wealthy businessmen, and ordinary citizens in Jinling City took refuge in the Shengyuan Pavilion. The Song soldiers set a fire, and:

> The sky is covered with smoke and the flames are blazing, it was an
>   appalling scene,
> and the towering Shengyuan Pavilion has since turned into ashes.
> The 240-chi tall building is no longer seen, but people have moved on
>   with their lives.
> Crows and magpies caw above, while underneath old vines and tree stems
>   tangle.

This is the site of the Shengyuan Pavilion in the eyes of the poet Liu Guo of the Southern Song Dynasty. It was heartbreaking to see it be ruined. The burning of the Waguan Pavilion symbolized the demise of the Southern Tang Dynasty. After the fire, the palace of the Southern Tang Dynasty became ruins, and there added several historical ashes on the ground in Nanjing.

After the Song Dynasty, the Yangtze River receded westward, and the phoenix, a symbol of imperial power, flew farther and farther. The Fengyou Temple was once rebuilt in the Ming Dynasty, but it used to be better than it was. There was no voice to suggest the re-construction of Shengyuan Pavilion, and this southwest area of the city was gradually forgotten, becoming an ordinary street. Since modern times, the city center of Nanjing has moved northward, and the Menxi area, which is rich in historical and cultural connotations, has become increasingly deserted. Some people rebuilt the ancient Waguan Temple on Hualu Hill a few years ago. The terrain there is narrow, and the building is simple. The couplets pasted on the columns have sloppy calligraphy, attracting few visitors. As expected, there is little attendance, and the temple is poor. It was not until recently that it gained more popularity.

> As I touch the moss print on the stone pillars,
> I am aware that the collapsed state will not rise again.
> There is no more 300-chi pavilion piercing through the clouds,
> but only its wind chimes echo in the world.
>
> —Zeng Ji, *Song of Jinling*

Unfortunately, even the wind chimes can no longer be heard in Kaiyuan Pavilion.

Chapter 14

Fine Alcohol of Jinling

Thousands of guests filled the hall,
exchanging fine wine in the spring of Jinling.
> —LI BAI, *To Wei Bing, When I Visited Him in High Spirits,*
> *and Came Across Yan Zhenqin, Thus This Gift*

Today, Nanjing does not seem to be famous for its alcohol. This city does not have fine liquor, yellow rice wine, and wine. Despite the presence of local brands such as Jinling and Longhu (dragon-tiger), no local alcohol is famous, let alone has a national reputation. However, in the history of this city, there are several memories and legends about wine worth reminiscing about. Let's start with Li Bai's poems.

There is a long history of winemaking in China. Unfortunately, knowledge about the famous wines before the Tang Dynasty needed to be recovered. History remembers the fine wines of the Tang Dynasty thanks to the chanting of some famous poets: *Ruoxiachun* (chun: spring) from Wucheng, *Lihuachun* from Hangzhou, *Tukuchun* from Xingyang, *Shidongchun* from Fuping, *Qumichun* in Yun'an, *Shaochun* from Jiannan, and *Jinlingchun* from Nanjing. Tang people liked to name their wines with the word spring. I wonder if poets inspired it. Those names sound rather poetic. *Qumichun* was famous because of Du Fu, *Lihuachun* because of Bai Juyi, and *Jinlingchun* because of Li Bai.

Li Bai went to Jinling more than once. Whether it was a journey to embrace nature, a nostalgic trip, traveling with friends, or seeing off guests or friends, drinking was one of his life's main activities and pleasures. He once said goodbye to a friend at a Jinling wine shop:

The spring breeze blew the willow catkins,
the fragrance of wine filled the room,
and the maid held out the fine wine, inviting me to savor it carefully.
My young friends from Jinling rushed to see me off.
Before I set off, we gulped down our joy and sorrow.
Let me ask, is our friendship longer than the river that runs east?

He also gulped wine on the Phoenix Terrace and expressed his feelings:

Today, we drink at the Phoenix Terrace in Jinling
to cherish time and life.
The Yangtze River flows forever below the terrace,
and we should be happy on the terrace.
Let me ask: who did the phoenix come for?
A thousand years have passed since the phoenix left.
It's time that it flew back today.

When Li Bai entered Chang'an for the first time, he received a resounding title from He Zhizhang: Exiled Immortal, which was soon extended to describe his drinking: "the eight drinking immortals." His good reputation during the Chang'an years was also brought to Jinling, and Li Bai's good friend Cui Chengfu called him "Jinling Wine Immortal." His wild and legendary drinking made him an "immortal." Li Bai himself also fancied this title. When he hung out with friends in Jinling, he used to call himself by it, such as in his poem *A Preface to Seeing off Quan Shiyi with Friends from Jinling*. Ren Si'an composed a short poem *Baixia Pavilion*, whose subject was Li Bai:

He took off his boots at the emperor's audience hall,
and demanded wine at the east of Baixia Pavilion.

Since the state has fallen,
who was there to enjoy the fragrance of flowers?

He must have loved wine deeply so that he demanded it. Even in the literary memory of later generations, the impression of "Jinling wine immortal" cannot be erased.

Li Bai had a poem inscribed *Appreciating the Moon in the Sun Chu Restaurant at the West of Jinling City, We Sung until Dawn Broke, And While Drunk, Wearing a Purple Fur Coat and Black Veil, We Chanted Songs on the Boat with Drinking Friends and Sailed to Visit Imperial Censor Cui.* The Southern Dynasty poet Bao Zhao also "appreciated the moon in the government office in the west of the city" and wrote the verse:

Rising from the southwest building,
the crescent hangs above like a jade hook.

However, Bao Zhao did not drink, so he did not seem as happy as Li Bai, who was appreciating the moon and drinking in the restaurant in the west of the city all night long and then with friends, while drunk, sailed a small boat along the Qinhuai River to the Stone City to visit Cui Chengfu. In the bright moonlight, this group swaggered through the city, and citizens on both banks of the river, seeing them, all clapped their hands and laughed. They compared Li Bai to Wang Huizhi, who visited Dai on a snowy night. In the title of this poem, Li Bai mentions his outfit, "a purple fur coat and a black veil." The purple fur coat was probably his usual outfit and seemed to be rather expensive.

One day, he bumped into a hermit from Pengchi near the Star Rock. They hit it off, and Li Bai "traded the purple fur coat for the wine of Jinling. The wine made them so happy that they started to sing, and it was such fun." This gown was probably never redeemed again. Henceforth, we never see this coat again in his poems. In *Invitation to Wine*, Li Bai shouted: "The fur coat worth a thousand coins of gold and a flower-dappled horse may both be sold to buy good wine that we may drown the woes age-old." His love for the wind was unparalleled, and his drinking experience in Nanjing proves that he was not exaggerating with the fur coat trade-off.

The place where Li Bai drank this time was called Sun Chu wineshop. It was named after Sun Chu, and its old site sits under Xiafu Bridge today, south of Xishuiguan, not far from Shuiximen Square. Sun Chu was a famous scholar in the Western Jin Dynasty. When he was young, he decided to be a hermit and didn't come out to take up an official post until he was in his forties. He died in the third year (493) of the Yuankang Era. He has never been an official in Jianye or been to the south of Yangtze. Several anecdotes about him in *A New Account of the Tales of the World* mention his deep love for his wife, his being self-conceited and insolent on account of his ability, his eloquence, and his liking to tease others. There is no record of his love for wine nor the restaurant named after him.

Among his descendants, Sun Tong and Sun Chuo were both well-known in the Eastern Jin Dynasty and also related to Nanjing and the Six Dynasties. However, it is unknown whether the restaurant had an association with them. Once, I read *The Anecdotes of Jinling*, compiled by modern people. It writes that Sun Chu inhabited Jinling during the Eastern Jin Dynasty and used to invite friends over for dinner. People admired his talent and fame, so the restaurant was named after him. This obviously does not match the time, and I am afraid it is just hearsay. Perhaps, Sun Chu is just the name of the restaurant owner and has nothing to do with the famous Jin scholar Sun Chu, and such a baseless assertion has been repeated. Or perhaps, there was another story behind the restaurant name, one that we cannot investigate to verify. This is like the cenotaph (monument) of Ruan Ji found on the Shangyuan No 43 Middle School campus in Hualugang, southwest of Nanjing. Ruan Ji was indeed addicted to alcohol, but he had never been to Nanjing in his life, so how could he be buried there? Could it be that his descendants miss their ancestor so much that they did this? Or was it purely fake? Times have changed, and it is impossible or necessary to clarify this mystery.

Sun Chu Restaurant later became almost synonymous with restaurant. Wine drinkers inevitably thought of Li Bai and Sun Chu when they went to the restaurant, adding elegance to the drinking. Wang Tinggui of the Song Dynasty wrote in the poem *Climbing to the Restaurant with Hu Guanguang*:

Li Bai climbed the Sun Chu Restaurant at night,
appreciated the moon and lingered.

Because of Li Bai's reputation, Zhou Yinghe of the Song Dynasty simply renamed it Li Bai Restaurant in *Records of Jiankang During the Jinding Period* (1260–1264). It is not uncommon for the customer to be more famous than the restaurant, but it is unbelievable that it was renamed after the renowned customer. In the early Ming Dynasty, people rebuilt a unique restaurant on the Sun Chu Restaurant's old site, named the Drunk Immortal Restaurant. It was one of the fourteen famous buildings in the capital in the early years of the Hongwu Period (1368–1398), but the citizens and the literati still liked to call it by its old name. And the new name seems to include both celebrities, Li Bai and Sun Chu. Yi Zhenji of the Ming Dynasty composed a poem, *Qing Ping Le*, which talked about nothing else but "the best Jinling wine is in the Sun Chu restaurant." Until the early Qing Dynasty, this restaurant stood on the banks of the Qinhuai River. It was listed as one of the Forty Scenic Spots of Jinling and the Forty-Eight Scenic Spots of Jinling in the Ming Dynasty and Qing Dynasty, respectively.

Li Bai got drunk in this restaurant,
and the flowers and trees next to it were quiet and beautiful.
It has become so desolate today,
and so has the late-blooming Yu Garden.

This is the description by Zhang Tongzhi of the Republic of China in *Inscriptions on Forty-Eight Scenic Spots of Jinling*. At that time, the restaurant had long since been abandoned, and even the Yu Garden, which was built afterward, became a forgotten hill.

The restaurant disappeared together with Li Bai, which is a significant loss for those who love wine and the ancients. However, in addition to Sun Chu Restaurant, there is another place where they can reminisce about the past: Xinghua (apricot blossom) Village.

Yes, this is the Xinghua Village in Du Mu's poems.

The constant drizzles drip all the dismal day,
so broken-hearted fares the traveler on the way.

When asked where a tavern bower could be found,
a cowboy points to yonder village of the apricot flower.

Since this poem's publication, the fame of Xinghua Village got bigger and bigger, like a rolling snowball. Many places wanted a share, either for business purposes or from a cultural stance. Since Du Mu's poem did not specify the exact location of Xinghua Village, it caused controversy among the curious. Some argued that it was in Guichi, Anhui Province because Du Mu worked there for two years as the prefect of Chizhou, and the poems might have been written there; some said it was in Fenyang, Shanxi Province, because it was home to fine wine; others suggested that it be in Macheng, Hubei Province. Nanjing joined the debate, too, but by this time, she had already lost its status as a political and cultural center, and her voice was naturally less powerful. In this debate, Nanjing neither won nor lost. In general, it had a bigger gain than loss. But more importantly, it shows this city's conscious cultural awareness.

Jiao Hong, a scholar of the Ming Dynasty born in Nanjing and affectionately called Jiao Zhuangyuan (number one scholar) by Nanjing locals, wrote in Inscription of *Reconstruction of Fengyou Temple* that the ruins of Xinghua Village in Jinling were in the west of Dark Gown Alley and Xinfu River in the south of the city, approximately the area of Phoenix Terrace. This number one scholar who fancied antiques did not get to the bottom of it. In fact, Xinghua Village of Jinling appeared at least in the Song Dynasty. Yue Shi of the Song Dynasty stated in *Tai Ping Huan Yu Ji* (a history series that documents the geography and territory of the Song Dynasty) that Xinghua Village stood in the west of Jiangning County in Shengzhou and that it was where Du Mu bought wine back then. Poet Yang Wanli of the Southern Song Dynasty also wrote in his poem *Climbing the Phoenix Terrace*:

The river weeds grow wild for egrets to feed,
while the apricot flowers are blooming
in the west of Dark Gown Valley.

Obviously, it was the scene of Xinghua Village. This further supports the city's claim to the ownership of Xinghua Village. In the Yuan Dynasty, there was an anonymous *sanqu* (non-dramatic song, a type of song popular in the Yuan, Ming, and Qing dynasties), *A Flower of Nan Lü* [fishing]. Its lyrics include:

Yesterday I left Stone Town,
today I am at Peach Leaf Dock,
and tomorrow I will reach Xinghua Village.

It is obvious that Xinghua Village was regarded as a real place in Nanjing. So far, Xinghua Village in Jinling has accumulated such a considerable amount of cultural capital that political power could not turn a blind eye to it. It is said that when Zhu Yuanzhang's army attacked Jiqing, he had an ultimate battle with the Yuan army in Xinghua Village, severely damaging the village. After Nanjing was made the capital of the Ming Dynasty, apricot trees were replanted, and the old gardens became prosperous again. Gu Qiyuan of the Ming Dynasty wrote in *Song of a Garden Life*: "Flags of wind shops were slanted outside Xinghua Village, while spring makes every tree in the wall bloom."

Yu Binshuo, a poet in the early Qing Dynasty, once described Xinghua Village *in See the Past from Jinling* as "during springtime, flowers bloom beautifully, and there are many gardens in the village." It seems that this village had not only flowers but also wine. Until the early Qing Dynasty, it was still a gathering place for ladies and gentlemen. In the Qing Dynasty, the Wine Fair at Xinghua Village was one of the Forty-Eight Scenic Spots in Jinling. Famous flowers, beautiful gardens, and delicious wine are naturally attractive. During the Jiaqing Period (1796–1820), when Chen Wenshu complied the *Chronicle of Places of Interests of Jinling*, he composed a poem:

Spring rain in the south of Yangtze
dreams without a trace,
and the wine shop flags at the market
waves white on the gate.

Since it was mentioned in the poem, people have been talking about the Xinghua Village to this day. In his eyes, Xinghua Village of Jinling seems to be the best of Du Mu's poetry.

The chilly water in mist; the beach, moonlight,
I moor on Qinhuai by a tavern one night.

This is a verse in Du Mu's *Moor on the Qinhuai River*. Unlike Sun Chu after all, Du Mu had been to Nanjing and was familiar with the city. According to his romantic and suave personality, he likely lingered at Qinhuai wine shops. It is unknown whether the Qinhuai wind shop mentioned in Du Mu's poems expressly points to one, but we at least know that there were wine shops by the Qinhuai River in the Tang Dynasty. Besides the Sun Chu Restaurant, there must be more alike. And this poem by Du Mu must have contributed to Xinghua Village's "settling" in Nanjing.

Whether it is the Sun Chu Restaurant, Ruan Ji's cenotaph, or Xinghua Village, there can only be one final conclusion from the perspective of historical facts. From the standpoint of literature and culture, the truth may not be so important, but what truly matters is the cultural psychology and historical meaning behind the facts. There were such a group of curious people in the history of Chinese culture. Their identities were complicated. Some were writers, some were local officials, some were squires who refused to move to another location, and some were foreign tourists who adored antiquity. They were seen on many occasions. They were obsessed with rumors and anecdotes and persistently spread and fabricated them. However, history has thus added some fun, and culture has thus added more weight. Stories such as the Sun Chu Restaurant, Ruan Ji's cenotaph, and Xinghua Village might be the cultural creations of these curious people.

To put it more profoundly, this incident reflects the tolerance and creativity of Jinling ancient city culture. It is a city that consumes culture but also a city that produces culture. It will make use of its own historical and cultural resources, exert the impact of cultural celebrities, create more cultural resources, and accumulate more cultural wealth. Nowadays, some people do not regard these cultural heritages as treasures but rather as burdens. In comparison, these people are truly worse than the squanderers. As I write this far, I can't help but sigh.

Chapter 15

Count the Falling Petals

The grass on Zijin Mountain is dense and luxuriant,
extending all the way to the pond.
Both the straight ditches and the winding pond are now sparkling.
I have been sitting here for a long time
to carefully inspect the fallen petals,
looking for the fragrant grass in my heart.
It is past time to go home.

—WANG ANSHI, *North Mountain*

One day in the summer of the fourth year (AD 1037) of the Jingyou Period under the reign of Emperor Renzong of Song Dynasty, Wang Anshi, a native of Linchuan, Jiangxi Province, who was under 17 years old, came to Jinling City for the first time with his father, Wang Yi. The latter was promoted to be a *tongpan* (an official that manages crop freight, local farming, water conservatory, etc.) of Jiankang. Although he had never been to the city before, he already knew its ancient and recent history. For three hundred years, the qi of an emperor resided in this city during the Six Dynasties, which is common historical knowledge. Over 60 years ago, this place used to be the capital of the Southern Tang Dynasty. Some of Wang Anshi's fellow countrymen and ancestors had served as officials in this regime, thus fairly familiar with the old stories of Jinling in that period. They used to tell those stories to the young lad. After many years, Wang Anshi still remembered such a story: in the Southern Tang court, Pan You and Xu Xuan, equally famous for their literary achievement, were on par.

Later, Pan You was sentenced to die because of his straightforward advice. Xu Xuan, who kept his nose clean, was just demoted to a *sanqi changshi* (an attendant to the emperor who went out with him riding horses) of the Song Dynasty. On the order of Emperor Taizong of the Song Dynasty, he compiled the history of the Southern Tang Dynasty as *Records of the South of the Yangtze*, where he spared no effort to cover up his errors, fabricate stories, and slandered Pan You. Years later, with these memories of his youth, Wang Anshi ruthlessly exposed Xu Xuan's false writing and hypocrisy.

It has been less than two years since the poet set foot in Nanjing. In the spring of the second year (AD 1039) of the Baoyuan Period, his 46-year-old father, Wang Yi died abruptly. As usual, the Wang family did not return the coffin to Linchuan to bury him in their hometown but temporarily buried him in Jiangning. It was not until nine years later that the deceased was buried on Niushou Mountain, and Wang Anshi's friend Zeng Gong was invited to write his epitaph. It seems that Wang Yi had already made arrangements for such a significant decision. After that, the Wang family settled in Jinling.

In ancient times, scholars who served as officials far from home usually returned to their hometowns after work ended. There were often special reasons for those who settled down where they worked. Some were subjective reasons, such as adoring the local scenery so much that they could not bear to leave; others were objective, such as the war or financial distress. It was, while unusual, not uncommon. Among the literati of the Song Dynasty, Ouyang Xiu adored the beautiful local landscape of Yingzhou (now Fuyang, Anhui Province).

Once, he made a pact with Zeng Gong to purchase a piece of land there for retirement. When he retired at the age of 65, he did stay there instead of returning to his hometown. Wang Yi, who earned a career thanks to studying hard, owned no land or family business in his hometown of Linchuan. Therefore, when he served as an official away from home, he was forced to take his entire family with him. In his will, he instructed his family to settle down where he worked, probably because of circumstances.

For Wang Yi, making this choice may have been accidental, or even with overwhelming helplessness, but for this city, it was a lucky opportunity. A literary genius inhabited Jinling, and his pen began to depict the natural beauty and cultural styles and features of the city.

From the age of 17 to 22, the five-year life in Jinling was the most unforgettable for Wang Anshi. Before the age of 17, he was a teenager, conceited and arrogant, high-spirited and vigorous, and talented. He claimed it was not until he turned 17 that he truly understood the truth of "A young idler, an old beggar." Hence, he halted interpersonal communications, studied hard, and read extensively, determined to be great. In his later poems, he recalled the situation at that time: "Less talented and less fortunate as I am, I aspire to make greatness."

The sudden death of his father hit him hard: "One day, bad news came, and I no longer have someone to rely on." He seemed to have matured overnight. Shortly after the mourning period ended, Wang Anshi traveled up north to the capital and was admitted as a *jinshi* (candidate in the highest imperial examination) with flying colors, fourth place among the first tier of candidates, to be precise, and embarked on an official career from then on. Three became prime ministers of all the *jinshi* that year: Wang Gui, Han Jiang, and Wang Anshi. No wonder Ye Mengde in the Southern Song Dynasty, called him unprecedented in *Shilin Yanyu* (a book of historical notes in the Song Dynasty).

Probably influenced by his childhood experience, after Wang Anshi passed the *jinshi* examination, he did not covet a high-ranking position in the office but took the initiative to ask for a foreign position as a local magistrate. From childhood, he followed his father and traveled all over the country, thus had an excellent understanding of local people's conditions and regional politics. He served in different local towns and counties, accumulating precious political experience. During those years, he came up with a political reform scheme. But he didn't stay as long in other cities as Jinling. Wang Anshi was reluctant to leave his hometown, Linchuan, Yinxian and Changzhou, where he worked. However, he had a far more profound love for Jinling.

I miss that old place three thousand *li* away;
when I lit the fire on Qingming Festival,

a sadness washed over me.
I might get drunk at a random wine shop
when I take off my court outfit.

This was the poem *Missing Jinling Under the Imperial Carriage on the Qingming Festival,* composed during his work at the capital. Looking from a distance of three thousand *li,* in his eyes, Jinling was the "hometown" that he missed.

The river goes around Guazhou Isle beside Jingkou.
Passing a few hills, I will arrive at my Zijin Mountain goal.
The spring breeze has turned the south riverside green,
when will the bright moon see me going back again?

This was *Mooring at Guazhou Isle,* which he wrote on his trip to his second term as Prime Minister. Instead of being complacent and arrogant, he was ready for a retirement as a hermit. His hometown was Jinling, and his mountain was Zijin Mountain.

In August of the eighth year (AD 1063) of the Jiayou Period, Wang Anshi's mother, née Wu, passed away in the capital. In October, she was buried on Jiang Mountain, also known as Zijin Mountain, in Jiangning Prefecture. The 43-year-old *zhizhigao* (an ancient official who drafts imperial edicts) Wang Anshi returned to Jiangning after working 20 years far away. This time, he stayed in Jiangning for five years. First, he was in mourning for two years, and from the fourth year (1067) of the Zhiping Period, he served as the Prefect of Jiangning. During this period, he gave lectures to apprentices at home, including Lu Dian, Gong Yuan, Li Ding, Cai Bian, etc. Middle age is such a rare period of indifference and tranquility for a man. For Wang Anshi, this was actually a turning point in life, and a new rise was brewing. In the first year of the Xining Period (1068), the newly ascended Emperor Shenzong favored Wang Anshi and recalled him to Kaifeng. At the beginning of the following year, he was promoted to Canzhi Zhengshi (equal to deputy prime minister). Henceforth, it has been a dangerous path up high, and Wang Anshi entered the most brilliant and unforgettable years of his life.

In the winter of the third year (1070) of the Xining Period, Wang Anshi was promoted to be Prime Minister. That year, he had just turned 50. "At the age of 50, one knows the mandate of Heaven." According to *Lin Han Yin Ju Shi Hua* (a book on poetry and poets) by Wei Tai, friends and family flocked to congratulate him when the news came, but Wang Anshi avoided seeing them and hid with Wei Tai in a small pavilion on the west corridor. Suddenly, he frowned, pondered for a moment, took a brush from the desk, and wrote:

The winter snow covers the bamboo,
and the bamboo forest houses the Zijin Mountain Temple.
This is the ideal destination for me
to retire for the rest of my life.

As soon as he reached the peak of his political career, he had already made a plan for the future. His body was in the court, but his heart was in the mountains. Four years later, in the seventh year (1074) of the Xining Period, Wang Anshi resigned for the first time and returned to Jiangning; he was asked to be the Prime Minister again in February of the following year; in October of the ninth year (1076) of the Xining Period, he resigned and returned to Jiangning again. At first, he carried an official title, "*Pan* of Jiangning Prefecture," commonly known as "*yishixiangpan* of Jiangning Prefecture." This was the system of the Song Dynasty. In *Ordinary Words to Warn the World*, "Whenever the prime minister is dismissed, he must be given an external title, and he will go to that place for retirement without the need to manage the place." The following year, Wang Anshi renounced that title, too. And the most leisurely ten years of his life began.

It was not until retirement that Wang Anshi seemed to start to pay attention to his personal life. From a young age, he had been always focused on national affairs, moral cultivation, and literary knowledge. He made little effort on the more minor points of conduct. He had a sloppy appearance, seldom changed his outfit, and even did not wash his face regularly. Legend has it that when he served under the Prefecture Chief Han Qi of Yangzhou, he studied all night. Sometimes, there was no time to wash up before an audience with the Prefect at the hall, which even led the Prefect to misunderstand that he led an unrestrained nightlife, which became a laughingstock for future generations. Having retired this time, he bought a piece of land in the east of Jiangning City and built it as a home in his later years. At first, this place was called Baitang, seven *li* from the east gate of Jiangning Prefecture and seven *li* from Zijin Mountain. Being in the middle-inspired Wang Anshi to name it Banshan (half mountain) Garden. He built a few houses, planted trees, dug a pond, and settled down. Here, he could always appreciate the beautiful wild scenery, such as

> Outside the courtyard, a small river surrounds the field,
> tightly embracing the green seedlings;
> two lush mountains greet people
> with the most refreshing green.

It appears that he was delighted with this place. There were many poems about this retirement home among his late years works, such as *The Things on a Spring Evening at Banshan*, in which he wrote about late spring, *The Things in the Year End Banshan*, which talked about the end of the year. This title *The Things at Banshan* included around a dozen poems. He felt like Tao Yuanming, who returned to the countryside, calm and comfortable.

In the past, when people mentioned Wang Anshi's calligraphy, they shared the conclusion that he tended to rush it, never taking it slow. At first glance, the calligraphy would suggest that he was a busy man. This was purely a personal habit. Zhu Xi, Yang Shen, and others associated it with his irritable and manic character, which sounded accusing and personal. However, as a ruling minister, Wang Anshi was on the cusp of implementing new laws and reforms, meaning he could not be nervous and impatient. In terms of relaxation, "He could not, not that he would not." Having started his retirement on Zijin Mountain, the poet stayed away from the political storms and had a new lifestyle for the first time, one that was relaxing:

> I have been sitting here for a long time
> carefully inspecting the fallen petals,
> looking for the fragrant grass in my heart.
> It is late time to go home.

And in another poem:

Sitting idle in front of green mountains,
reading a book and dozing off in the company of orioles.

How relaxed and comfortable he sounded. And reading the poem *To Chang'an*, which he wrote to his eldest sister Wang Wenshu in the fifth year (1060) of the Jiayou Period, will tell us even more that he always was an affectionate individual:

The feeling of parting when we were young was deep;
now that I am old, even seeing each other saddens me.
I prepared some food and wine as I pleased,
so as to chat as we ate; when the lights went dim,
we shared what we had seen and thought about until late at night.
As I was feeling sorry that it had been three years since we were apart,
I am leaving you for the Liao Kingdom,
thousands of *li* away, braving the sandstorms.
You asked me when we would meet again, how can I tell?
When you see the wild goose flying south,
there will be a message that I am well from me.

But people held a too deep bias against him. It was the profound helplessness and sadness of the politician Wang Anshi. In addition to the vicious cursing at him in Ao Xianggong (his nickname among the people back then) *Regrets at the Banshan Hall*, there were so many rumors, so much nonsense, and deliberate distortions and attacks among the Song Dynasty's poems. For example, Shao Bo not only wrote *On Identifying the Treacherous Court Officials*, slandering Wang Anshi for being unsympathetic, but also fabricated a story in *Records of What the Shao Family Heard and Saw*, where Wang Anshi was said to be employing a veteran in his Banshan Garden to help him with his daily life. He praised to soldier when he was satisfied, but whenever the tiniest thing did not go his way, he became furious and chased the soldier away. This was nothing more than to portray Wang Anshi as a moody villain, tainting his image. Another example is the quarrel between

Wang Anshi and Xie An. Wang Anshi's name was exactly the same as the style of Xie An, and the humorous poet took the opportunity to joke with the ancients, hence his two four-line poems, *The Xie Mound*:

Accidentally, my name is the same as your style,
but this mound is so in my house
that I wake up to see it.
It belongs to me and should not be under your name.
The old story of Xie is difficult to find;
the mountain, the moon,
and the clouds were only memories from the past.
The past is gone and never to return;
he could only shed tears in his twilight years.

According to an old legend, the Xie Mound sits near Banshan Temple. It was said that in the Song Dynasty, Banshan Temple was named Kangle (health and happiness) Alley, and Xie Xuan was bestowed the title Duke of Kangle. Therefore, Kangle Alley was probably where Xie Xuan and his descendants lived and had nothing to do with Xie An. Some ancients said that the Xie Mound was the high place where Xie An and Wang Xizhi climbed in the Chaotian Palace region. No matter where it really is, for Wang Anshi, this was just an innocent joke between literati, but he was accused of being so small-minded that he even teased the ancients. This only shows that those people were small-minded and nothing else.

When life changes, poems change, too. Wang Anshi's lyrics in his early years were arrogant, and he liked to be unconventional and sharp. After retreating to Nanjing, his style of poetry has undergone significant changes. Between his two dismissals from being the prime minister, his younger brother Wang Anguo and his son Wang Xu passed away one after another. Their sudden deaths devastated him much more severely than the political ups and downs. In his later years, his state of mind gradually turned peaceful, and his poems also became calm. He was no longer arrogant, and there were no longer long poems like *Song of the Ming Concubine*, which was a pure showing-off of his talent, sharp edges, and clear arguments. His poetry became shorter, too. He used to be good at the seven-character-per-line long poems, but now he seemed to prefer the succinct four-line poems.

But despite the different forms, he still excelled at composing poems as ever, or even better. He should thank Nanjing and Zijin Mountain. If Nanjing is compared to a poetic city, Zijin Mountain is simply a wonderful poem. During the Yuanfeng Period (1078–1085), Wei Tai paid Wang Anshi a visit and asked about his recent poetry writing. Wang Anshi replied that he had not written poetry for a long time because, according to Buddhism, chanting was also deemed as oral creation, but occasionally he felt something, and he couldn't help but compose some poems. He recited a recent piece to his guest:

> The east hill of southern riverside in February,
> so beautiful that it inspired me to compose new poems.

The beautiful scenery of the eastern suburbs put him in the mood to write, and this old man in his fifties couldn't resist the eagerness nor bothered to care about the Buddhism prohibition, but instead, reached a new peak in his poetry writing. This was another harvest period for Wang Anshi's literary creation. Among the poets of the Song Dynasty, perhaps only Su Dongpo in his Huangzhou period was his match.

Since the Northern Song Dynasty, people in all dynasties have slandered and scolded Wang Anshi. They never got tired of it, as if not doing this would fail to prove that they were gentle, honest, and righteous, but nobody could deny Wang Anshi's literary talent or poetic achievements. As early as the first year (AD 1056) of the Jiayou Period, his predecessor Ouyang Xiu gifted a poem to Wang Anshi:

> Your poetry shows you are just as talented as Li Bai;
> Your article, like Han Yu's, a minister of the Ministry of Officials,
> has been handed down to later generations.
> Although I am old and sad alone, my ambition remains;
> Who can compete with you in the future days?

On the one hand, he praised Wang Anshi's literary talent; on the other, he expected him to have a bright future. From the age of 17, Wang Anshi did not seem to take his literary talents too seriously. In his reply to Ouyang Xiu's poem, he confessed: "I wish I could understand more of Mencius in the future, and I dare not to ever compare myself to Han Yu." His biggest ambition was to be a Confucian scholar instead of a man of words. This orientation involuntarily affected his life and his literary creation during his administration. When he thought as a politician, as a minister in power, his ideas may have lacked imagination, or there was no poetic nature at all. It was said that on November 11, in the eighth year (1074) of the Xining Period, he presented a memorial to the emperor, proposing that Xuanwu Lake be turned into farming land since there were more mountains than farming land in Jinling, a city that was densely populated. There, the rich had enormous fields while the poor had nothing. In this way, for the short term, the food supply in the lake could save the poor and hungry; for the long term, farming would happen, and taxes could be collected annually to increase public revenue. This plan reminds me of the verses of a foreign poet:

Flowers bloom on the grassland,
but when the cattle and sheep come,
all they find is food.

According to Chinese tradition, this can really be included in *The Trivialities*, listed as the first article of a killjoy.

Such unpleasantness did not actually start with Wang Anshi, and it happened for a reason. In the first year (1017) of the Tianxi Period, Ding Wei, the Prefect of Shengzhou, reported to the court that 76 mu of Xuanwu Lake had been converted into civilian land due to the drought in previous years. After Ding Wei took office, he gradually found that the lake was shrinking, aggravating the drought and endangering the city, so he turned waterways back into ponds to store water. When the people were distressed and the land was in short supply, the lake was made for farming. Although it sought immediate success instead of long-term benefits, there was no other choice. It is forgivable to make such an extreme choice when this choice is the only choice because the motive is positive. Having resigned from the position as prime minister, Wang Anshi probably did not have to make these kinds of plans anymore. In his later years, he seemed to have recovered his status as a poet. This is not what Tao Yuanming called "Now I have come to realize how wrong I have been all those years," nor what

Qu Boyu called "Forty-nine years of my fifty years were so wrong." Perhaps it is Wang Anshi's return to literature, a poetic life, and his true self. This is worth celebrating for literature, for Jiangning, and for Wang Anshi.

The wind blows by, and the petals fall, spiraling down. To appreciate the beauty, one should sit in silence and count them carefully.

Chapter 16

Autumn Leaves at Banshan

"One leaf's falling tells the coming of autumn."

—Chinese idiom

Having endured the ups and downs of life, the old poet Wang Anshi became much calmer, except some of his character had not completely changed, which was not reflected in life but in literature.

Wang Anshi, a prime minister, was also stubborn in literature. He enjoyed jokes, preferred balanced sentences, liked to compose *jiju* poems (a literary form where verses of different famous poems are extracted to make a new poem), was a gambler who bet on Chinese chess, on poetry, on couplets, welcomed challenges, and rarely admitted defeat. There was a story about him betting on poetry with Su Dongpo. Allegedly, Wang Anshi once wrote a poem:

The autumn wind blew through the garden last night,
and the yellow chrysanthemum petals fell all over the ground.

Su Dongpo raised an objection: "Autumn flowers do not fall like spring flowers; I implore the poet to think it through."

Wang Anshi quoted *Sorrow after Departure* to refute:

Dew from magnolia leaves I drank at dawn,
at eve for food were aster petals borne.

This was a widely circulating saying from Song Dynasty notes on poets and poetry such as *Cang Hai Shi Hua* (shi hua: notes on poets and poetry) by Wu Ke and *Gao Zhai Shi Hua* by Zeng Xing. It was expanded and became the story of *Wang Anshi Making It Difficult for Su Dongpo Thrice in Ordinary Words to Warn the World*. When he was in Banshan, his poems remained feisty. In the past, he seemed to love writing articles that reverse a verdict and creating new ideas, and now, he fancied singing a different tune, too. He once wrote a poem called *Zijin Mountain Quatrain*:

The mountain stream runs quietly around the bamboo forest.
The soft flowers and grass swayed in the spring breeze
on the west side of the bamboo forest.
I sat under the thatched roof,
appreciating the splendor of spring all day long;
The sun was setting in the west, and with no birds chirping,
the mountain became extremely quiet.

Wang Ji, a Southern Dynasty poet, wrote in *Visiting Ruoye Creek*:

With the screaming cicadas, the forest becomes quieter,
with the birds chirping, the mountain, too.

Wang Anshi deliberately sang an opposite tune to it. Allegedly, Wang Anshi also quoted from two poems from the Southern Dynasties:

The petals still fall when the wind does not blow (by Xie Zhen),
and the mountain gets quieter when the birds sing (by Wang Ji).

In his eyes, "the mountain gets quieter when the birds sing" was undoubtedly a witticism. From the bottom of his heart, he admired it. However, his character and poetic style prevented him from following his predecessors' rules and steps.

In *Wang Anshi Making It Difficult for Su Dongpo Thrice*, he wrote that Su Dongpo was demoted to Huangzhou because of Wang Anshi, which was the novelist's opinion. In July of the seventh year (1084) of the Yuanfeng Period, Su Dongpo returned north of Huangzhou, passing through Jinling, and stayed there for three months. Accompanied by Wang Shengzhi, the prefect of Jiangning, he made a memorable trip to Banshan Garden to visit Wang Anshi and Zijin Mountain. Wang and Su both studied from Ouyang Xiu.

During the Xining reign, they used to be capital officials, but they communicated little with each other. This time, the two masters of literature finally had the opportunity to exchange ideas. They stayed together for over a month. They talked, traveled, chanted, and sang, deepening their understanding of one another. Time passed as if two pieces of sky, right after the baptism of a storm, became extraordinarily clear and calm. In an instant, the two great minds reconciled and understood each other. Su Dongpo admired Wang Anshi deeply. Reading *The Fragrance of Cassia Twig: Jinling Nostalgia*, he sighed: "He is as smart as a wild fox." After leaving Jiangning, Su Dongpo reached Yizheng and sent a travel poem about Jiang Mountain. After reading it, Wang Anshi was amazed and praised the following verse:

The many peaks block the sun,
the long river connects the sky.

He sighed: "I have never in my life written any poem as good." His admiration was sincere. After he left, Su Dongpo wrote twice. In the letters, he mentioned the joy of traveling together and the sadness of parting and sincerely confessed his disappointment and hope: at first, he wanted to live in Jinling so that it would be convenient for him to hang out with Wang Anshi, trekking in the beautiful scenery of eastern suburbs. Later, he hoped to purchase a house in Yizheng. Once the wish came true, as Yizheng and Jinling were not far apart, it would be easy to travel between the two places by boat.

It was Wang Anshi who first suggested spending the last years of their lives in Zijin Mountain. Both the *Four Songs to Wang Anshi* by Su Dongpo and one of the *North Mountain* poems by Wang Anshi mention this:

Riding a donkey into the wilderness,
I should have come earlier to visit the ill.
Suggested imploring the emperor for a piece of land,
I should have done that ten years ago.

However, the turbulent political situation often forces people to make choices they do not want. It was not easy for Su Dongpo, who was still in a political vortex, to get out. As a result, the reunion of two literary stars fell through. It was a memorable reunion in the history of literature, which blew some fresh air into Jinling in the warmth of July.

With *Riding a donkey into the wilderness*, the poet Su Dongpo was sharp, and his memory was reliable: riding a donkey was indeed the standard image of Wang Anshi in his late years. At first, Wang Anshi occasionally traveled on horseback, and Emperor Shenzong of the Song Dynasty bestowed the horse. After the severe illness of the seventh year (AD 1084) of the Yuanfeng Period (1078–1085), the old poet's vitality was severely reduced. Next, when the horse died, he changed to riding a donkey. And he had a soft spot for this donkey. He once wrote a poem for it.

As strong as tigers and dragons
and no less eloquent than the immortals.

From Banshan Garden to the city or Dinglin Temple outside the city, he relied on it to travel. Initially, in the eyes of people of the Tang and Song Dynasties, donkeys had long been a special mount for poets. Jia Dao recited poetry on a donkey, Zheng Qi believed that poetry was written on the back of the donkey, and Du Fu "has ridden a donkey for thirteen years, touring the capital." Lu You rode a donkey through Jianmen in the drizzle, feeling like a poet.

When painting Li Bai and Du Fu, painters could not help adding a donkey to the painting, which was almost the cherry on top. Given Wang Anshi's identity and age, riding on a sedan chair was naturally more suitable and comfortable, but he preferred a donkey. It was not for show, but he explained: "Since ancient times, terrible as some were, none dared to use people to replace livestock for such labor." It turned out that he had a benevolent heart for the people. During the Yuanfeng Period, there was a painting called *Duke Jing (Wang Anshi) Riding a Donkey* by the famous painter Li Gonglin. Huang Tingjian saw it and inscribed it. What did a poet on the back of a donkey look like? It is said to be wearing a hat and a strap. In the fifth year (1106) of the Chongning Period, when Fuzhou Prefecture in Jiangxi built the Wang Anshi Ancestral Hall, a portrait was painted and passed down from generation to generation. In the painting, Wang Anshi wears a hat, and the strap is well tied, like a typical Chinese old farmer, genuinely unattractive. Judging from the image, this might be a copy of Li Gonglin's painting.

Imagine that over 900 years ago, on the road from Banshan Garden to Zijin Mountain, an old man in plain clothes on the back of a donkey. That was Wang Anshi. Through the description of notes on poetry and poets in the Song Dynasty, scenes at that time emerge before our eyes: Wang Anshi rides a donkey to go out, one man leading the donkey, and sometimes one more attendant. Once, Wang Dingguo inquired about his entourage curiously; where was Wang heading? One attendant replied when the man leading the donkey was in front, it was up to him; when the man leading the donkey was behind, it was up to the donkey. Sometimes, when the poet wanted to stop for a while, the animal was halted, or he would sit on a rock under the pines to rest or stroll to a village farmhouse, or the nearby temple. Every time he went out, he had to bring a bag of books, sometimes reading them on the donkey, sometimes during breaks. He always brought a pack of food, too. If there was leftover, he gave it to the donkey leader; if the donkey leader couldn't finish it either, it was rewarded to the animal. Sometimes, he ate the food sent by the villagers. In short, he was like a cloud, free to move about.

Before the seventh year (1084) of the Yuanfeng Period, Wang Anshi was most interested in traveling. His footsteps covered the city, and he composed poems wherever he went. His lyrics are seen in the cemetery of Sunquan, Jiuri Terrace of Southern Dynasties, Baixia Pavilion of the East Gate, Changgan, Taicheng, Qixia Temple, etc. Sometimes, when he saw poems by his old friends inscribed on the wall, he couldn't help writing one, too. Sometimes, he also took a canoe along the Qing Creek, around the tidal channels, entered the Qinhuai River, and reached the Terrace of Raining Flowers in the south of the city, or the Qingliang Mountain and the Appreciation Pavilion in the west of the city. The mountains, rivers, small bridges, flowing streams, green willows, and spring plums made him linger and forget to go home.

"Longguang Temple under Fuzhou Mountain, Wulong Hall by Xuanwu Lake" used to evoke his nostalgia as well. Wang Anshi was a person with a great sense of history, but his nostalgic poems in his later years were not as good as his landscape poems. He wrote in his *Jinling Nostalgia* poems:

Ancestors built the regime from scratch,
most descendants surrendered hundreds of cities instead.
Under the lonely mountain is buried the qi of an emperor,
in the monk's windows floats the soughing smoke.
A Yellow flag has been waving for three hundred years,
purple clouds ended up with nothing but a pair of swords.

Certainly, these ideas make sense, but they come straightforward, thus not as good as those poems on landscape tours, they are vivid and interesting, which can also help us reconstruct Nanjing's cultural relics in our imagination.

The place Wang Anshi frequented the most was Zijin Mountain outside the city. He especially adored this mountain, and it was all he thought about. In one of his four poems titled *Visiting Zijin Mountain* he wrote:

Looking at the mountain all day long but never tired of it,
purchase land in the mountain for the last days.
The flowers wither, but the mountain remains still,
the creeks run busy, but the mountain remains free.

It was the mountain that he kept talking about. He wrote poems whenever he visited the mountain alone or with friends. In *Accidental Poem at Jinling Junzhai* he wrote:

Move the bed to face the autumn wind alone,
lying and watching the spiders weave their webs.

In front of the busy spiders, he had a taste of the leisurely retirement in the autumn wind. Wang Anshi believed that the white clouds in Zijin

Mountain stood in opposition to everything in the city. They represented the quietness of the mountains and forests, seclusion and purity, and another value orientation. In his writings, Zijin Mountain seems to be the Shangri-la of Tao Yuanming. The grass was greener there, the mountain flowers bloomed, and the water lucid. The sound of roosters and dogs was often heard from the sparse houses, which made the surroundings appear more peaceful. He described such a scene in *Fifteen Extempore Poems*, and his twilight years were immersed in such a scene.

Banshan Garden sat in the middle between the forest and the city, both inside and outside the mountains. The wonderful thing was the perfect distance. "Ban" (half) was a word carefully chosen by Wang Anshi himself and also a symbol of his mentality in his later years. He seemed to like it very much. In one of the *Two Gift Poems To Duan Yuezhi*, he wrote:

Half in the mountain and half in the city,
  dust in your house and clouds in mine.
Never stain mine with dust,
  I have the clouds for you.

Yuezhi was the style name of his friend Duan Feng, whose address was on top of Qing Creek River in the northeast of Jinling, not far from the former residence of Jiang Zong. It was a lively place, with dust and noise, and Wang Anshi deliberately avoided it. However, a man who had fought in political storms all his life might fail to be free from the city dust when he grows old, although he was fonder of the white clouds above Zijin Mountain. "Cut half of my green in Zijin Mountain," he only wanted half, humble and compromising. Between the city of the past and the forest of today, there was the freedom to both advance and retreat.

One midsummer day, Wang Anshi rode a donkey from Banshan Garden and came across Li Maozhi, a Criminal Judge who came to visit him. He got off the donkey, sat on the side of the road with Li Maozhi, and chatted casually. Li Maozhi ordered his subordinates to shade the sun via an umbrella, which was not wide enough, and the sunlight hit Wang Anshi. Li Maozhi quickly instructed his aides to move the umbrella closer to the poet. Wang Anshi declined, "No need. If I become a cow in the next life, I will have to plow the fields in the sun." In his later years, he enjoyed hanging out with monks, and the speech on reincarnation was from Buddhism. However, it shows how free, easygoing, and serene minded he was.

In the Zijin Mountain area, Wang Anshi visited Bagongdeshui, Fayun Temple, and Dinglin Temple the most. The Dinglin Temple was built in the Southern Dynasty. Surrounded by new pines and old cypresses, it was quiet. In front of its gate, the monks built a new flat road so tourists could easily visit it. Wang Anshi had a private room in the temple called Zhaowen House. He usually read there and sometimes stayed overnight there in Dinglin Temple. During this period, most of his contacts were people with poetic minds, including many eminent monks.

Among them was Zen Master Zanyuan, a good friend of Wang Anshi in his early years. When he lived in Dinglin Temple in his later years, he sought peace from Zanyuan whenever he felt irritable. The two sat silently facing each other, a similar image to what poet Wang Wei described, "Zen pacifies the most vicious dragon."

"I intend to stay focused when I am old, but I am easily distracted when people come." He also said, "I still dream about the ups and downs in this world because I know that I have not forgotten all my old habits." It seems that there was restlessness behind the tranquility. It confirms this point that he used to seek peace in the temples.

Once, Wang Anshi visited Banshan Temple with his old friend Yu Xiulao. It must have been after he fell severely ill in the seventh year of the Yuanfeng Period. This disease seriously harmed his vitality. Emperor Shenzong sent an imperial physician to treat him. After he recovered, he donated his own house in Banshan Garden to be a temple, and the emperor bestowed upon it the name Baoning Zen Temple, also known as Banshan Temple. At noon, while Wang Anshi took a nap in the facility, Xiulao secretly rode his donkey to visit Zen Master Baojue at Fayun Temple. When Wang Anshi found out, he punished his friend by asking him to compose the poem *Voice of Pines*. Unfortunately, such fun did not last. After a couple of years, Wang Anshi died and was buried in Baoning Temple near Banshan Garden.

The singing oriole woke me up from a noon nap,
leaving me to wonder whether I am still in Banshan Garden.

In this way, he stayed in Nanjing forever. Let me take it literally: Banshan and Baoning are two words that can at least sum up his later life.

For political reasons, he was once cursed, and also, for political reasons, he was once forgotten. His former residence was closed for a long time. When it opened, only a few people visited it. Back then, when Wang Anshi saw a clump of chrysanthemums beside Chengdong Temple, he once wrote,

I cannot bear to be the only one awake,
thus, keen to take one flower home.

Today, how many people share the same taste and elegance as Wang Anshi? One evening when the autumn wind blew, I stood alone in front of the old site of Banshan Garden and couldn't help feeling gloomy: Wang Anshi gave the city a lot, but the city returned him too little.

One leaf's falling tells the coming of autumn. Perhaps, he was fundamentally a person who never asked for anything in return.

Chapter 17

Love in Jinling

Nanjing is the favorite of literature. From ancient times, the literati have been writing about it, and famous verses about this city in poems and songs of the past dynasties are still remembered by countless people today. In operas and novels, there are also plenty of stories that take place in Nanjing and that are themed around Nanjing. As a realistic background in many literary works, Nanjing is important; as an imaginary landscape, Nanjing is beautiful. Coincidentally, the two greatest novels of the Qing Dynasty, *The Unofficial History of the Scholars* (儒林外史 *Rúlín Wàishǐ*) and *Dream of the Red Chamber*, (红楼梦 *Hónglóumèng*) are both based on Jinling. Whether explicit or implicit, the novels are an added cultural background and a classical humanistic atmosphere. In the narrative of novelists, in the words of characters in the novels, in the expression of the mountains and rivers and customs, the city also highlights its own image, including fictional illusions, a charming imagination, a conceptual imprint, and a realistic texture. In this place, the colors and shadows of an era condense and emerge. The excellent works of the previous generations are a window for future generations to look back at the past. And what do we see from it?

In the words of Cao Xueqin (author of *Dream of the Red Chamber*), Nanjing seems a deep and distant memory. The writer spent his youth in Nanjing, and then he drifted farther and farther. As time rolled forward, his childhood impression of this city became hazier and hazier and more and more beautiful. The rich colors in his memory have settled, dispersed, and painted the *Twelve Hairpins of Jinling*. Fascinating memories tinkle like a jade pendant. With the unique antique scent of Jinling, they are blurring and melancholy. All of these are sets, as if in the dark, in the background, thus so vaguely hazy that they inspire people's wildest imaginations. In contrast, Nanjing in *The Unofficial History of the Scholars* is more realistic. It is given a clearer image, more complete, and more down-to-earth. This is the necessity of the novel's aesthetics, as well as the crystallization of the author's personal life experiences.

Wu Jingzi held contradictory attitudes towards Nanjing. His book *The Unofficial History of the Scholars* mentions Nanjing in Chapter 24. From there, the city became the center stage of the novel's characters. The second half of this book basically revolves around this center. Sometimes, the story's clues seem to drift away, but eventually, it returns to this center. It is the city of Nanjing that holds the structure of this book together.

Purportedly, there was an *anchasi* (ancient official title, equivalent to the chief justice of today) surnamed Cui, who died of illness right after being promoted to serve at the capital. He had a pupil who was an actor called Bao Wenqing, a native of Nanjing. "With nobody to lean on in the capital, he had to pack and return to Nanjing." When writing this story, Wu Jingzi gave a detailed account of Nanjing:

> Nanjing is the capital that the Emperor Taizu established. With thirteen inner city gates and eighteen outer city gates, it stretches forty *li* and has a circumference of 120 *li*. The city has dozens of streets and hundreds of alleys, all of which are crowded with people and buildings. There is a river, the Qinhuai River, in the city that extends ten *li* from the east to the west. When the water is full, boats are sailing, and are busy day and night. Inside and outside the city, palaces and towers stand tall everywhere. In the Six Dynasties, there were 480 temples; now, there are more than 4,800. In the streets and alleys are 600 or 700 restaurants, large and small, and over 1,000 tea houses.
>
> However remote an alley is, there is always a tea shop where lanterns hang. Decorated with seasonal flowers, tea is boiled in the finest rainwater. The tea houses are full of tea drinkers. In the evening, the thousands of lanterns on the restaurants on both sides of each street are lit so bright that citizens need no extra light to see the way. When moonlight is on the river, the darker the night, the louder the singing

heard from the boats, desolate, euphemistic, and touching. The girls living in the river houses on both banks, in light gauze garments and with jasmine flowers on their heads, roll up the curtain, lean on the railing, and listen quietly. So, when the drum on the boat sounds, the curtains on both banks are lifted, and the fragrant mist in their rooms spreads out. Together with the moonlight, they took a heavenly picture of the river. There are exclusive brothels of prostitutes for government officials, with new make-up and attire, entertaining their customers from all over the country. What a splendid scene! (see Chapter 24)

Flowers bloomed, and people partied every night, so bustling and lively that it seemed surreal. There is a detailed description in both the beginning and middle of Chapter 41. The first paragraph depicts the dazzling scenery of the Qinhuai River in the latter half of April, where the boats and lanterns waltzed on the surface. The middle paragraph writes a different scene of the Qinhuai River in the early autumn, the grand gathering of worshiping Ksitigarbha Bodhisattva on Qingliang Mountain. The most succinct words outline a vivid picture of Nanjing's urban life.

People's usual first impression of Nanjing is that it is enormous and prosperous. Just as people like to call Shanghai "the Big Shanghai" in modern times, people used to call Nanjing "*dabang*" at that time, which in today's words, translates as "the Big Nanjing." In the eyes of the villagers and newcomers, Nanjing was an absolute metropolis. In the novel *The Unofficial History of the Scholars*, Zhuge Tianshen of Xuyi, Lou Taiye of Tianchang, and Shen Qiongzhi of Changzhou all confirmed this idea. People who were used to life there, even the commoners, were sophisticated. Needless to mention, the bigger aspects, even in the smaller aspects, such as behavior and daily diet, they seemed to have seen the world. In Chapter 41, the actor Bao Wenqing and Ni Laodie, who repairs musical instruments, walk into a random restaurant.

The waiter introduced a dozen meat dishes to them while the two listened calmly. In Chapter 28, Ji Tianyi randomly ordered four dishes. Zhuge Tianshen, a hick who had just come from Xuyi County, didn't know half of them. He mistook sausages as bacon and thought jellyfish would taste "crispy." This is probably a kind of cultural shock. With different knowledge, one naturally demonstrates a different demeanor and style. Therefore, it was common for the yamen runners in the city to bully the villagers by flaunting their powerful connections. In Chapter 41, it is written that Shen Qiongzhi, who escaped from a Yangzhou salt merchant, had seen the world after all. The two Jiangning County policemen who came to arrest her were snarling. She exposed their fake faces mercilessly: "You could only fool a villager who has seen nothing."

In a metropolis like this, there are all sorts of people, high-ranking officials, free-minded heroes, well-learned scholars, romantic poets, famous prostitutes, actors, etc. It is a mixed lot, lively and bustling. In the market, there are *guqin* (Chinese zither) repairers, umbrella repairers, bamboo fan makers, sellers of ancient books, calligraphy and painting vendors, wood and stone sculptors, etc. Guo Tiebi used to engrave books in Wuhu but later moved to Nanjing; Ni Laodie, who lives in Sanpailou, is a repairer of musical instruments. These characters have strong skills and a humble background, but they are simple, gentle, and kind, and they find happiness in a poor life. Their existence makes the city in the novel warm and enables the readers to feel the city's friendliness.

In real life, Wu Jingzi was familiar with such people. According to *Bo Shan Zhi*, Volume Four by Gu Yun, during his years in Nanjing, Wu Jingzi once "grew vegetables at home, and worked with the servants" and experienced the simplicity and roughness of urban life and the fun of "servant's work." The history and culture of Nanjing are spread among the ordinary alleys and streets, among the common citizens, and inevitably among some literati and celebrities. In Chapter 29, on the top of the Terrace of Raining Flowers, Du Shenqing and others sat until the sun started to set and saw two people carrying two empty dung buckets taking a break. One patted the other on the shoulder and said: "Brother, we are sold out today. Let's drink at Yongning Spring and return to Terrace of Raining Flower to see the sunset."

Du Shenqing laughed: "It's so true that even the working class retains the lifestyle of the Six Dynasties." This is a very famous sign that the city remembers to this day and that people who live in this city are happy to quote.

In this sign, the most important is "the lifestyle of the Six Dynasties." The history and culture of the Six Dynasties originally belonged to the whole nation, at least the entire South. In fact, this history is particularly attached to the city of Nanjing. In other words, Nanjing stubbornly monopolizes this part of the cultural heritage. The Six Dynasties are gone, but the city stands still. At the distant historical horizon, the Six Dynasties and Nanjing are indistinguishable in time and space. They are seen as one. In legends and imaginations, the city is deeply associated with the Six Dynasties, and there are more imprints of the Six Dynasties in this city, and then they become a tradition of the city. Classical glitter and charming luster, light and unrestrained, romantic and frail, almost all of these in Nanjing come from the Six Dynasties. This made Wu Jingzi hold a mixed love-hate attitude toward Nanjing. He loved its romance and passion but hated its weakness and depravity.

In Chapter 29, Du Shenqing concludes: "Had this dynasty not pulled itself together during the Yongle Period, under the weak reign of Emperor Jianwen, it would have ended the same as the Qi and Liang Dynasties." Qi and Liang are beautiful scars on the face of Nanjing. It is a pride as well as a sore point, just like the frown of Xi Shi. In fact, what Du Shenqing points out is exactly what Wu Jingzi believed deep down. And Wu Jingzi, in reality might have made a harsher accusation. He was a heroic man with a dashing brilliance. In his eyes, Du Shenqing, although elegant, "is still girlish." This is what he wrote in Chapter 30. He prefers heroic characters and cities, but at last he chose beautiful and affectionate Nanjing, which is contradictory.

Wu Jingzi chose this because of his preference for the city's cultural traditions. Since ancient times, many literati fell for this city. They knew their bias, but they didn't abstain from it. Zhao Yi concluded that Yuan Mei "loved to live in Jinling for the Six Dynasties," and Lin Zexu's *Inscription on the Painting of Yang Xueqiao (Qingchen) Riding a Horse in Jinling* also writes: "The officials love the south of the Yangtze for the Six Dynasties." In their eyes, the Six Dynasties are undoubtedly the shining point of Nanjing. Interestingly, local and foreign people seem to have forgotten that there was Southern Tang Dynasty after the Six Dynasties, possibly because they believe that the cultural style and historical meaning of the two are exactly the same.

The Six Dynasties outshone the Southern Tang Dynasty and replaced it and the history of the entire city and even the entire history of China. Yu Qiuyu wrote about Nanjing in *Tales of Five Cities*: "For the Chinese man of letters who has the same passion for landscape and history, one of the best final destinations is Nanjing. Except that the summer is too hot, and the local dialect does not sound pleasant, I never hide my love for Nanjing." He actually translated the ancient Chinese words of Zhao Yi and Lin Zexu into a modern sentence. The difference is that his praise is reserved. After all, this is a statement from an outsider. People like Wu Jingzi, who has lived there long enough, I am afraid that they have nothing to complain about.

In the eyes of people like Wu Jingzi, Nanjing is a city that dislikes grand publicity. Her prosperous face still shows the restraint of the past without the vulgarity of the nouveau riche. This city still keeps the lifestyle of the Six Dynasties and therefore holds historical connotation, cultural heritage, and distinctive style. Compared with other cities, Nanjing's quaint and cultural ambiance is self-evident.

For example, Yangzhou. In the eyes of poor literary celebrities like Xin Dongzhi and Jin Yuliu, Yangzhou is a city full of salt vendors, rich and abominable. The debtors sitting in the sedan chairs, the ass-kissers carrying and following the sedan chairs, the liars guarding their gate, and the residents in the fancy mansions are all snobs. People in this cynical place always need to understand how to respect literati and poets. In Yangzhou, the scholar Ji Weixiao had to swallow his pride and marry and live with his bride's family, surnamed You, next door to the salt merchants. Being so poor and wretched certainly makes them so indignant that they cannot help teasing and cursing. They make up their minds to move to Nanjing one day in the future. In their eyes, Nanjing is where there are many literati, many famous officials, and a strong cultural atmosphere. It holds a cultural center status that no surrounding cities can compare.

Therefore, in Chapter 28, Mr. Mu'an (Zong Ji), who claimed to have been in the capital and studied with Mr. Xie Maoqin, finds Ji Weixiao and volunteered to inscribe her self-portrait. He promised to take it to Nanjing so literary scholars could inscribe it. It seems a necessary step to becoming famous. In Chapter 40, after Shen Qiongzhi escapes from the salt merchant, her first idea is to sell poetry in Nanjing for a living: "Nanjing is a wonderful place. There are so many celebrities there. I can write, so why not make a living there? I may have some luck." See how charming Nanjing's literary circle is and how appealing Nanjing's celebrities are?

For example, Wuhe. Chapter 47 revolves around this county in northern Anhui. In the eyes of Yu Huaxuan, it is a place of vulgarity. There is no poetry nor etiquette at all, and locals are unkind, "In terms of local customs, he laughs when a local is described as virtuous; when the past noble families are mentioned, he snorts; when a common villager is regarded good at poetry, his eyebrows oppose furiously."

Yu Huaxuan was born into a rich family and was well-read and proficient in poetry and essays. He could have ridden on the crest of success, but he was disappointed. In the end, he can only sigh together with the Yu family brothers, lamenting that it is not Nanjing after all, "In our county, a sense of propriety, justice, honesty, and honor is dead. Following the example of the imperial court, all local officials are corrupt. In Nanjing, this would never happen." Nanjing houses a great many talents, and has a sophisticated cultural taste, which is admired and envied by talents and scholars from the small county in northern Anhui.

For example, Tianchang. Here, Du Shaoqing was respected because he was wealthy. He was charitable and generous, but he soon ran out of the money from his ancestral family, and local gossip spread wild, making it difficult for him to stay there. In the end, Lou Taiye advised him to move to Nanjing because "Nanjing is a metropolis. Someone as talented as you might find your luck and make a difference." Only a place as grand as Nanjing can enable him to unleash his talents and lofty sentiments. As expected, after Du Shaoqing arrived in Nanjing, he rented a riverside house near the Lishe Bridge and gradually made some friends with shared hobbies. In the second half of March, the guests were invited to dinner, and when the guests were all in place, he opened the gate facing the river. "Guests are scattered, appreciating the running water, or chatting while sipping fine tea, or reading, or sitting as they please," so free-minded. This kind of life is unimaginable in Tianchang, but in Nanjing, especially on the banks of the Qinhuai River, it is so common that everybody behaves with grace and calm, giving out a vibe of pursuing an artistic lifestyle of the Six Dynasties.

Chapter 18

The Elegance of the Literary Celebrities

In *The Unofficial History of the Scholars* era, there were scores of literary celebrities in Nanjing, many of whom were distinguished and admirable. Soon after Du Shaoqing arrived in Nanjing, he makes a shocking literary pursuit. In Chapter 33 of the book, he accompanies his wife to visit Qingliang Mountain. In the spring splendor, he drinks jovially and holds her hand while holding a wine glass in the other hand, laughing loudly. They stroll around for one *li* on the hillside of Qingliang Mountain. There are three or four women behind them giggling, and the people on both sides of the road are so dazzled that they do not dare to look up at them. In the lushness of Qingliang Mountain and the mellow spring light, Du Shaoqing is extraordinary and glowing. He releases the romance of Nanjing's landscape and history.

It is well-known that the prototype of Du Shaoqing in *The Unofficial History of the Scholars* is the author Wu Jingzi himself. The happy laughter on the hillside of Qingliang Mountain is the author's, and the social standing of the character's family is the author's as well. Wu Jingzi was discriminated against and ostracized by his clan because he treated people equally, befriended people extensively, and donated money generously, so he had to move to Nanjing. I assume that had he not moved, he probably couldn't have written *The Unofficial History of the Scholars*. Freed from the shackles of old rules and the ancient environment and breathing the romantic air of Nanjing, Wu Jingzi was relieved and relaxed, and nothing could persuade him to leave the city.

In Chapter 34, Du Shaoqing learns that the letter that offered him an official post has arrived, and he immediately pretends to be sick to dodge the job about to be his. He explains to his wife: "I could not be happier than us together in Nanjing. Every spring and autumn, we will go out to see the most beautiful flowers and taste the finest wine. Why want me in the capital? Even if you come with me, it is cold there. The chilly wind will break your weak health. It is better that we stay put." Nanjing is not comparable to Beijing as a southern metropolis and then-southern capital, so they can always be free and enjoy life there. It is warmer, and there are fewer rules to follow. Du Shaoqing sees the city as fun, delightful, and unrestrained. Here, he can take his wife to a wineshop for a sip, although some fail to understand this elegance of his, he cannot care less. He can calmly hang out with Shen Qiongzhi, unlike ordinary people who either regard Shen as a snobbish prostitute or suspect that she steals. This is him being distinguished and admirable as a literary celebrity.

Those who get along with Du Shaoqing are all these kinds of romantic literary celebrities. One of them is Zhuang Shangzhi, who applies for a job as an official in the capital Beijing, where he has some achievements, but in the end, he "implores to return to his hometown." The emperor bestows him Xuanwu Lake so that he has a place to write. After returning to Nanjing, he moves to Xuanwu Lake overnight to enjoy his gift. Henceforth, he lives an almost hermitic life in the middle land of the lake, often refusing to receive guests. He just leans on the railing with his wife to appreciate the calm lake. They read together as if they are walking on air. Yu Boshi is another who shares the lifestyle of Du Shaoqing. Du Shaoqing calls him "indifferent to fame and wealth."

After Yu passes the *jinshi* exam, he could have stayed in the capital and become a *hanlin* (member of the imperial college), but he seeks no fame. He wants nothing but to be an idle official of the imperial college in Nanjing so that he can live an everyday life with his family by his side. After Emperor Chengzu of the Ming Dynasty moved the capital to Beijing, Nanjing became the *liudu* (the old capital), and officials of various ministries in the *liudu* were commonly known as *nancao*, which had always been a sinecure that allowed the employee to work while enjoying life. And Nanjing is the perfect place for this position. With these people around, Du Shaoqing, or to be precise, Wu Jingzi, would not feel lonely.

These literary celebrities' first literary pursuit in Nanjing is to worship the *taibo*. Chi Hengshan first advocated it, and Du Shaoqing seconded it without hesitation. It is something that two literary celebrities supported the ritual together. The ritual passage is detailed in Chapter 37, and readers must take it seriously. In reality, Wu Jingzi once gathered like-minded friends to build a pantheon at the foot of Yuhua Mountain. To raise funds, he did not hesitate to sell the old house in his hometown. The novel's pantheon became the Taibo Temple, but the cultural significance remains the same. Taibo was the first to cultivate the people south of the Yangtze and the foremost sage in Nanjing. This plot of setting up a temple mainly reflects the author's personal wish to revise rites and music and restore ancient learning.

The ceremony was huge. There were a total of 76 attendants, including Yu Boshi, who made the first libation, Zhuang Zhengjun who made the second libation, Ma Er who made the last libation, and Chi Hengshan and Du Shaoqing who guided the ritual, plus those who shouldered various responsibilities, such as music and dance. The people participating in the sacrifice dressed like and thought about the ancients, the utensils used were also antiques, and the ritual music was even older. The old onlookers were amazed, saying that they had never seen such a thing over their seventy to eighty years living in Nanjing. Many years later, people in the south of Yangtze still talk about this ritual with great relish, and those who have experienced it are proud of this experience, and those who have missed it naturally regret missing it.

When Taibo worshipping takes place, it is the heyday of Nanjing culture. In this then-capital city, so many elegant literary scholars gathered with such noble aspirations that they could not care less about social status or wealth. With Dr. Yu, Zhuang Zhengjun, Du Shaoqing, and Chi Hengshan as the center, they often got together, forming a group to help each other, exchange ideas, and share secrets. There are some genuinely moving details. In the novel, there is one of the most nostalgic days. In reality, it reflects the most pleasant and unforgettable period of Wu Jingzi's life in Nanjing. It's a pity that the good times don't last long. In Chapter 48, Wang Yuhui goes ashore from Shuiximen, settles down in Niugong'an, and begins to search for these literary celebrities, "Yu Boshi serves as an official in Zhejiang, Du Shaoqing goes to look for him, Zhuang Zhengjun returns to his hometown to repair the ancestral tomb, Chi Hengshan and Wu Zhengzi become officials in far-away places. I can't find anyone." The literary celebrities are scattered, and the famous city seems empty. "The play ends, and the audience disperses." A desolate atmosphere gradually shrouds the city.

Among all the scholars in the world, when Wu Jingzi arrived in Nanjing, he immediately searched for his own kind. He kept his eyes wide open, looking for the talented among the ordinary. This was the need for reality as well as the need for the art of fiction. Perhaps there are too many fake literary celebrities, fake poets, snobbish squires, and treacherous officials in the first 24 chapters. The circle of scholars is so corrupt that it is suffocating. The appearance of a rare talent, like a gust of fresh wind, enables a fresh breath. He first found Father Fengsi, a heroic man. He knew martial arts skills and was charitable and righteous. He does what the frail scholars find difficult to do, catching liars, competing in martial arts, and collecting debts. His prototype is Gan Fengchi, a legendary Nanjing martial artist in the early Qing Dynasty. He was proficient in inner- and outer-family boxing, earning him a reputation, thus his nickname Hero of the South of the Yangtze. Wu Jingzi named him Feng Mingqi in his book. Like the phoenix cried on the Qi Mountain, this name adds a mysterious vibe. The emergence of this rare talent adds a heroic vibe to the scholar's circle in the novel, which suffices to boost the morale south of Yangtze. The Four Men in the last chapter are also rare talents discovered by Wu Jingzi among the ordinary.

One of the Four Men is Ji Xianian, whose calligraphy skill was fantastic, homeless since childhood, and makes a living in a temple; another is Wang Tai, who excels at going and selling firework wrap; the third is Gai Kuan, who used to run a pawn shop, but later changes to operate a teahouse; the last is Jing Yuan, who runs a tailor's shop on Sanshan Street and plays the guqin beautifully. These four men have their own strengths and noble pursuits despite their common profession in society. *Old Tales of Yecheng* by Lu Qian writes that there was a guqin master called Wang Binlu in the late Qing Dynasty, who was a rare talent like Jing Yuan. He settled down in Nanjing. Dressed in Taoist attire, he burned incense and played the qin in Plum Nunnery daily. After the song was over, he left immediately. For several years, he reminded people of the ancient sages. After the sages and gentlemen had gone, these rare talents were the real literary celebrities in Nanjing, who retained the city's Six Dynasties atmosphere and kept its reputation for literary celebrities.

When there are real literary celebrities, there are fake ones; when there is real literary pursuit, there is vulgar pursuit. Fake literary celebrities pose as cultured people among men of letters. In fact, they cannot appear more vulgar. The literary stars at the Xiaoshan Yingdou Lake Poetry Gathering were all phoneys who could not be tackier. The fake knight-errant Zhang Tiejie, who used a pig head to pretend to be a human head, was a pure deceiver. The fact that this kind of thing did not happen in Nanjing does not mean that there are no vulgar people and things in the city. It was just when Wu Jingzi wrote the book, he was merciful.

It should be noted that at that time, the textile industry in Nanjing was developed, many silk merchants were coming and going, and the city was home to plenty of silk shops. Merchants in Nanjing sought profits, and so did prostitutes. They were snobbish and gold-digging, as expected. Among the prostitutes, Pin Niang from the Laibin Tower was a representative of snobbery, Mao'er Huzi was an example of the con artists in silk shops, and there were plenty of rascals like Long San in the market. When writing about the *gongyuan* (the venue to hold the imperial college exam) and brothels, it is inevitable to mention such public morals and mores. However, Wu Jingzi only picked out a few typical examples, without criticizing them hard. Maybe he wrote too much of this in other cities, or perhaps he didn't want to stain the image of Nanjing in his heart. Chapter 42 details the imperial examination that Tang You and Tang Shi take. These two young masters of the general military commander of Guizhou travel from Yangzhou to Nanjing to take the exam. "They have four servants tagging along. In broad daylight, a pair of lanterns are lit. One reads *Military Commanders*, and the other reads *Exam in Nanjing*. They go in for ostentation and extravagance instead of studying hard. Before the exam, they visit brothels in Yangzhou, and after the exam, they cannot wait to see some local plays. Apparently, they are fake literary celebrities. These two phoneys are foreign, passers-by, thus incomparable to celebrities who have been living in the city for a long time and have never been regarded as local literary celebrities.

Regarding the deeds of local literary celebrities, not to mention the grand ceremony of worshipping Taibo, the Mochou Lake Pavilion Conference differs significantly from the Yingdou Lake Poetry Gathering. Du Shenqing is no local either, but after all, he was there long enough, so he had the idea of turning vulgarity into elegance: together with other literary celebrities, referring to the practice of commentary, he could judge the famous actors in the different troupe who are both attractive and skilled. This caused a sensation and made Du Shenqing famous in the south of Yangtze. It takes place in Nanjing, the capital of the Six Dynasties, and has the background of Mochou Lake, where the beauty of the Six Dynasties is inhabited. Therefore, everything feels proper and elegant.

There is a price to be paid to enjoy a free and unconventional life. Whether it is the Jiajing era set in the novel or the prosperous years of Emperor Kangxi and Emperor Qianlong when Wu Jingzi lived, it is a challenging task to survive in the metropolis of Nanjing. The city can be so cruel, which Ji Weixiao profoundly understands. He is generous, giving Bao Tingxi enough money to return to his hometown in Nanjing. Ji Weixiao knows a fellow countryman, Ji Tianyi, who comes from a different clan despite their same surname. The two leave Anqing together to make a living in Nanjing. Ji Tianyi, a scholar, comes from little and is no catch in the employment market. Nanjing is, of course, "no easy place to survive in" for him. Therefore, Ji Weixiao instructs Bao Tingxi: "When you come to Nanjing, you must find and persuade my friend Ji Tianyi to return. In Nanjing, people can starve to death, and staying long is not a wise option." I shudder every time I read his comment.

"Chang'an is so expensive that it is a challenge to survive." This is what Gu Kuang said to Bai Juyi in the past. We might think he was making a fuss or half-joking. Bai Juyi also used his talent to prove him over-worried. But for Wu Jingzi, this comment in the novel is by no means alarmist. It is his wisdom after learning the lesson the hard way. After Wu Jingzi moved to Nanjing, like Du Shaoqing, he was fine at first, but soon his money ran out, and life became more and more challenging. As Cheng Jinfang wrote in *To Yan Dongyou*, "When the pockets are empty, the belly rumbles like thunder." "I heard that there are no more clothes to pawn, and no smoke rises from the stove, for there is no coal to cook." In such circumstances, selling books for the coal to make fire was inevitable. He was too broke to get charcoal on a cold night, so he "invited friends to walk around the city to keep his feet warm." Those who know nothing about the background of this story often praise him for such literary pursuits, but for those who know, it sounds bitter. Before, the author had tasted the gentle warmth of the city, but at that moment, he was suffering from the freezing wind.

The last chapter of *The Unofficial History of the Scholars* is a *ci* (a classical form of Chinese poetry), to the tune *Qin Yuan Chun*:

I remember that time, and I loved Qinhuai so much
that I left my hometown for it.
I sang at the top of my lungs in Meigenye several times;
I lingered at Xinghua Village several times.
The phoenix perches on the high Chinese parasol,
while the insects sing in the low bushes.
When I was young and ambitious,
everything was a competition for me.
But that is gone.
Why don't I take off my shoes
and step on the waves in the river?
What boredom!
How about I make some new friends to have a drink with?
One hundred years pass in a blink of an eye.
Why am I so depressed?
We can discuss everything, however significant it is.
When I write about the misty drizzle in the south of Yangtze
and the aging literary celebrities in the south of Anhui
it breaks my heart.
From now on, my heart is focused on nothing but Buddhist scriptures.

This *ci* is the confession of this literary celebrity. He has been to Meigenye, been to Xinhua Village, and therefore been to Nanjing. What's there to regret? In the end, Wu Jingzi died in Yangzhou and was buried in Nanjing. Some say that his tomb is at the foot of Qingliang Mountain, while others believe it is near Fengtai Gate, not far from the Qinhuai River, which confirms his honesty in the words, "I loved Qinhuai so much."

Chapter 19

Free and Content

Yuan Mei might have realized it very early: Nanjing was his paradise.

In 1737, Yuan Mei was 22 years old. The year before, he took the imperial college examination in the capital, failed, and was ashamed to return home. This year, Yuan Mei, poverty-stricken in the capital, came across a kind man from Jinling named Tian Gunong. Tian Gunong was concerned about the poet's well-being. He offered him food and wine, for which Yuan Mei was deeply grateful. This might be his first bit of luck in Nanjing. Five years later, the 27-year-old poet was dispatched as a *hanlin* (member of the imperial college) *shujishi* (an excellent scholar, a short post in the imperial college) to serve as the magistrate of Lishui in the southern suburbs of Nanjing. The following year, his position was changed to Jiangpu Magistrate in the northern suburbs of Nanjing, thus officially kicking off his short-lived career in the city.

Two years later, Yuan Mei, who had just turned 30, was transferred from Shuyang to Jiangning as its Magistrate. Thus he began to serve as an official in Baixia (another name for Nanjing). At this time, his Jinling benefactor Tian Gunong had long passed away, but another benefactor, Yin Jishan, was in power as the Governor of Liangjiang. Yin Jishan was Yuan Mei's examiner for the imperial college exam. He appreciated Yuan Mei's talent and was always kind to him. With the appreciation of such an immediate boss, Yuan Mei was in his element at work. However, at this time, even he himself did not expect that he would choose to live in Nanjing. After retiring from officialdom, he lived there until he died, becoming one of the most famous residents in Nanjing's urban history in the 18th century.

Before retiring from officialdom, Yuan Mei was a diligent county magistrate who cared about the people. In his leisure time, he was most relaxed, lingering in the mountains and rivers, appreciating the beauty of mist and clouds in the twilight. Nanjing is home to Six Dynasties and the ten-*li*-long Qinhuai River. To Yuan Mei, everything here seemed kind and natural. Two *li* to the west of Beimen Bridge stands the beautiful Xiaocang Mountain. This is one branch of Qingliang Mountain. The mountain is divided into two ridges, north and south, winding eastward, embracing a long and narrow valley in the middle dotted with ponds and fields. Those low-lying areas are the river courses of the past, which the locals call *ganheyan* (dry river course). Near the north peak of Xiaocang Mountain, weeds and flowers surround several houses and restaurants, and multiple sections of ruins stand in the setting sun.

This is the Sui Garden, which once thrived during Emperor Kangxi's reign. Sui Garden, whose real name was Cao Garden, belonged to Cao Fu, the uncle of Cao Xueqin (author of *Dream of the Red Chamber*), who once served as head of the Jiangning weaving department in Nanjing. After the Cao family's property was confiscated, the garden fell into the hands of the new head of the Jiangning weaving department, Sui Hede. Soon, Sui Hede's property was confiscated by Emperor Yongzheng. When Yuan Mei arrived there, the Sui Garden was deserted. The descendants of the Sui family had no intention of repairing it and were looking for an opportunity to sell it. It was priced at merely three hundred taels of silver, which was indeed a good bargain. Having heard the news, Yuan Mei was decisive. He bought it with his savings, renovated it, and changed the name of Sui (隋 suí, a surname) Garden to Sui (随 suí, casual) Garden. Later, it turned out that the 300 taels of silver were an extremely wise and absolutely worthwhile investment, both for Yuan Mei and Nanjing.

This happened in Yuan Mei's third year as the magistrate of Jiangning. The 32-year-old official was overjoyed to obtain this piece of land. For him, Sui Garden was a completely different living space from the yamen, which meant a lifestyle completely different from the officialdom. If he had to choose between officialdom and the garden, he would definitely give up his official position. He confessed in a poem he composed that year: "In the future, I will trade my position for this garden." It was a declaration of his desire and an announcement in advance of his life plan with the position of Jiangning County magistrate. In fact, buying the Sui Garden with official salaries was already an attempt at a trade-off, except it was not done through a monetary transaction. This young county magistrate's seemingly accidental purchase of land changed his life path as well as the fate of the abandoned garden. And the re-birth of this famous garden remade the cultural map of Nanjing.

After the garden became his possession, Yuan Mei started to repair it, which took great effort. This task ran through his life, and garden planning and renovation became an essential part of his life, daily concern, and long-term hobby. He planned the garden according to its topography. He built a tower at a high place so that he could overlook the Yangtze River and built a creek pavilion at a low place. A small bridge over the flowing stream was a scenic spot. Yuan Mei attended to everything in the pavilion, tower, winding corridors, rockeries, flowers, and trees. He planted plum blossoms extensively in the garden, up to 700 at most. On such a large scale, it became a scene in the garden and a plum blossom viewing spot for those with literary pursuits in Nanjing at that time. In the first three to five years of construction, the carpenter Wu Longtai contributed the most, building most of the pavilions and towers. After he died, Yuan Mei buried him on the west side of the garden to commemorate his contribution. His friends and disciples also contributed to the repair of the garden with ideas and gifts. A dying garden was given a new look in just a few years. As depicted in Yuan Mei's poems, the garden had twenty-four scenic spots. In the mountains were Cangshan Cloud Cottage, Nap House, Green Dawn Pavilion, Panzhizhong, and Little Qixia, and by the water were Double Lake and Echo Casket, Lucid Spring, Crane Bridge, Fragrance World, as well as Bamboo Treats with sloping bamboos, Willow Valley with graceful willows, Jade Hills with plum blossoms, Cypress Pavilion surrounded by a forest of cypress, etc. In front of such a poetic and picturesque garden, Yuan Mei couldn't be prouder and more content. He placed the cultural relics and antiques collected over the years around the garden and casually displayed them. It was not far from the city and relaxing without the urban hustle and bustle. Yuan Mei was enjoying the fun of living in his urban forest.

Yuan Mei was only 33 when he first tasted the pleasures of this leisurely life. In the second autumn since he purchased the garden, he resigned from the official position because his mother was old and ill and moved his family into the Sui Garden. They led such a leisurely life for more than three years. Four years later, he entered the capital again and took a new post as the magistrate of Shaanxi. He had no choice but to take this job at first.

Additionally, he didn't get along with the then-governor of Shaanxi and Gansu Provinces, Huang Tinggui, who was quite indifferent to him. As a result, he couldn't be more determined to resign. "There, the clouds idle away from their mountain recesses without any intent or purpose, and birds, tired of their wandering flights, will think of home." His father died of illness this autumn, and the poet finally had a proper reason to retire. He returned home, putting an end to this brief comeback. After that, the 37-year-old man lived in the mountains with his old mother, never to return to work again. He embraced another busy life in the leisurely mountain days. Cheng Zongluo, a poet in Tongcheng, sighed with great envy, "Need a crane to walk thousands of *li* away, but never had to work for fifty years." He was referring to this kind of busy but leisurely life.

"Being free tastes better than being rich and being smart doesn't guarantee happiness." This is a quote from Zhao Yi, a Qing Dynasty literary scholar. He could relate to the pursuit of Yuan Mei. Yuan Mei was truly fortunate. He lived during the prosperous years under the reign of Emperor Kangxi and Emperor Qianlong and in Nanjing, a rich and flourishing city in the south of the Yangtze River and the place he was most lucky. In his will, the poet recalled his life. When he compared himself with Su Dongpo, he felt fortunate. Undeniably, Su Dongpo was a literary giant, but he "profited nothing from his talent in writing." Instead, he was imprisoned frequently for it. Yuan Mei was the exact opposite. Back then, when he started his retirement in the Sui Garden, he had little savings left from his years of work as a magistrate after paying for the garden and daily expenses. Still, his reputation and literary talent quickly brought in a steady stream of income. He wrote travel notes, biographies, and inscriptions for people, making a fortune from dignitaries and wealthy salt merchants. This laid an essential economic foundation for him to retreat to the forest and enjoy a happy fifty-year retirement.

Yuan Mei was most fortunate in Nanjing, so fortunate that he could bring his talents to the extreme. In his thirties, he used Nanjing as his base and Sui Garden as the stage to perform his self-written life drama. As described in his biography written by his contemporary Sun Xingyan, Yuan Mei "was tall and strong, his teeth white as shells, and his voice melodious like a bell." The owner of the Sui Garden was a talented performer, which is consistent with his image. Before officially taking the stage, he had accumulated rich performance capital. The first was his experience as a government official, and the second was his growing literary fame. He made full use of his prestige and literary talent to invite friends over to his Sui Garden, where they chanted beautiful poems. Years later, a rendezvous venue with Sui Garden as the center quietly took shape, and the garden owner's reputation grew stronger and stronger. Whether it was local officials or dignitaries passing through Nanjing, they were willing to mingle with men of letters and pose as a lover of culture, rushing to present their poems at the poem exchange party, trying their best to squeeze into this circle.

Yuan Mei once counted in his later years that he had received over 1,900 poems from people. Younger poets were more eager to attend his gathering. Visiting him at the Sui Garden has almost become an important ceremony for entering the poetry circle. Also, Yuan Mei spared no effort to comment and praise, to open doors wide, and to support the younger talents. He had many disciples, including prestigious nobles and young men and women from all walks of life. In the eyes of the Taoist defenders at the time, this obviously violated feudal gender ethics. Even today, the poet would be deemed too "ideologically emancipated," and his behavior was definitely ahead of his time. His good friend Zhao Yi teased him that "he befriended the Three Councilors of State and the Nine Ministers, believed bravery warriors to be potential poets, lured the descendants of good families, and took women as his disciples." "Unrestrained as it was, he was violating the social rule." Yuan Mei would not take such jokes among friends seriously. However, at that time, a group of people represented by Zhang Xuecheng could not bear his behavior. They criticized him openly and harshly, calling him a sinner. At first, Yuan Mei fought back and defended himself, but after hearing it too much, he decided to let it be.

This slander caused little trouble for Yuan Mei in the end, thanks to his personal connections. He excelled at pulling strings for self-protection and developing new "connections." He paid great heed to keeping good relations with the successive viceroy of Jiangnan Province and Jiangxi Province in China's Qing Dynasty and local bureaucrats at all levels, from governors to magistrates. For every new viceroy, he composed poems of praise, or with his excellent parallel prose skills, he drafted important documents on their behalf and wrote biographies, travel notes, inscriptions, and other texts for them to consolidate their friendship. The most important figure among them was Yin Jishan. During the Qianlong Era, this mentor of Yuan Mei served as viceroy of Jiangnan Province and Jiangxi Province four times, and he took great care of his old disciple. Certainly, Yuan Mei drafted documents and wrote extensively for him.

With the support from this high-ranking mentor, Yuan Mei could afford to be "fearless." In general, Yuan Mei maintained a friendly relationship with the local government. The "expulsion" incident that happened when he was 54 was an exception. He was more scared than hurt, after all. When famous Qing calligrapher Liu Yong, whose ancestor was a prime minister, was appointed as the prefect of Jiangsu, he may have heard some rumors, and Yuan Mei did not take the initiative to visit him. He was so annoyed that he ordered the poet to be expelled from the garden. Yuan Mei stated in a poem to his younger brother Yuan Shu: "Having spent 20 years in Baixia (another name for Nanjing), I had no choice but to return to my hometown. Now that I have been expelled, I might as well go to West Lake, my new hometown." Of course, this was him whining when helpless and depressed. However, Yuan Mei later wrote a *Memorial on Thanking for Blessing Jiangnan* for Liu Yong, and the two reconciled. When Liu Yong was promoted and left Jiangsu, Yuan Mei composed a long poem of praises to see him off. The Sui Garden has always maintained its elegant reputation, and its owner's life improved daily.

In the urban legends of Nanjing, there is never a shortage of stories of exiled talents. As an ancient capital, it is natural that Nanjing was particularly attractive to outsiders. In the poem Arriving at Jinling Yuan Mei on his first trip to Nanjing, he sighed: "Being the capital is an easy path to fame." However, when he settled down in Sui Garden, Nanjing was no longer the capital, and there was nothing but old imperial memories. Amid these historical memories, Yuan Mei cared the most about the Six Dynasties. When he was only 15, he wrote this verse in the poem Spring Willows: "The old rain pours as if in the six dynasties" He had a special liking for that period. "The talented are demoted to Sanchu (Hunan, Hubei, Anhui, and Jiangsu Provinces), and the beautiful were born in the Six Dynasties." There were beautiful women and plenty of talented people in the Six Dynasties, so it is no wonder he fancied it the most. His articles are also in the style of the Six Dynasties. In *Biographies of the History of the Qing Dynasty: History of the Literary Circle* it is called "an epitome of the Six Dynasties lilt." His poems often quote the Six Dynasties facts, such as *A Letter to His Majesty, Bei Shan Yi Wen, An Idle Life, Mourning The Deceased, Biography of the Learned Persons*, and *A Suburban Life*. He borrowed to express his personal feelings.

He proudly compared himself to Xie An of Dongshan and Yuan An of the Southern Dynasties. He claimed that the Sui Garden was the place where Xie Mound was; therefore, he was roaming where Xie An and Wang Anshi once walked. Having resided in Sui Garden for years, Yuan Mei still had a psychological obstacle he could not overcome. That is Hangzhou, the city where Bai Juyi and Su Dongpo lived, where there is West Lake and Su Xiaoxiao, where his former residence and ancestral tombs were located. At age 54, with his mother's consent, he buried his father in Sui Garden, showing his determination to die there. "I made my West Lake in Jinling so that I pretend to see it from home." He comforted himself, "isn't there a lake that imitates the West Lake in my garden? Isn't Mochou Lake, where boats sail busily, better than the West Lake?" Su Shi once wrote, "I have no home. What better choice do I have than settling down here? Even in my hometown, there is no scenery as beautiful." That happened to be Yuan Mei's hometown, so it does seem wise to quote it as a response; otherwise, it would degrade Hangzhou. A better response is the words with profound historical connotation by Zhao Yi, a historian, and poet, "The Six Dynasties are the best time to live in Jinling" (Notes on Reading Sui Garden Poems Inscription).

Purportedly, when Yang Jian, Emperor Wen of the Sui Dynasty, was the prime minister of the Northern Zhou Dynasty, he first named the new dynasty "sui (随)." For fear that it would repeat the same mistakes of the Song, Qi, Liang, and Chen Dynasties in the south and Zhou and Qi Dynasties in the north and be easily defeated, "辶 (foot)" was removed and sui (隋) was chosen." Yuan Mei renaming the Sui (隋) Garden from Sui (随) Garden was just an opposite action. Chinese have always attached great importance to the form of Chinese characters, and names must be restored. This suí (随) with "辶 (chuò, foot)" seems to symbolize an unrestrained attitude towards the world and a relaxed attitude towards life. With feet, one can wander around, so Yuan Mei left officialdom and went into society, pursuing an idle life; with feet, one can run, so Yuan Mei had a casual style of writing; with feet, one can travel, so Yuan Mei left footprints all over the southeast of the country, building a fine reputation. His two sons were named Tong (tōng, 通) and Chi (chí, 迟), both with "辶 (foot)." Perhaps, it is not a coincidence. Or is it? Suí (隋) and suí (随) have formed an interesting contrast: a steady political pursuit to a casual life pursuit.

From age 34 to 55, in two decades, Yuan Mei wrote six pieces of *Diary of Sui Garden*, in which he made a detailed and authoritative explanation of the meaning of Sui in all aspects. Still, he could have explained the point mentioned above. It's too careless, isn't it?

Chapter 20

Obsessed with the Dream

This is a story about Li Xiangjun, narrated by Yang Chaoguan, owner of the Yinfeng Pavilion and a talented Wuxi playwright, and written by Yuan Mei, poet, owner of the Sui Garden, and a gifted Qiantang scholar. A beautiful woman and two talented men, almost two hundred years apart, made a wonderful literary tale in Nanjing. The two talented men even stirred up a storm for her, which is known as the Li Xiangjun and examination paper case.

In the 35th year (AD 1770) of the Qianlong Reign, Yang Chaoguan, a Wuxi native serving as the Prefect of Qiongzhou, Sichuan Province, came to the Sui Garden. Yang and Yuan had been old friends for decades, getting along well with one another. Around that time, Yang Chaoguan specially sent 300 taels of silver from Qiongzhou (the price Yuan Mei paid for the garden estate that year), asking the poet to purchase a house in Jinling on his behalf. He intended to spend his late life with Yuan Mei in Nanjing. This time, on a business trip to the east, the Prefect naturally visited his old friend in the Sui Garden. Having been apart for many years, they naturally had plenty of stories to tell when they finally met again. And Yang shared a personal experience.

Eighteen years earlier, in 1752, the 41-year-old Yang Chaoguan was the magistrate of Gushi County, Henan Province. That year in the Henan Township Exam, he served as the co-examiner. When all examination papers had been reviewed, and the results were to be announced, he flipped through some failed papers at the test site. He fell asleep, bending over the desk, probably because of exhaustion from days of work, and had a dream. He saw a 30-year-old woman with light makeup, wearing a black and red skirt, with a black scarf around her forehead. She was not tall, but beautiful, a typical type in the south of Yangtze. She walked to Yang Chaoguan's bed, lifted the bed curtain, and whispered, "There is a paper with osmanthus fragrance; I beg your help, please." As soon as she finished the sentence, the woman disappeared.

Yang Chaoguan woke up in surprise. He shared this dream with other examiners, and they jeered at him, arguing that it was too late for that examination paper when the results were about to be announced. He agreed with them but still paid extra attention to the examination papers. As expected, he noticed one with "osmanthus fragrance spreads in the season of apricot blossoms" on a failed paper. Shocked, he read it carefully and found that it answered the exam questions rather well, especially the answer to the five questions on politics was particularly detailed. It showed that the candidate was a learned man and talented, but he failed the exam because his eight-legged essay (a fixed literary form for imperial exams) was not good enough.

Because of his dream, Yang Chaoguan wanted to recommend this paper to the chief examiner, but he felt that the timing needed to be better to mention it. As he was stuck in this awkward position, the chief examiner, Qian Rucheng, discovered that the discourse on politics was poorly written on some of the papers and asked the examiners to select some suitable substitutes from the failed papers. Yang Chaoguan immediately recommended the osmanthus-fragrance exam paper, and the chief examination was satisfied with it and ranked it 83rd among all papers. When the candidates were revealed to announce the test results, it was discovered that Hou Yuanbiao, an old tribute scholar from Shangqiu, was the candidate, and his grandfather was Hou Chaozong, whose story with Li Xiangjun was well known.

As a result, everyone believed that the woman that appeared in Yang Chaoguan's dream must be Li Xiangjun. Yang Chaoguan was even more proud when he heard this opinion and boasted to people everywhere that Li Xiangjun showed up in his dream.

Among the people Yang Chaoguan boasted to was Yuan Mei. However, when he vividly told the story to Yuan Mei, 18 years had passed. In that

18 years, Yang Chaoguan must have told it many times. He might have improvised each time he told it, thus the many versions of this story. Except for the satisfaction from boasting, the narrator wanted to gain nothing else, but the listener took it seriously. Yuan Mei always had a special liking for such mythical stories. At that time, he listened to it with great interest and wrote about it twice without great enthusiasm.

As a result, the story of Li Xiangjun recommending an exam paper took on the form of a text as an article in Volume Three of *Zi Bu Yu* (*What the Master Would Not Discuss*) and a paragraph in *Sui Garden Notes on Poetry and Poets: Volume Eight*. After the publication of *Zi Bu Yu*, Yuan Mei, enthusiastic and good-hearted, sent a special copy to Yang Chaoguan. He was so excited that he did not expect his old friend to be irritated and rain on his parade.

Normally, no one takes such stories seriously. There is no problem if the narrator and the listeners confine such a narrative to a private conversation. Once it is documented and passed on, it becomes a completely different situation. As Yuan Mei's works were published, the boastful narrative of Yang Chaoguan in private conversation entered public space. Therefore, a private story is exposed to public criticism. The readers can exaggerate, misinterpret, and distort it, while the creator can never control them. In a word, he was terrified of what people would think of it. No wonder Yang Chaoguan was so anxious that he immediately sent Yuan Mei a handwritten letter, scolding him for his inaccurate writing and demanding Yuan Mei to immediately "remove it." More than two hundred years later, when rereading the letter, we can still feel the palpable rage of Yang Chaoguan, who was over sixty years old when he wrote it.

Texts have always been more decorative and suggestive than a verbal description. Perhaps Yang's own narrative back then has already been embellished. After his literary friend's polishing, the story was even more charming. In his enthusiastic and vivid texts, Yang Chaoguan saw Yuan Mei's proud expression. He was so irritated that he could not bear it, especially in two sections: one section wrote that he dreamed of Li Xiangjun lifting his bed curtain and whispering, and the other called him complacent, "Every time he boasted about the dream, he sounded arrogant." And "lifting his bed curtain" and "whispering" might mislead readers, and they might even consider it a carnal case, which not only "slandered an innocent soul" but also "an old friend."

It shamed Yang Chaoguan terribly. Certainly, he had to defend himself. He did not deny telling the story but accused Yuan Mei of inaccurate writing, which caused the misunderstanding: "First, you wrote that it happened in 1752, but that year I was not the County Magistrate; second, even I had forgotten who the chief examiner was, given that the test took place many years before I told you the story. How could you be so sure that it was Qian Rucheng? Obviously, you fabricated this fact; third, there were only 71 candidates that took the exam. Where is the 83rd place from? Obviously, you added it yourself; fourth, Hou Sheng, who was selected at last, was only a grandchild in Hou Fangyu's clan, not his direct grandson. In a word, all of these are your fabrication that could not be farther from the truth."

The letter started with polite remarks, mere self-defense, but as it continued, Yang Chaoguan became so increasingly furious that he couldn't help accusing Yuan Mei of being too mean to an old friend, "harshly insulting" him. He snarled, "What is Li Xiangjun? Nobody but Hou Fangyu's bitch in the late Ming Dynasty. Even if I met her alive, I would never take pride in our meeting, let alone if it were just her ghost in my dream. In addition, I am a man with libido, but no lust comes from me towards this bitch. I hate nothing more in my life than famous prostitutes. How dare you write that she lifted my bed curtain and whispered that I boasted about it? How could I stoop so low? The nature of this matter was originally "a righteous soul helping a talented exam candidate in a dream." It had nothing to do with Li Xiangjun, the famous prostitute of Qinhuai, or anyone else. I have written an article about this matter and sent you a copy. This article is the real truth of the story."

I am curious about when Yang Chaoguan wrote this article and whether he wrote it after reading Yuan Mei's texts to right the wrong, but unfortunately, I can't get to the bottom of it now. At the end of the letter, Yang Chaoguan, as an old friend, kindly advised Yuan Mei, "Book titles such as *Zi Bu Yu* expose your blatantly "contradictory" and "absurd" ideology. In front of your high prestige, no one dares to give you their honest opinion. Today, as a respectful friend (there is a saying later that Yuan Mei regarded him as a respectful friend), I give you my honest opinion that is not music to the ears." These words seemed to persuade Yuan Mei to wake up to the danger at the last moment. In the end, he went straightforward, demanding the poet to reflect on it and "reply" as soon as possible.

Yang Chaoguan was an excellent writer, as evidenced by his 32 kinds of *Yinfeng Pavilion Drama*. However, I don't think the letter was just. It was true that he over-boasted back then. Once he told the story, there was no untelling it. Regretting it doesn't take it back, does it? Defending himself by listing the four points, none of which hit the bullseye, and fussing over the details cannot erase what has already happened. Even I, a bystander, stand unpersuaded, let alone Yuan Mei, the party involved at the time. When the poet read the letter, he was both irritated and amused by his old friend's stubbornness. He immediately replied, sending three consecutive letters back, whose lengths were at least five times that of Yang Chaoguan's. He refuted point by point, sometimes sneering, sometimes joking, almost sinking their friendship.

In the letters, Yuan Mei wrote, "What is written in *Zi Bu Yu* is all unwarranted and jokes. You could not be more pedantic in taking it seriously, scrutinizing every word like textual research, and even getting mad about it. Dreaming is normal and not surprising or shameful to dream of a woman like Li Xiangjun. You told the story yourself when you were in your prime of life. You speak justly and honestly, without any scruples. When you are old, you have a hard time worrying about what your epitaph will be. Isn't this the reason you defended yourself so strenuously?" These few words hit the nail on the head, pointing out what Yang Chaoguan most cared about, "reputation." What a sharp remark!

"Indeed, Li Xiangjun was a prostitute, but must a prostitute be underestimated? Not to mention every trade has its masters, it was challenging to be a famous prostitute, and her steadfast integrity in the face of eunuchs such as Ma Shiying and Ruan Dacheng sufficed to make many so-called scholar-officials ashamed. Today, there are still people who know your name. In 30 to 50 years, everyone in the world will still know Li Xiangjun, but who will know you? You call yourself lecherous, but never for a famous prostitute like Li Xiangjun. I believe you are basically pretending to be so. Ming Dynasty scholar Wang Ji once said: 'It is a shame that a poor scholar tries to prove himself lecherous by having sex with his faded old wife.' This is exactly you, isn't it? Or is your wife so intimidating that you dare not to dream?"

Yuan Mei then quoted the article Yang Chaoguan sent along with the letter, using Yang's words against Yang. "How ridiculous that you should say Li Xiangjun 'knelt under the bed and begged' instead of 'lifted your bed curtain and whispered'! You have not been an official for years, and Li Xiangjun is no arrested criminal. Why should she kneel before you? Should you have an innocent mind, what's the harm in her lifting your bed curtain and whispering? If you have evil thoughts, you will still drag her to your arms even if she kneels. What's the point of your argument? You described she was "dressed elegantly and neatly made up." If you didn't stare, how could you see it so clearly? Didn't you violate the no-stare rule? You claim to have been practicing Taoism and Zen for years, but I don't believe you have made any progress. Before advising others, I suggest you wash off the filth and rot in yourself with ten buckets of spring water on Mountain Hui in Wuxi."

Yuan Mei reacted so aggressively, which was beyond my expectations, and probably beyond Yang Chaoguan's expectations as well. Frankly, Yang Chaoguan was no Taoist, let alone a defender of Taoism. Judging from *Yinfeng Pavilion Drama*, most of his scripts are about the trivial life of the general public to reflect the national economy, people's livelihood, and the state of the world. His words were humorous, meaning he was no rigid man. His life was also full of romantic stories. On his 70th birthday, "He and his wife held a wedding ceremony again, his children helped them into the bridal chamber, and they consummated their marriage again."

Seldom do people of his age make this romantic love. Based on the fact that he built the Yinfeng Pavilion on the former site of Zhuo Wenjun Chamber of Powder and Rouge when he was serving in Qiongzhou, Sichuan Province, he could be regarded as "lecherous." Otherwise, he would not have ignored the constant slander and abuse of others and befriended Yuan Mei. When this debate happened, Yang Chaoguan was already 80, enjoying the last years of his life, and Yuan Mei, who was younger, was 76. It was unusual for two elderly people to quarrel over a dream decades ago so seriously and so aggressively. Yang Chaoguan had been sophisticated all his life. He had served as an official for over 30 years. He was diligent and has an "upright and incorruptible reputation." In *Chronicles* he writes that he enjoyed writing in his life as if he were committed to making his words immortal. In fact, in addition to that, he also wished to establish a reputation and create meritorious deeds to be remembered, and this wish became stronger and stronger as he aged. This is human nature; Yuan Mei's words were a bit harsh but true. To Yang Chaoguan, when life was coming to an end, the charm of the self-admiring suave talent had been exhausted; to Yuan Mei, the 76-year-old elderly man was still roaring in the garden, and the older he got, the more stubborn he became. To Yang Chaoguan, this was a matter of great importance to his reputation, and it was necessary to "follow the rules" and "advise an old friend;" to Yuan Mei, this was "nothing important" but a "squabble with an old friend for fun." In the twilight of life, on the values of life, the differences between the two old friends surfaced at last.

This debate has shown me the Sui Garden owner's frankness, argumentativeness, and savageness, as well as his personality, style of writing, and brilliant ideas, which cannot be underestimated. He fought against literary celebrities and heroes from all walks of life and never gave up, sweeping away countless rivals with a sharp pen. There are still many similar writings of his in *The Letters Written in the House on Xiaocang Mountain*. The first article of the surviving *Extra Words Beyond the Letters* is his defense of Wang Anshi and several other Song Dynasty literati. It was not enough for him to sit on the sidelines of the debates hundreds of years ago. He had to join them. One could not be more contentious. However, this time, after all, it was an old friend, so obviously, he had to restrain himself. Although he criticized his friend harshly and attached the letter from the friend on the back of his reply as if "to be preserved as a basis for verification," in the end, he made a concession and compromised; otherwise, decades of friendship would absolutely sink. I noticed a detail that Yuan Mei might have revised the texts of this story in *Zi Bu Yu* later. In the letter from Yang Chaoguan, it was mentioned that she "lifted his bed curtain and whispered" in the story of Li Xiangjun and the examination paper. In the current edition of *Zi Bu Yu*, the verb whisper is changed into a murmur. Although a murmur also implies some kind of intimacy, it is less sexual and dubious than a whisper. After all, everyone knows the famous verse in *The Everlasting Regret*:

On the seventh day of the seventh moon
when none was nearby,
at midnight in Long Life Hall
he whispered in her ear.

However, whispering was still used in *Sui Garden Notes on Poetry and Poets*. In addition, at the end of the story, in the current edition of *Zi Bu Yu* is written: "It is suspected that the woman in the dream was Li Xiangjun." The word "suspected" is wonderfully chosen. *Sui Garden Notes on Poetry and Poets* only asks, "Is it Li Xiangjun?" I assume that the original wording was not so vague, and there was no little room for imagination. Unfortunately, there is no earlier version to verify that. At least for the previous example, what Yang Chaoguan saw at that time differed from the present version.

Yuan Mei's compromise and Yang Chaoguan's death prevented the two friends from drifting apart, but they moved closer again and forged another literary bond. Before that, they had frequently exchanged poems. According to the *Revised Wuxi County Chronicle* by Qin Xiangye of the Qing Dynasty, Yuan Mei once performed his *Yinfeng Pavilion Drama* in Sui Garden, leaving the audience in awe. Allegedly the handwritten copy of *Yinfeng Pavilion Drama* today stored in the Xieyun Building was revised by Wu Qiongxian, a female disciple in the Sui Garden.

In addition to the letters, another bond was made between Yinfeng Pavilion and Sui Garden. When he was dying, Yang Chaoguan invited Yuan Mei to write his biography, which is *The Biography of Yang Chaoguan* in of *Die Xian Lei Zheng*, Volume 232. In the biography, Yuan Mei wrote that he and Yang Chaoguan had been friends since childhood. "We have totally different personalities. I am arrogant while he is irritable; I am unrestrained while he is loyal; I never believed in Taoism and Buddhism while he fancied Zen. For that reason, he set strict rules for himself in his last years, thus was defensive often." It seems to allude to their debate. "People in the world are both different but similar. Isn't that you and me?"

In the end, they sought common ground while reserving differences. The storm subsided, and Yang Chaoguan and Sui Garden had another bond of life and death. His long-cherished wish to die together with Yuan Mei in Nanjing was not fulfilled, but because of this case, he forged an indissoluble bond with Sui Garden, with Li Xiangjun, and with Nanjing.

As the proverb goes: never talk about a dream in front of the easily obsessed. Even in Nanjing, even on the banks of the Qinhuai River, where Li Xiangjun rose to fame, there is no exception, which, after this storm, Yuan Mei and Yang Chaoguan should have both realized. One was uninhibitedly "obsessed," while the other was pedantically "obsessed." They were both adorable, weren't they?

Chapter 21

Through Common Eyes

Perhaps you have never read *Peach Blossom Fan* (a musical play and historical drama in 44 scenes that was completed in AD 1699 by the early Qing Dynasty playwright Kong Shangren after more than ten years of effort). Still, it's unlikely that you have never heard the name Li Xiangjun. Maybe you have never read *Banqiao Zaji (Miscellanea on the Slate Bridge)* by Yu Huai, and it's unlikely that you have heard of *the Eight Beauties of Qinhuai.* These two works were written after earth-shaking upheavals during the Ming and Qing dynasties, and hidden in their intricate plot and beautiful sentences is the heavy weight of recalling a painful experience. However, people take pleasure in reviewing history. When the prosperous times return, and parties are held again, the unbearable pain in the vicissitudes of the past life will be rinsed off by time and one by one become conversation topics at people's leisure.

As a result, the charm of the long Slate Bridge, the parties at the old courtyards, the lights on the painted boat, the beauties' makeup, the elegance of Li Xiangjun, and the brothel of Gu Hengbo all have become faint memories. Plus, the charming ancient legends, as early as Wang Xianzhi gifting his concubine with peach leaves at the ferry beside Huaiqing Bridge, as early as Du Mu staying the night in Qinhuai, listening to the girls singing *A Song of Courtyard Flowers* across the river, the ancient past seems to come back to life. This slump under the autumn willows today used to be so prosperous.

Indeed, as the old capital of the Ming Dynasty and the new capital of the Southern Ming Dynasty, Nanjing was briefly flourishing during the Ming and Qing Dynasties, brief as the last radiance of the setting sun. In *Banqiao Zaji*, Yu Huai called this romantic place "heaven on earth" and "the kingdom of happiness." At that time, countless refined scholars lingered there and regarded it as a paradise.

> Parties continue, painted boats keep sailing late at night,
> boy meets girl, and a love story begins.
> It takes generations of good deeds to be this lucky
> that every woman's husband is a government official.

Qin Jitang's poem titled *Notes on Banqiao Zaji by Yu Zhanxin* precisely summarizes the satisfying experience of the refined scholars in Nanjing and also depicts their "common imagination" of the old courtyard at Banqiao. As time went by, even if the realistic background on which these experiences are based ceased to exist, the literati could still use their literary imagination to continue to build their elegant and mysterious literary buildings. Outsiders are usually stunned when they see it and inevitably get sucked into a hazy romantic dream: looking at the houses on both banks of the Qinhuai River, it seems that it is all such a romantic vibe, and what lingers in the heart seems to be all the literary undertakings, all the fascinating "makeup," and all the memorable "anecdotes."

This is probably the so-called "refined taste of the refined scholars," who naturally have a pair of "refined" eyes that see only the refined things. They disdain vulgar people, vulgar affairs, and vulgar things, let alone care about them. When they cannot avoid vulgarity, they refine it.

In the autumn of the 26th year (1846) of the Daoguang Period, Wang Tao, a 19-year-old scholar from Luzhi in Suzhou, came to Nanjing and lived under the roof of the Gongs in Diaoyu Lane, east of the Confucius Temple. Around it was plenty of brothels. Wang Tao made full use of this advantage, going in and out of the fun venues, so happy that he had totally forgotten the township examination. In the memoir *Late-Year Wandering Jottings*, he simplified his trip to Nanjing decades earlier to only three memoirs, titled *Delivering Letters in Baixia*, *Visiting Brothels in Nanjing*, and *Jinling Travel Journal*. At the end of these three paragraphs, he appended a number of beautiful poems, trying to portray himself as a romantic, self-appreciating, and amorous young man. As for his failure in the township exam, he omitted it, as expected.

There was a Wenyi Building west of the Gong Family Water Pavilion on Diaoyu Lane. In the brothel, there were two prostitutes, Ren Suqin and Miu Aixiang, whose beauty was rivalled and whose names were well-known. They were his favorite. He claimed to have visited them five times. Supposedly, they were no strangers to him. But the strange thing was that one day, Wang Tao traveled to Miaoxiang Nunnery, "Where he met Suqin and Aixiang, sitting quietly, sipping tea, and enjoying their moment of leisure. They noticed him, smiled, and cast me an amorous glance. I walked past them, but they pretended not to know me, afraid to be exposed and judged." (*Wandering Jottings, Jinling Travel Journal*) This encounter was too dramatic. Both parties being so reserved and raising serious doubts: Was Wang Tao really familiar with the two women? Were they really close? Was his memory real? Otherwise, was this reserved and subtle demeanor concealing something, such as he had no more money to afford their service, so when they met again, they pretended to be strangers to avoid awkwardness?

This kind of speculation is undoubtedly cynical. I am also afraid that I might slander the ancients and ruin the "refined taste of the refined scholars," becoming a buzzkill if I am careless. However, although the world has become used to "seeing things through refined eyes," there might be a new meaning if we do that with a pair of "common eyes." The texts of "refined eyes" are not difficult to find, while the texts of "common eyes" are, especially those with illustrations. "Fancy finding by sheer luck what one has searched for far and wide." Just as we were making a comprehensive search, *Dianshizhai (Touchstone House) Pictorial*, which has been forgotten in the dust for over a century, stepping on the loud drumbeat of the advent of the visual age, "makes a grand entrance," and enters our field of vision.

First, let's talk about a piece of news from this publication, and the new title is *Unrequited Love*.

Purportedly, a lady named Ru was in a mansion in the Jinling Pigment Factory. She was a famous hooker in Goulan and once "shone brightly" in Diaoyu Lane. Later, she married a high-ranking official as his concubine. She was so much his favorite that she couldn't be cockier in front of his other women. One day, Lady Ru, dressed in a bright and gorgeous dress, led a group of servants to the Temple of Fortune to pay respect. It was such a grand outing that it attracted a crowd of people from the neighborhood, and she couldn't be more proud. There was a scholar among the onlookers, who happened to be her old client from the past, and because of their history, "She strode forward, whispered to him, reminiscing about the good old days and confiding in him her secrets."

Unexpectedly, the beauty, "ashamed into anger" afterward, ordered the servants to escort the scholar back to the mansion and implored her high-ranking official husband to send the man to the yamen for severe punishment. It was undoubtedly a mistake for the scholar to be sentimental, and it was ruthless enough that she and he parted ways, but it was too much that she regarded him as an enemy and bullied him. Looking back at the encounter between Wang Tao and his two prostitutes, both sides' restraint and subtlety were just perfect, enabling them to retain a little "refined taste of the refined scholars."

Dianshizhai Pictorial was a news pictorial in the late Qing Dynasty, explicitly referring to the period from 10th to the 24th year of Emperor Guangxu's reign (1884–1898) in this book. This time span was also the later years of Wang Tao. Measured by a long-term historical scale, it was also the time of Wang Tao's "Visiting Brothels in Nanjing." When it comes to news, most of the news in *Dianshizhai Pictorial* was taken from *Shen Bao (Shanghai News)* because illustrations can be easily added to the materials of *Shen Bao*. In addition to Shanghai itself and the capital Beijing, news about Nanjing, Suzhou, Yangzhou, and other surrounding cities also accounted for a considerable weight in *Dianshizhai Pictorial*.

Regarding illustrations, over the 15 years of *Dianshizhai Pictorial*, there were over 4,000 illustrations, including more than 200 about Nanjing. They added great fun to the reading. In Chen Pingyuan's words, the literary form was between journalists' reports and literati's articles. Compared with *Shen Bao*, it was more kitsch, obviously, and closer to today's tabloids and supplements. In my opinion, being kitsch is the key. A news pictorial certainly relies on a pair of "news eyes. For *Dianshizhai Pictorial*, its "news eyes" are, in fact, the common eyes that observe the everyday world.

After 1889, *Dianshizhai Pictorial* opened distribution points in various places, called Dianshizhai Branches. Its distribution point in Nanjing sat in the east archway of the Confucius Temple, which is adjacent to Diaoyu

Lane. In addition to distributing the publication, it shouldered other responsibilities and functions, such as providing news or clues to the Shanghai headquarters. It is impossible to get into the details now. What is certain is that among the news on *Dianshizhai Pictorial* about Nanjing, a lot happened near the east archway and Diaoyu Lane, most of which was related to brothels. I ran rough statistics and found there were as many as ten. And the news headlines are as follows:

Uneven happiness, gambling ruins people, bathing when dirty, beaten customers, indulging in alcohol, drinking and drowning, escape from the flower cave, suddenly a grown man, reckless trouble, humiliation when protecting the hooker, humiliation from negligence, stealing from the hooker, frivolous and humiliated, procuresses tour around the lake, the infatuated painter, beaten up, grand gathering in Qinhuai, and unrequited love.

Only from these headlines can we see the taste and "news orientation" of *Dianshizhai Pictorial*'s editors. Except for "grand gathering in Qinhuai," none has the slightest sense of elegance and couldn't be farther from the refinement mentioned in Yu Huai's *Banqiao Zaji*. The beginning of the new article, *Uneven Happiness* seems to be a tad refined:

"The spring tide is not there yet, the Qinhuai River is still shallow, the boats, lit and painted, come and go, and the melody of the flutes back up the singing of *A Song of Courtyard Flowers* across the river."

Then, it writes that in such a comfortable ambiance of the music, a manure boat tries to get out of the East Water Pass before night falls, thus sailing hurriedly, but when it reaches Peach Leaf Dock, the river is crowded, and the manure boat gets stuck. After some struggle, it finally capsizes, and all the filth falls into the river. This ruins the beautiful scenery, and the aesthetic mood is swept away entirely.

Escape from the Flower Cave is about an elderly brothel customer staying overnight at a prostitute's house in Diaoyu Lane. At night, the river lights burst, causing a fire. He made a fool of himself during the escape. Although the headline "The Infatuated Painter" sounds elegant, it tells a ridiculous and pitiful story: a painter surnamed Pan from Jinling, ". . . is in his thirties, and still single. He feels lascivious and thinks of hiring a prostitute, but he is broken, so he tries to bargain with a private hooker and ends up humiliated." Such behavior is, of course, disdained by refined scholars.

In *Dianshizhai Pictorial*'s prostitution news, humiliation seems to be the most common theme. The situation deteriorated to the point of humiliation; disgrace prevailed, and undoubtedly no elegance was left. *In Frivolous and Humiliated*, a well-off second lieutenant invites guests to a feast on the boat in the Qinhuai River. As they drank with great delight, a gaily-painted pleasure boat paddled towards them, and a gorgeous woman was on the ship. The host starts to judge her frivolously. However, she turns out to be a favorite prostitute of one of his guests, who reprimands him harshly. This is definitely self-inflicted criticism and has nothing to do with the prostitute. Prostitutes are snobbish. Once they are taken advantage of in terms of money, they will do whatever it takes to retaliate, including resorting to violence. One descendant of an old family got intimate with a prostitute. He was richly dressed, but stingy. The procuress finally sees his stinginess. She has him "stripped and drowned to vent her anger" (Drink and Drown). How vulgar! There are many brothels in the area of Diaoyu Lane.

A regular customer or not, whoever pays is welcomed warmly. Humiliation is inevitable if one without money pretends to be wealthy, trying to exploit the sex workers. Even the sons of aristocratic families would be beaten for pulling the trick (Beaten Customers). One inspector claims to be romantic and unrestrained and enjoys acting as a "lady's savior," buying back the prostitute's freedom. After one night banquet, a famous prostitute named Lan was hidden away. The procuress is furious when she finds out her cash cow has been taken away. She discovers where he hides the brothel's top earner and sends hatchet men to teach him a lesson. The poor inspector is dragged two or three *li* by his hair, parading through the street. Ultimately, he has to agree to return Lan, so that it ends (humiliation when protecting the hooker).

Outside Diaoyu Lane, there are also private and local prostitutes elsewhere. Although these prostitutes are illegal, messing with them would be a mistake. The nephew of Hu Daling in Jiangning County once passed by Zhu Er's house, which was on the Xinfu River. The coquettish prostitute at the door laughed at him for being stingy and unwilling to pay for fun. The two have a verbal dispute. Zhu Er's servant works at the Southern Police Station. She takes advantage of her connections and sends her servant to beat him terribly. Later, the nephew realizes that he is "bearding the lion in his den," too late to regret but to let it go. (Beaten Up) The servant of a local prostitute is merely a policeman, which suffices to make him become violent. The procuress in Diaoyu Lane must have a much stronger backing, thus their more rampant violence. In *Dianshizhai Pictorial*, this sexual place in Nanjing shows its more snobbish, despicable, and filthy side. These stories of being humiliated by prostitutes point directly at the ferocity of the procuresses, shocking and eye-catching.

However, everything has its vanquisher. There are times when procuresses suffer and cannot tell it to another soul. The news of the Procuresses' Tour around the lake tells the story of a few procuresses pretending to have refined manners. As they row in the middle of the lake, they get carried away. As a result, they are scolded loudly by some tourists who claim to be righteous. Only their own arrogance makes them suffer, and they can still tell it to others. In another piece of news, a son of an official family in Zhejiang, who had found out in advance that a prostitute in Xinfu River saves a considerable sum of money, "orders her service and shows her great care." He is generous, winning the trust of everyone in the brothel. And the prostitute is charmed, fails to see all his lies, and tells him where she keeps her savings and other secrets.

Suddenly one day, a young woman shows up at her doorstep with six or seven brawny men, claiming to be looking for her disgraceful husband. The man inside the house pretends to be scared and hurriedly escapes through the back door under cover of the prostitute. The wife makes a punitive expedition, and during the chaos, she loots the savings of the prostitute. (Stealing from the Hooker) It turns out that the couple works in tandem to scam her. These prostitutes usually outsmart others. One of the news in the *Dianshizhai Pictorial* tells the story of a prostitute in Qingyunli setting up a gambling scam to steal from people (Gambling Ruins People). This time she becomes the victim, which is nothing but karma. This story alone shows that the moral degeneration of the world is worsening day by day.

Speaking of moral degeneration, there are more interesting examples. *Dianshizhai Pictorial* reported the news called *Bathe When Dirty*. The headline seems refined, but it is actually about several teenagers and a young prostitute. They took her to a public bathhouse to enjoy a bath together. When the owner found out, he chased them away. Even in northern Shanghai, where promiscuity prevails, this kind of debauchery is unheard of, but now it happens in Nanjing, which is truly astonishing. As an ancient cultural capital and famous old city, Nanjing's remaining little sense of moral superiority in the face of the emerging colonized and commercialized city of Shanghai was instantly shattered. Nothing could stop it. Nanjing was one of the earliest trade ports to open and one of the first cities to receive everything from the West. *Grand Gathering in Qinhuai* is about a Cantonese man named Chen, who ran a photo studio diagonally opposite the examination compound. To entertain foreigners, he hired a Western-style light boat called Qinhuai Laixi, organized foreign banquets, and recruited dozens of famous harlots from Diaoyu Lane. They sang and drank, swaggering across the river. This can be regarded as a kind of Chinese and Western integration. The background of this news was the Sino-Japanese peace treaty, the Treaty of Shimonoseki, had just been signed. Generally, tabloids such as *Dianshizhai Pictorial* paid little attention to national affairs but sometimes included news of the turbulent times.

In 1864, Zeng Guoquan led the Hunan Province army to attack Nanjing. After they broke into the city, they burned, killed, looted, and robbed, and a group of them became rich overnight. After that, Zeng Guofan, Li Hongzhang, and Zeng Guoquan successively became Nanjing's Viceroy of Jiangnan Province and Jiangxi Province. Thus, many civil and military officials with Hunan and Anhui accents appeared on the streets of Nanjing. A brothel client with a Fengying accent "proclaimed himself a bureau director." He went to his favorite prostitute Jin Bao in Diaoyu Lane but was rejected. Instead, he gulped wine until he was drunk in another harlot's chamber. As he left the brothel, he fell into a big bucket for rinsing rice by the roadside, making a fool of himself (indulging in alcohol). Certainly, this kind of behavior is no example to be followed. Still, it was an important opportunity that shouldn't be ignored because such people frequented Diaoyu Lane and flourished the Nanjing prostitution industry in the late Qing Dynasty.

It is said that after Zeng Guoquan became the Viceroy, he took bribes. To avoid being caught, the bribes were always handled through intermediaries in the brothels of Diaoyu Lane. At that time, the yamen of the Viceroy had two outer gates, east and west, on which were written the four characters of "两江保障" (liǎngjiāng bǎozhàng, guardian of Jiangnan and Jiangxi) and "三省钧衡" (sānshěng jūn héng, balance among three provinces). Some people split the character "衡" (héng) into two characters, "鱼" (yú, fish) and "行, (xíng)" and the two characters for "钧" (jūn) and "钓 diào) " have only one stroke difference. In this way, "三省钧衡" (sānshěng jūn héng) became "三省钓鱼 (Diaoyu) 行," (sānshěng diàoyú 'Diaoyu' xing) alluding to the fact that Zeng Guoquan was the head of the "Diaoyu (profit-making) business." Many years ago, I read Shi Sanyou's *Unofficial History of Jinling*. I was so profoundly impressed when I saw this story that I could not forget it for long. Today, when I skimmed through *Dianshizhai Pictorial*, I noticed that when Zeng Guoquan was leaving Jinling, he earnestly admonished his subordinates to "abide by the law and work diligently" as if he were a Neo-Confucianism scholar. (*Parting Words*) I smiled, knowing that Zong Zongzhu had this side. This again comes down to the difference between "refined eyes" and "common eyes." The "refined eyes" seem hot, ethereal, and concealing, while the "common eyes" are cold, real, and exposing. Looking at the world with both types of eyes may enable us to see it more comprehensively.

According to Shi Sanyou, the famous poet Fan Zengxiang wrote a poem about the "Diaoyu Business":

Qinhuai painted boats are warm and sexy,
sometimes fishermen come to visit.
Sitting in the house on the river bank
thinking about what is wrong,
about who runs the Diaoyu business.

Fan Zengxiang was absolutely talented. His writing blurs the boundaries between elegance and vulgarity. He teased both the fishing (Diaoyu) "heroes" and the "beauties" who accompanied him in a different way. In the poetry circles of the late Qing Dynasty, Fan Zengxiang was known as "Fan Beauty," and his poetry was beautifully worded. I believe it matches the topic of this chapter by using his poem as the ending.

Chapter 22

Wine Lover

One year ago, I absolutely dare not touch this topic. Despite Huang Kan's (also known as Jiangbei) wine-lover reputation, I was born much later than him, so most of what I know about him was just ambiguous hearsay. Since he passed away, getting more accurate materials has been more challenging. Fortunately, *Huang Kan Diaries*, which has been sorted and checked, has finally been published by the Jiangsu Education Publishing House. With over 1,000 pages, this book starts on June 20, 1913, and ends on October 7, 1935. And the diaries after 1928, in which he settled in Nanjing and taught at Central University, are incredibly complete. There is abundant content about his life and reading. With the help of this book, I am confident to give a brief discussion about the topic Huang Jigang and Wine.

I believe there are two couplets that can sum up this topic. Jigang made the first in 1922, which quotes and combines poems from the Tang Dynasty:

I wish to go up to the blue sky to pluck the bright moon,
needing the finest wine, to sum up my life.

The first half is quoted from *Bidding Farewell to Librarian Shu Yun at Xietiao Tower of Xuanzhou* by Li Bai, while the second is quoted from *Search for Flowers Alone at the Riverside* by Du Fu. It is a rather neat couplet from the two greatest poets. Although they are quotes, the inclination of Jigang is vividly conveyed. The other couplet comes from Zhang Taiyan in July of 1931:

No one to drink with,

all the money for the books.

Unsurprisingly, as a scholar, he read extensively; his love for wine shows his literary pursuits and celebrity bearing. In his own words, "delicious wine and rare books make me the happiest." No one knows the disciples better than their teacher. Zhang Taiyan's two lines, which quote Jiang Ximing from Qing Dynasty and highlight the two, books and wine, hit the spot.

Jigang had long been a wine lover. After settling in Nanjing at a later age, he had more opportunities to drink, either gulping down wine in a restaurant with his best pals, sipping in the suburbs with family and friends, or drinking alone at home. He once jokingly claimed that he indulged himself in the pleasure of alcohol. The sea is open to all rivers without discriminating against the trickles. Jigang didn't seem to prefer a specific brand when he drank. Whatever wine got him drunk was good enough for him. In addition to the usual rice wine, beer, Moutai, brandy, German or other foreign wines, he was open to all sorts of alcohol. At the beginning of 1932, to avoid bandits, he left for Beijing, where his disciple Lu Zongda hosted a dinner for him at the Red House, a Russian restaurant in Santiao Hutong, Pailou, Dongdan District. It was foreign wine that he had, and he returned drunk. In Nanjing in the 1920s and 1930s, finding a few decent restaurants with Western food and wine was not difficult.

The German restaurant in Pingcang Lane and the Youth Association in Neiqiao were restaurants that Jigang frequented. One afternoon in August 1935, he and Wang Dong and other friends made an appointment to travel to Xuanwu Lake. Before leaving, a thunderstorm struck, but they still "enjoyed German food, drank German wine in Pingcang Lane, got drunk, and in the darkness and rain, visited the tea pavilion on the lake, appreciating the lotus and discussing plays, and returned at ten o'clock." Authentic western food and wine and the leisure and ease of authentic traditional literati can probably be called an integration of western and eastern lifestyles. In the darkness of the rainy night, a couple of confidants sat relaxed in the tea pavilion on the lake, listening to the sound of raindrops on the lotus while chatting cheerfully. It must take alcohol to nurture such a mood.

Jigang lived in Nanjing for eight years. These eight years were a short-lived prosperous period in this city's modern history. Back then, eminent scholars and excellent teachers gathered where he taught at Central University and Jinling University. He had a group of like-minded friends and colleagues. Among them, Chen Hanzhang (Botao), Wang Xie (Bohang), Wang Dong (Xuchu), Wu Mei (Qu'an), Wang Yi (Xiaoxiang), Wang Guoyuan (Pijiang), Hu Jun (Xiangdong), and Hu Guangwei (Xiaoshi) hung out with him the most in the companion of poetry and wine. The restaurants they used to dine at included the Grand China Restaurant on North Gate Bridge, Laowanquan on Lishe Bridge, Shuxia Hotel on Tangfang Bridge, Liuhuachun on Gongyuan East Street, Green Willow in Peach Leaf Dock, and Ma Xiangxing Muslim Restaurant in Bao'en Temple in the south of the city, Minsheng Restaurant and Bean Jelly Village in Chengxian Street, Guangzhou Wine Restaurant in Songtao Lane, and others. By sorting out the names of restaurants in his diaries, it is almost possible to restore a food map of Nanjing seventy years ago. At that time, drinking beer in Laowanquan and eating authentic Nanjing cuisine cost two yuan per person for a group of seven to eight customers. For professors with higher incomes, it was not a problem at all. As they relished in the drinking, a poetry club was formed, the poetry bell was sounded, and poems were composed together, and everyone became drunk and elated. On such occasions, some students sometimes waited for them around. Observing their teachers having fun with poetry and wine was the best way for them to learn.

Jigang and his friends often took advantage of tipsiness to travel together, visiting ancient times and seeking hidden paths. As a result, the fragrance of wine and poetry spread from the bustling city to the verdant suburbs. On December 2, 1928, Wang Dong invited Jigang and his colleagues Wang Pijiang and Wang Yi had a drink at the Great China Restaurant of the North Gate Bridge. Tipsy, the four of them hired a car and visited the ancient forest temple in the west of the city. Along the Qingliang Ancient Road, they passed Sanbuliang Qiao (Three-Steps-Two Bridge), crossed Huayangang Gate, and reached Guiyun Thatched Cottage. Not until dawn broke, they returned to Huang's residence by car along Matai Street. In the evening, they continued to drink and chant poems at Jigang's place, and a total of 16 heptasyllabic quatrain poems were composed. They were all in their forties, their prime years, at that time, and this literary gathering of theirs became a favorite topic of the general public.

Jigang, Wang Dong, Wang Yi, Wang Pijiang, and Wu Mei visited Xuanwu Lake the day before the Double Nine Festival in the second year. There is no restaurant at that tourist spot, so Jigang prepared in advance, "bringing wine and crabs himself." Sitting in the Chau Shan Tea House, "they wrote ci together in front of the lush Zijin Mountain, the smoke rising in the north, and the withered lotus and the yellow willows in the depressing autumn, returned while the moonlight was bright, drank again, and began to disperse at ten o'clock. Qu An wrote a heap of poems. Today's trip was best friends appreciating the beauty of nature." Lingering in the lake and mountains, immersed in poetry and wine, drinking under these kinds of circumstances is most inspirational, revealing the true spirit and talent.

One can drink far more than usual with a bosom friend. Jigang's love for wine is actually loved for "the fun of traveling and appreciating the beauty of nature with best friends," and the confrontation of talents and the cultivation of friendship in the companion of poetry and wine. "With dogs barking and donkeys screaming around, drinking can never be pleasant." He had no interest in such a party. At times, it might even be said that he valued the ritualized meaning of drinking. In the poem *Drinking*, Tao Yuanming wrote: "If one doesn't drink one's fill, it is a disgrace to one's towel for filtering wine."

When autumn came, when the chrysanthemums bloomed and crabs grew fat, Jigang used to hold a wine glass in his right hand and a crab in his left, an image of a literary celebrity. His refined taste can be seen from time to time in his diaries. Once, he walked into a restaurant by himself, chatted with an old man he didn't know sitting next to him, and happily got drunk. Another time, he was with several friends, drinking and laughing while sharing a round table with other customers, having a good time. This elegant and unconventional demeanor made people miss the Six Dynasties.

It is great that alcohol makes people bolder and more expressive, but it is also inevitable that people behave foolishly and arrogantly when drunk. Certainly, such arrogance should not be taken seriously. It becomes interesting and adorable if it is seen as revealing true temperament. For example, once, after drinking at Laowanquan, the tipsy Jigang and two friends toured the Qinhuai River by boat. He stepped into the river, wetting his shoes and socks when he went ashore. Luckily, the water was shallow at the bank, so he didn't drown.

Another example is the drinking dispute between Jigang and Wu Mei. The two gentlemen taught at Central University, often hung out, and drank and composed poems.

One year, Wu Mei also made a memorable trip to gift Jigang with smoked fish and lent him a rare edition of *Classical Interpretations*. Jigang immediately gave his friend the book *Mao Shi Zheng Yun* as a return gift. Unexpectedly, one day in June 1933, graduating students invited their teachers to feast at Laowanquan in the Confucius Temple. The two gentlemen talked wildly after drinking, offending each other. They even got physical. Luckily, they were pulled away in time. The next day, after Wang Dong's mediation, the two reconciled as before. In the poem *Drinking* by Tao Yuanming, he writes: "Mistakes are made when people are drunk, we should forgive the drunk." It is a perfect summary of this case.

The general public believed that Jigang's indulgence in drinking was associated with his irritability and cursing. In fact, he himself might not be unaware of the intoxication and harm of alcoholism. In his diaries, he repeatedly reminded himself to abstain from drinking, speak prudently, and exercise self-discipline. Even if it would be difficult to achieve right away, he should avoid going to drinking parties as much as possible. For a few years, he did arrange to control his drinking, keeping a healthy diet and regular lifestyle.

Before November 1928, he paid attention to drinking less. It was on November 4 of that year he decided to quit drinking. In those days, his two-year-old daughter, Nianhui, was in critical condition; her weak life was on the line. Deeply worried, he picked up wine again to drown his sorrow. On November 5, when his little girl passed away, Jigang was devastated. He wrote several poems in a row to mourn his daughter. In the following month, he hardly ever lived a day without drinking. He relied on alcohol to anesthetize himself. Judging from the diaries, this was the period when he was the most inebriated.

After the September 18 Incident, the Japanese imperialists accelerated their aggression against China, and the nation was in danger. The enemy was aggressively coming. Seeing the difficult situation, he was so worried that he couldn't help but write. After he left for Beijing to dodge the aggressors in 1932, his anxiety about the times intensified. He wrote more and more about his alcoholism in his diaries until he died. At this time, Jigang, just like Ruan Ji in the Wei and Jin Dynasties mentioned in *A New Account of the Tales of the World*, Rendan "tried to drown his sorrow with alcohol." In 1936, Wang Dong gave a eulogy on the first anniversary of Jigang's death that "He indulged himself in drinking when he was devastated, and that killed him." It was just another way of summarizing it, but more clearly.

Chapter 23

The Distinguished and Admirable Wang Bohang

Old Nanjing rests in the south of the city. Since the Six Dynasties, this has been a well-off place that has brought forward men of talent. From the east of the city gate to its west, there are historical relics and cultural landscapes all the way. Little of the Phoenix Terrace, the Xie Ancestral Hall, the Yu Garden in the west, the Zhou Chu Reading Terrace, and the Jiezi Garden in the east can be seen today, but these names still possess a genuine classical charm, and calling them charming is enough. We wonder how many literati and refined scholars lingered here, chanting poems to nature. Without walking the path, they walked, our thoughts run wild, nostalgic about the past. If we visit what they visited, the unexpected discoveries and gains will leave us in awe of the heroic, talented, and distinguished men it has bred. This is how I felt when I walked into the Wang Bohang and Zhou Fagao Memorial Hall for the first time.

I recall that it was on November 8, 1998, the day when the Wang Bohang and Zhou Fagao Memorial Hall opened. I went to offer my congratulations as a representative of the Chinese Department of Nanjing University. The building stood at. 3 Renhouli, Gate East (now 98 Bianying), not far south of Zhou Chu Reading Terrace. This used to be the ancestral house of Bohang. He was both born and buried in its yard. The beginning and end of his life converge, drawing a perfect circle of life. Bohang once taught at Nanjing

Higher Normal School, Southeast University, and Central University. Therefore, he qualified as one of the founders of the Chinese Department of Nanjing University, highly respectful. But it is a shame that I knew so little about him then.

Mr. Bohang (1871–1944), whose style name was Xie, called himself Dongyin in his later years, so scholars also called him Mr. Dongyin. Dongyin Hangxie refers to the evening mist. There is this verse *Travel Far* in *Songs of Chu*:

> Swallow the six essential qi and sip the lucid dew,
> rinse the breath with the light of the morning glow.

And in *Ling Yang Zi*, its annotation, is written: "*Dongyin hangxie* refers to the evening mist in the north." The evening mist, pure and noble, just like the familiar Mulan dew, Qiu Ju petals, and Zhengyang morning glow, are symbols of the nobles like Qu Yuan and nourishment for their minds. Unfortunately, few people know this origin now. In modern Chinese, when the word 沆瀣 (hàngxiè) is used, people immediately think of the idiom 沆瀣一气 (hàngxiè yīqì, to act in collusion with) of the story about the imperial examination in the second year (875) of the Qianfu Period in the late Tang Dynasty: a candidate named Cui Xie participated in the imperial examination of that year and passed. The examiner, Cui Hang, happened to come from the same clan, so people made it a joke: "Hang and Xie acted in collusion." Under the negative influence of this story, the original pure and noble meaning of the word 沆瀣 hàngxiè was gone, together with its classical context, leaving us only vagueness, just like Wang Bohang.

This detailed account of the name is given because Bohang lived up to this name. He was a clever child who studied *Shuowen Jiezi* (*Words and Expressions*, an ancient Chinese dictionary) from Gao Zian, a famous scholar in Jiangning, who taught him everything he knew. Before the teacher died of illness, he entrusted him to other teachers via poems. Bohang studied at Nanjing Zhongshan Academy in his early years. He was outstanding and a favorite student of the academy Director Huang Xiangyun of Qichun. After he turned twenty, he indulged in alcohol, often "dressed up, drinking and composing poems with rich friends." Once, having gulped alcohol, he was so drunk that he "threw the oil lamp on the desk" (*Qian Kunxin Stories of*

Mr. Dongyin by Qian Kunxin, the same below), almost burning down the study. And he quit drinking after that. Twenty years later, the wine-loving boy grew into a famous scholar in the Southeast. Even when he was partying with a group of wine-loving celebrities in Nanjing at that time, he never touched a drop.

Bohang spent his life learning. He was so erudite that it was difficult for ordinary people to imagine how he knew so much. His academic path differed significantly from that of ordinary people. It can be roughly divided into three stages: when he was young, he studied ancient writings and poetry, taking the usual path of the traditional scholars and showing promising talent; in his prime, he studied country management, was quite ambitious, including spending extra effort on the law, but his mother believed that his firm and morally upright personality would make him offend his supervisors often, and get him in trouble, thus firmly forbade him from becoming a government official.

Respectful of his mother's wish, he never made any attempt in that direction; after turning forty, he devoted himself to Confucianism in the Song and Ming Dynasties and studied Buddhism and Taoism, becoming an expert in Buddhism, Taoism, and Confucianism. At that time, Lay Buddhist Yang Renshan established the Jinling Sutra Engraving Office in Yanggongjing, Nanjing, to spread Buddhism. Bohang and Yang got along well, and he often attended his friend's lectures at that office. Bohang also had the nickname of Lay Buddhist Wuxiang, an excellent name; it not only shows his ambition clearly, and his understanding of Buddhism, but also his origin background from Lishui—he was an expert in words and expressions. This nickname reminds us of Zhou Bangyan's famous *Man Ting Fang: Xiari Lishui Wuxiang Shanzuo*. In terms of roots, the Wang family of Lishui originated from the Wang family of Langya, who moved from Lishui to the south of Nanjing at the end of the Ming Dynasty, closer to their ancestor's Black Gown Lane.

It is legendary that Bohang devoted his life to the Taigu School. It was a sect of Confucianism founded in the Jiaqing and Daoguang years of the Qing Dynasty by Zhou Taigu, a native of Shidai, Chizhou, Anhui Province. It mainly focused on Confucianism, especially Song Confucianism, and included Buddhism. In real life, this school advocated "following the examples of those of intelligence and integrity, the examples of sages, the examples of gods" by "expounding one's theory in writing, rendering meritorious service, and fostering good virtues" and pursuing "making a great contribution to the nation without being a hero." It was more tolerant than other schools of thought.

Judging from the academic orientation of integrating Confucianism, Taoism, and Buddhism, Bohang bore similarities to the Taigu School. At that time, Huang Baonian from Taixian, a student of the Taigu School, was giving lectures at Guiqun Thatched Cottage, on Shiquan Street in Suzhou, attracting more than a thousand people to attend. When Bohang learned about it, he made a special trip to Suzhou to pay homage to Huang Baonian and be formally apprenticed to him. That year, he was already over 40 years old. He had long been a famous scholar with an upright personality. It surprised many around him, including old friend Chen Sanli and family friend Huang Jigang, that he was willing to be an apprentice.

However, Bohang did not change his mind. Later, whenever he was free, he traveled to Suzhou to serve Huang Baonian and listen to his lectures. Huang Baonian, well aware of this student's temperament, changed his name to Boqian (humble), hoping that he would soften. After that, his thinking and even his character changed drastically. Based on integrating the theories of Confucianism, Buddhism, Taoism, and the Taigu School, he proposed "to cure the heart with Buddhism, to protect the body with the Taoism, to administer affairs with Taigu School, and to educate people with Confucianism." This unique ideological connotation makes him stand out both as an individual and as a scholar.

Knowledge and understanding are the biggest shining points of Bohang's legendary life: he was so well-read that he mastered a plethora of ancient books; he was so abundant in ideas that four schools were integrated; he was proficient in poetry, calligraphy, painting, and carving; even in the academic circles in the early years of the Republic of China, such a comprehensive talent was rare.

For example, adept at poetry with beautiful rhetoric, he exchanged poems with Wu Mei on the subject of New Year's Eve up to ten times, and it became a favorite topic among his teachers and friends. However, he did not cherish his own poems and articles, discarding them often. He read extensively and was a real bookworm. He had a deep understanding of history, theories, and poetry. His lectures at the Central University were so eloquent that students from all departments flocked to attend them. He was most famous for his analysis of the Four Books (four Confucian classics: *The Analects, Doctrine of the Mean, Great Learning*, and *Mencius*), which earned him the nickname "Four Books Man."

However, he strictly adhered to the teachings of Confucius throughout his life that one narrates and does not write. He was cautious with his writing, a typical old-schooled scholar. However, he made various annotations and corrections in his family book collection, like pearls scattered, shining with the brilliance of talent that the dust of history can't cover up. His commentary on *Dream of the Red Chamber* is the most famous of these. Having a soft spot for this novel, he read it no less than 20 times in his life and reviewed it with hand-written notes five times. After the Japanese invaders occupied Nanjing, he had to stay in his ancestral home because he was too old and sick to escape. He would rather die than take the lucrative offer of the Japanese. His honorable death was the perfect ending to his legendary life.

Purportedly, someone once teased him that a teacher from a private elementary school was not qualified to teach in an institution of higher education. This is another point of his legendary life experience. Indeed, Bohang was a teacher at the private elementary school teacher of poet Chen Sanli. From the 26th to 27th year (1900–1901) of the Guangxu Period, the Chen family moved from Nanchang in Jiangxi Province to Nanjing and settled in Toutiao Alley. Chen Sanli had long admired Bohang, so he invited him to teach students at his place. However, the relationship between Bohang and the Chen family was more than just guest-host. He and Chen Sanli and his eldest son, Chen Shizeng, used to discuss poetry and paintings and chant together, becoming close friends.

On May 13, 1913, Chen Sanli and Chen Renxian, Yu Keshi, and the Shou Cheng brothers decided to visit the Jiaoshan Temple in Zhenjiang together and also invited Wang Bohang. The next day, Bohang left Nanjing to join them, stayed there for a few days, and left several poems. Six years later, in the autumn of 1919, Bohang went to Beijing, and Chen Shizeng showed him around the Tanzhe Temple on the West Mountain, among other scenic spots. Chen Sanli's sons, Chen Longke and Chen Yinke, were all taught by Bohang. Their profound foundation of Chinese studies must give credit to Bohang's hard work.

In the Republic of China's fourth year (1915), Jiang Qian was the head of the Nanjing Higher Normal School. He visited Bohang in person, imploring him to take the job as a professor. Back then, Bohang was employed by the Nanjing Library, wandering happily among the rare books. At last, he said yes to the invitation because they insisted that he take the job. However, he made a unique requirement: he did not want a letter of appointment, so if the school showed any disrespect, he could walk away free. Huang Kan concluded that he had uniqueness, a temper, and a style. In this way, Bohang was distinguished and admirable. In today's words, he showed the upright disposition of traditional scholar-officials and adhered to the dignity of a teacher, a scholar, and a life that he had never wavered throughout his life.

From that time, he taught for nearly 30 years from Nanjing Higher Normal School to Southeast University to Central University. "He set up his teaching with Confucianism as the body and Zen as the application. He taught ancient poetry and prose and discussed the books of five masters (Xunzi, Yang Xiong, Wang Tong, Laozi, and Zhuangzi), enchanting the students."

He guided the students to explore the depth of knowledge, inspiring and encouraging. Students worshipped him, and his prestige expanded in the southeast of China for a while. His best students, such as Tang Guizhang, Duan Xizhong, Wang Huanbiao, Shu Shicheng, and Zhou Fagao, later became famous scholars in China. Among them, Zhou Fagao also married Bohang's daughter. He first studied at Central University and inherited the traditional style of study of Nanjing Higher Normal School. Cultivated by the good conventional Chinese academics, he studied at the Institute of Literature at Peking University and the Institute of Linguistics at Academia Sinica, absorbing the new Western theories, and finally became a famous linguist who "integrated the best of south and north, ancient and modern, Chinese and foreign teachings."

After the government of the Republic of China made Nanjing its capital, especially from the mid-1920s to the mid-1930s, famous scholars gathered in the city. There were many great Confucians in the academies. Bohang and his close friends Liu Yimou, Wu Mei, Huang Kan, Hu Xiangdong, Wang Dong, and Hu Xiaoshi often hung out, traveling together, chanting poems, and discussing art and literature. It was such fun. In *Dongyin Hut Poems* and *Dongyin Hut Ci*, there are many pieces chanting about the ancients. For example, verses are written about the Leaf Sweeping Tower, Xuanwu Lake, the Huomeng Tower of Jiming Temple, the Banshan Pavilion, Qing Creek, the Ming Forbidden City, etc. In the winter of 1929, scholar and poet Ye Gongchuo came to Nanjing and gifted Bohang a copy of *The Posthumous Poems of Wen Daoxi (Tingshi)* through Huang Kan. Huang Kan kept it in his hand for a few days. Inspired, he wrote a heptasyllabic quatrain at the end of the book and asked Wang Dong to do the same before giving it to Bohang.

The refined taste of these senior scholars was fascinating. Hu Xiangdong wrote an article, *Three Songs of Ziyi Building*, which used the dwarf pine as a metaphor for teachers, the boxwood for friends, and the spider plant for maidens. Bohang appreciated this interesting idea. Unexpectedly, in 1937, Bohang suddenly had a stroke. The boxwood withered and never recovered (Hu Xiangdong's *Preface to Boxwood*), deeply saddened his old friend. Seven years later, the unyielding boxwood died and was buried in the backyard of his ancestral house. When he was alive, he stood in front of the bayonet of the Japanese invaders with his head held high; when he died, he never gave in to the Japanese invaders. This boxwood tree was standing when it withered.

Over half a century has passed, and the old appearance of the yard has hardly changed, but people have grown old. On that day, at the opening ceremony of the memorial hall, I met Xu Fu, a student of Wang Bohang, a linguist with gray hair and high spirits, and Wang Mian, his daughter and widow of Zhou Fagao. Bohang had two sons, both of whom died early. After Bohang passed away, his daughter worked hard to collect and organize and publish his manuscripts. She traveled across the Taiwan Strait to build this memorial and worked tirelessly to see it happen. Later, she also contacted me and donated the works of his father (Wang Bohang) and her husband (Zhou Fagao) to the reference room of our department to spread them widely and keep their studies passed on. After decades of separation, the father-in-law and son-in-law finally reunited in the memorial hall. From then on, they could accompany each other day and night by the Zhou Chu Terrace and read to each other. In an ancient poem is written:

Zhonglang has a daughter to pass on his career,
Bo Dao has no son to keep the family line.

Of course, it is a pity that Bo Dao had no son; if Bohang could see from above, he should feel relieved when he returned to the old house in Renhouli in the bright moonlight.

Though I have written so much, my views have not been fully expressed, so a poem is attached below:

The old Confucian beside the Reading Terrace,
his traces help us recognize his old residence.
Wind howls but the wall of poetry stands still,
and the flowers and trees keep growing lush.

Postscript

1

If a city is compared to a person, Nanjing ought to be a silver-haired elder with a youthful appearance and spirit. In his eyes, the past prosperity, bloody wars, the gathering, separation, and reunion of the ordinary, the achievements of heroes are nothing but a flash in the pan. Moving stories reflect his unique personality in every stage in his tortuous life. In front of this ancient city, this thousand-year-old elder, all the literati and celebrities can't help rhapsodizing about their imaginations and feelings. Probably, what attracts them is the temperament of this city.

Over time, the stories of these people become the stories of the city. From ancient times to today, many people have never been to Nanjing. Still, whenever they mention it, a literary feeling arises in their hearts, adding a classical and romantic excitement. Probably, what excites them is the temperament of this city.

I once expressed my willingness to vote for Nanjing if we were to select the most quaint and literary city. A few years ago, I was so itching inside that I taught a semester of *Nanjing in Literature* at Nanjing University. Later, based on the lecture notes, I organized a series of articles titled *City Legends*, which were published in *Knowledge of Classical Literature*. Now that I think about it, probably, what drives me is the temperament of this city.

Such temperament gives it a legendary life. How can we not love this city? Although fundamentally speaking, in its history, I am just a passerby, in its present, I am just a foreigner who has lived there in exile for many years.

2

So, what is Nanjing's temperament like?

Some time ago, I was invited to write a few words for its urban image planning in the form of duality, perhaps revealing its urban temperament in my subconscious. One is:

A pleasant city;
A sorrow-free home.

Needless to say, they are puns with Shangxin (pleasant) Pavilion and Mochou (sorrow-free) Lake. I wanted to highlight the living environment and cultural atmosphere of the city. Nanjing is a livable city.

Another one is:

Ancient and modern wealth is buried in Jinling;
Southern and northern auspiciousness is gathered in Jiqing (another name for Nanjing in ancient times).

The name Jinling has been used for thousands of years from ancient times to modern times; in the Yuan Dynasty, Nanjing was called Jiqing Prefecture. Northerners traveled southwards to this city. Culturally, it connected the north and the south. Located in the north-south communication center, Nanjing is a transportation hub today. In the era of the global economy, it is inevitable to join in the fun and say a few words of wealth and auspiciousness. However, as an ancient city of culture and famous capital east of the Yangtze River, it cherishes the most and takes the greatest pride in its cultural capital. For example:

Zijin Mountain towers high,
and the purple clouds float from the east;

Stone City stands upright,
and the phoenix flies to the west.

The auspiciousness is highlighted by its geographical advantages, and
the noble status of a capital is stressed from the purple clouds. It is believed
that the phoenix can be reborn from the ashes. Nanjing has experienced ups
and downs for more than 2,000 years. Today, it still has the virtue of staying
new every day, just like the phoenix. Combining the classical context with
modern Nanjing, we can say:

Among the three mountains and two rivers,
the thousand-year context extends;
In the north and west of the rivers,
the old appearance changes.

Certainly, if one only pays attention to its historical identity and
geographical environment, it can also be:

The prosperous capital for ten dynasties;
The number one city south of the Yangtze.

If the modern consciousness is highlighted, the vast space there is
available for greatness to be made. When the geographical location of
Nanjing is combined, we can say:

In the wide rivers, the hero braves the wind and waves;
Under the vast sky, the career takes off and soars.

Or:

Zijin Mountain is towering,
and we look up at it;
The sky is vast above the river,
and the new swallows fly far away.

Certainly, we look up to the Sun Yat-sen Mausoleum in Zijin Mountain, and the ever-new Swallow Rock injects people with the urge to fly.

Nanjing has always been known as "a city of mountains and rivers" and "an urban mountain forest." In the form of acrostic poetry, I wrote two sets of words. The first is:

With famous mountains;
With green rivers;
This thousand-year-old city;
Has gardens everywhere.

The other is:

This thousand-year-old city;
South of the Yangtze River;
Houses several famous mountains;
And countless gardens.

They can be regarded as a simple explanation for the two titles above and incidentally highlight the city's historical tradition and regional positioning.

Speaking of historical tradition, there is:

A coiling dragon and a crouching tiger,
the thousand-year royal qi;
A white egret and a blue sky,
the poetic urban image.

The first sentence aims to present the imperial atmosphere of Nanjing as a capital. A bit outdated as it is, it is okay to have some old titles to praise. Every Chinese is familiar with Li Bai's poems, and the egret in the blue sky evokes poetic imagination. It is a poetic city.

In terms of geographical advantages alone, we can say:

The rivers run free, and the scenery is magnificent;
The mountains stand tall, and the atmosphere is majestic.

Or:

The rivers and streams run on the ground,
and the Yangzi River is surging with majesty;
The sun and moon hang in the sky,
and the Zijin Mountain shines the light of benevolence.

In this way, Nanjing has not only a humanistic temperament, but also a strong spirit.

3

The city is not only a concept of geography and space but also one of culture and time. Every city has its own personality, its own image, and its own charm. True and false stories in history are repeating and deepening these urban expositions, and nobody bothers to care about their authenticity.

History is trivial, complex, and vivid, but the usual narration is inevitably general and abstract, thus losing its original flavor. I hope to look at the city's image from a different angle, that is, from the narrative of literature. Let the city narrate literature and history instead of the usual heroic protagonists; at the same time, let literature and daily life stories depict a city instead of boring statistics.

There are various ways of talking about history. "Explore the interaction between natural phenomena and human society, understand the development and evolution of all dynasties from ancient times to the present, and form our own unique historical theory," this is the way of Sima Qian.

The once magnificent ancient palace is desolate,
and the beautiful flowers in the palace are blooming in loneliness.
The surviving silver-haired palace maids, sitting idle,
have nothing but the anecdotes of the emperor to gossip about.

This is the way of poets.

Reunited with friends at last.
Over glasses of wine,
we talk about past and present history.

This is the way of fishermen. There are more ways of talking about history. No matter which one, I always believe that talking about literature and history should involve a little more emotion, story, and fun. Every city has many allusions, many legends, and many stories. This is the condensation of the urban cultural spirit and the root of the city. And investigating the documents and digging up the ancestral stories is seeking the cultural roots of a city.

4

Cities with a bit of history have unique landscapes, labeled as ten scenes, twenty scenes, twenty-four scenes, and even forty-eight scenes and sixty scenes. The number keeps going up. Nanjing had *Forty Scenes of Jinling* in the Ming Dynasty and *Forty-Eight Scenes of Jinling* in the Qing Dynasty. Behind every scene is a legend, which is full of humanistic warmth. I love the old names of those scenes. They have a certain cadence to pronounce, are carefully worded, and are full of classical charm. It is a pity that today's new names sound flat and lack literary charm, failing our ancestors. I prefer the *Forty-Eight Scenes of Jinling* painted by Xu Hu in the Qing Dynasty, so when I selected illustrations for this book, I took them all without leaving one behind. When there needs to be more text, pictures come to the rescue. I am no exception. A book of words supplemented with images is pleasing to the eye and stimulates the nerves numbed by the words. I don't boast of the presence of both illustrations and texts, but I hope that readers will understand my intention with the illustrations.

A restaurant in London puts out the candles and lights before dining because it intends to enable the diners to be free from visual disturbances and enjoy the gourmet food wholeheartedly. However, reading differs from dining, although books are often compared to spiritual food. Reading is, first and foremost, the activity of the eyes. Without light, we cannot read.

In addition, the torrent of the visual era is unstoppable. As insignificant as me, naturally, I dare not stop it, so let's go with the flow.

These two dozen articles are only part of my original plan. Because I am a fan of Jinling's forty-eight scenes, I borrowed their names' cadence to title my chapters. It's not a difficult task. To my dismay, after years of work, I am ashamed to admit that only half of the forty-eight scenes have been completed.

CHENG ZHANGCAN

August 26, 2005

In Longjiang, on the other side of Stone City

Postscript to the Revised Edition

Most of the chapters in Ancient Swallows were first serialized in a column called "city legends" *of Knowledge of Classical Literature,* sponsored by Phoenix Publishing House. Thanks to President Jiang Xiaoqing for allowing me to publish them in a collection. As a fan of *Five Poems of Jinling* by Liu Yuxi, I chose *Ancient Swallows* as the title of the book, and inspired by the column, I created a subtitle, *The Legend of a City.* I recall that after submitting the manuscript, I was on an academic visit abroad. So, when the proofs came out, I could only read the PDF file on the computer. Time flies. It has been fifteen years since the first edition of this book.

In the postscript to the first edition, I wrote, "These twenty or so articles are only part of the original plan." It is a pity that some of the "original plans" fifteen years ago remain uncompleted. Fortunately, part of it has been completed. However, it is presented to the readers in another way, meaning *The Mountains around the Homeland,* published by Nanjing University Press in July 2019, and *Tide in the Stone City,* published by Phoenix Publishing House in June 2020. Together with *Ancient Swallows,* they are my three Nanjing books. It has been 40 years since I moved to this city in 1983. How time flies! All I can gift to this city are nothing but my words.

Thanks to Nanjing University Press for publishing this revised edition.

CHENG ZHANGCAN
August 9, 2020
In Xianxialu, Jinling

List of Political Powers with Nanjing as Capital

Dynasty/ Period	Capital City	Time	Emperors/ Rulers	Notable Events
Eastern Wu	Jianye	AD 229–280	Sun Quan, Sun Liang, Sun Xiu, Sun He, Sun Hao	Establishment of the State of Wu, Three Kingdoms period, relocation of capital from Wuchang to Jianye in AD 229, eventual surrender to the Jin Dynasty in AD 280.
Eastern Jin	Jiankang	AD 317–420	Emperor Yuan, Emperor Ming, Emperor Cheng, Emperor Kang, Emperor Mu, Emperor Ai, Sima Yi, Emperor Jianwen, Emperor Xiaowu, Emperor An, Emperor Gong	Unification of China under the Western Jin Dynasty, rise of Buddhism, establishment of the Southern Dynasties.
Liu Song	Jiankang	AD 420–479	Emperor Wu, Emperor Wen, Emperor Xiaowu, Emperor Ming, Emperor Shun	End of the Sixteen Kingdoms period, cultural and economic development, eventual collapse and conquest by the Southern Qi Dynasty.

(Continued)

Dynasty/ Period	Capital City	Time	Emperors/ Rulers	Notable Events
Southern Qi	Jiankang	AD 479–502	Emperor Gao, Emperor Wu, Emperor Ming, Emperor He	Founding of the Southern Qi Dynasty, the flourishing of art and culture, conquest by the Liang Dynasty in AD 502.
Liang	Jiankang	AD 502–557	Emperor Wu, Emperor Jianwen, Emperor Yuan, Emperor Jing	Establishment of the Liang Dynasty, the spread of Buddhism, and the conquest by the Northern Zhou Dynasty.
Chen	Jiankang	AD 557–589	Emperor Wu, Emperor Wen, Emperor Xuan, Chen Shubao	Founding of the Chen Dynasty, struggle for supremacy with the Northern Zhou Dynasty, eventual defeat by the Sui Dynasty.
Southern Tang	Jiankang	AD 937–975	Li Bian, Li Jing, Li Yu	Founding of the Southern Tang Dynasty, cultural and economic prosperity, eventual collapse and absorption by the Song Dynasty.
Ming	Nanjing	AD 1368–1421	Emperor Hongwu, Emperor Jianwen, Emperor Yongle	Founding of the Ming Dynasty, construction of the Forbidden City in Beijing, relocation of capital from Nanjing to Beijing in AD 1421.
Taiping Heavenly Kingdom	Tianjing	AD 1853–1864	Hong Xiuquan	Revolution against the Qing Dynasty, establishment of the Taiping Heavenly Kingdom, eventual suppression by the Qing Dynasty.
Republic of China	Nanjing	AD 1912–1949	Sun Yat-sen, Chiang Kai-shek	Overthrow of the Qing Dynasty and founding of the Republic of China, relocation of capital from Beijing to Nanjing, period of political instability and Japanese invasions, eventual victory of the Communist Party of China and establishment of the People's Republic of China in 1949.

Index

ABOUT THE AUTHOR

CHENG ZHANGCAN is a celebrated author, historian, and professor of literature at Nanjing University. He holds a Bachelor of History from Peking University and a Ph.D. in Literature from Nanjing University. As a recipient of the prestigious Changjiang Scholar Award, he is recognized as one of China's leading scholars in the field of literary studies. Zhangcan has published over thirty books, including the acclaimed *Ancient Swallows: Nanjing, the Legendary City of Literature*, *Mountain-Encircled Homeland: Tales of Old and New Nanjing*, and *The Tides of Stone City*. His works have been widely translated and are highly regarded for their depth of research and engaging storytelling.